Praise for *You Ought to Do a Story About Me*

"Consistently complex and absorbing. . . . A rich and rewarding narrative about the possibilities—and the challenges—of redemption."

—*Kirkus Reviews* (starred review)

"Gut-wrenching yet hopeful, Jackson's work is a bracing look at the struggles and triumphs on the road to redemption."

—*Publishers Weekly*

"From football victories to enduring injuries, valiant recovery to lost years, Jackson pieces together Wallace's story with care. Bound by faith, his biography is a painstaking portal into the human condition and how we care for one another."

—*Booklist*

"*You Ought to Do a Story About Me* is elegant in its detail, abundant in its humanity, and poignant in its truth. Jackie Wallace is real—and stunningly realized in these pages—and so his path zigs and zags, driven throughout by the unbroken will of the many loving—and also flawed—people orbiting around him. Ted Jackson, the author, is among this constellation, and in his hands the story gracefully encompasses all the messy nuances of sports, fame, romance, male friendship, and the competing angels and demons that reside in us all."

—Jeff Hobbs, author of *The Short and Tragic Life of Robert Peace*

"This masterpiece of dogged and loving reporting will astonish you and touch your heart. The struggles and quest for redemption of football star Jackie Wallace make for a fall-from-grace tale that's both unsettling and uplifting."

—Walter Isaacson, author of *Steve Jobs*, *Leonardo da Vinci*, and *Benjamin Franklin*

"This book will melt your heart. The story of Jackie Wallace is an unforgettable tale of hope, grace, and the miracle of the human spirit. Ted Jackson writes with searing honesty and deep love for a troubled man who started as his subject and became his lifelong friend."

—Jonathan Eig, bestselling author of *Ali* and *Luckiest Man*

"When Jackie Wallace was my teammate with the 1970s Baltimore Colts, I knew him as a man of great talent and great heart. Now, thanks to the powerful work of Ted Jackson, we see every haunting detail as Jackie struggled to navigate the decades that followed. It is a story defined by both the brutality of drug addiction and the beauty of friendship, and this book allows us to explore our own thoughts about each."

erback

T0025587

You Ought to Do a Story About Me

Addiction, an Unlikely Friendship,
and the Endless Quest for Redemption

TED JACKSON

DEY ST.
An Imprint of WILLIAM MORROW

For Nancy

HarperCollins books may be purchased for educational, business, or sales promotional use. For information, please email the Special Markets Department at SPsales@harpercollins.com.

A hardcover edition of this book was published in 2020 by Dey Street, an imprint of William Morrow.

FIRST DEY STREET PAPERBACK EDITION PUBLISHED 2021.

Designed by Paula Russell Szafranski

Library of Congress Cataloging-in-Publication Data has been applied for.

ISBN 978-0-06-293568-7

21 22 23 24 25   LSC   10 9 8 7 6 5 4 3 2 1

Contents

Prologue

Jackie Wallace stumbled out of the New Orleans Mission a broken and defeated man. He wore three shirts to protect against the cold, but the wind pierced the thin fabric of each. As he wandered toward downtown, a cold, damp blast reached through his bones and sunk him.

He staggered past St. John the Baptist Catholic Church, and when he came to the entrance for the Pontchartrain Expressway, he turned. Walking up the ramp, hemmed in by commuters and tractor-trailers, he felt momentary relief. He leaned against the quivering railing for balance.

To his left, if he had looked, he would have seen the gleaming towers of commerce, a statue of Robert E. Lee and the riverboat *Natchez*—vestiges of old Dixie. To his right, he would have seen the neighborhood where he enjoyed Carnival as a boy and the wharfs where his father earned a living and his family's respect. But his eyes were fixed on the Mississippi River bridge. As he approached, he could see the plaque of a selfless mother pelican bolted to the structure's crossbeam.

In his sixty-three years, he had been the pride of his hometown, the envy of his childhood friends and schoolmates, a true American success story, a Super Bowl hero. But a life full of accolades and praise meant nothing to him now. He had come undone. Living low and getting high had become as common as taking a breath. He had come to the Mississippi River bridge to die.

Jackie instinctively dodged cars as he crossed the last ramp. No one seemed to notice him. Just a little farther and it would all be over. One hundred fifty feet below, the muddy Mississippi would swallow his soul and his wretched life. He bundled tighter and walked on, convinced that neither height nor depth could separate him from the love of God.

But before he reached the span, an especially cold crosswind caught his face. Maybe it was the chill of death or the wing of an angel. Fear and grace gripped him. He stood frozen between earth and eternity.

I WAS ONLY one block away, shooting an assignment for *The Times-Picayune*. A crowd cheered as I trained my camera lens on a beautiful restored fighter plane while a crane lifted it into a museum showcase. If I had refocused my zoom in another direction, I might have seen my old friend. If I had known, I could have made a difference. I would have moved heaven and earth to help him.

CHAPTER ONE

The Prodigal Son

1990

The heavyset, gray-brick building and the iconic clock tower that housed *The Times-Picayune* newspaper bore a resemblance to a lighthouse set upon a rock—a reliable guiding light, a beacon of truth that overlooked the Pontchartrain Expressway, the Louisiana Superdome, and the New Orleans skyline beyond.

Inside, the cavernous newsroom on deadline surged with a boisterous channeling of facts and figures, reporting and opinions, and features and scandal moving in a syncopated rhythm. It was a beehive of activity, noisy with hundreds of staffers: each day, the assembled team built another massive shipment of news, features, sports, classifieds, comics, debutante introductions, and obituaries—not to mention the endless investigations and revelations of the latest crooked Louisiana politician. We were the preeminent watchdog of state politics—the state's paper of record. Of our staff of twenty-four photographers, most still considered me a rookie. I'd seen a lot in six years, but I still had a lot to learn about big city journalism.

I would soon get my opportunity. On a particularly hot summer day in New Orleans, one of those soaking, sweaty days when breathing hurts, I'd spent the morning chasing down false leads on a celebrity murder case. If the afternoon turned out like I hoped, I'd spend the afternoon developing film and making prints in the cool of the darkroom.

But my photo editor, Kurt Mutchler, had other ideas.

Over the weekend, he had noticed a curious homeless camp under the Pontchartrain Expressway, near Carrollton Avenue, just twelve blocks from the office. While frequently short on pleasantries, he had a knack for sniffing out great ideas.

"It's a homeless camp," he said, "unlike any you've ever seen. It's just where the ramp comes to ground level. Look quickly to the right. There, tucked under that space, you'll see it."

"What makes it so interesting?" I asked, intrigued and fishing for details. I had worked on several homeless stories since the mid-eighties, when the oil bust sent Louisiana's unemployment rate over 13 percent.

"It's got a couch, end tables, chairs—all arranged like a living room. It's right where the bridgework meets the ground, in that little wedge space."

I've always loved arbitrary ideas like this—a random notion to fill my afternoon—nothing much expected, nothing more in mind. I thought of them as simmering adventures. I tried to imagine the pictures I'd shoot—guys huddled around a cooking fire, their weary faces cast in beautiful light.

How many homeless men and women had I wandered by in the past six years? Thousands, maybe? Most of them at the time slept alone, curled into a hidden spot under tattered blankets, trying to attract as little attention as possible. A camp sounded like a community, like a family, like something different—and journalism thrives on different. "Let me know what you find," my editor said as I hustled out the door.

I drove the twelve short blocks from the office to the spot he described, where Mid-City met Gert Town, past old warehouses and through the heart of Xavier University. I crossed Carrollton Avenue and parked near the overpass beside a group of closed businesses. My two-hundred-thousand-mile Honda, with its chipped paint, split cowling, and ridiculously noisy suspension, blended into the landscape. It made a great decoy for the expensive gear concealed beneath the hatchback, easily worth five times the car.

The space under the bridge looked ominous. A few shadows moved slowly in the distance, which made me nervous. The roar of traffic overhead drowned out any warning sounds I might have otherwise heard. Cars, trucks, and eighteen-wheelers rumbled over the concrete sections with an irregular *ca-thunk, ca-thunk* beat. Those were people with someplace to go.

I picked my way through steel supports where weeds suddenly gave way to rock and dirt, and I then spotted a railroad track that suggested an alternative walking path toward downtown. I worked my way past the rusted remains of forgotten cars and debris—unrecognizable as once useful. I practiced how I would approach the men, now only a hundred yards away—what I would say and how I would say it. I wanted to be compassionate and understanding. But this hidden realm was so different from my own. How could I adequately relate to people living on the streets, estranged from family, numbed by addiction—ignored, or worse, forgotten?

My cameras were prepared for whatever might happen. The exposures were preset, the lenses prefocused halfway to infinity. I tugged on the rewind knobs to make sure I'd loaded film. I'd experienced this rush of uneasiness many times before, remembering that some of my most meaningful photographs had been made while treading similarly unpredictable terrain.

As I turned the last corner, my previsualized concept evaporated.

The sofa was overturned. Tables were smashed against a pile of broken concrete as if marauders had ravaged the place. There was garbage everywhere. The people were gone.

I exhaled and surveyed the scene. I meandered a bit, looking for any clues as to what could have possibly wrecked the scene. What had driven the homeless to this desperate space in the first place? Where would I have gone if I had run out of choices? I started back toward my car. Time to move on.

As I rounded the next support column, a small movement caught my eye. When I looked closer, I spotted a half-naked man sleeping on a rusty box spring covered with cardboard. He was wrapped in a sheet of thick, clear plastic that opened around his arms and chest. His head rested on a wadded yellow jacket, also wrapped in plastic. He slept in the fetal position in only his briefs and an undershirt. I took a few photos with my long lens, then came closer and climbed the pier for a few overhead frames. Then I climbed down and tried to wake him.

"Hello," I said. He rustled a bit.

"Hey, man," I said. "Hello."

This time he lifted his head. He squinted his eyes into focus and rolled toward me. He didn't seem startled. When you sleep under bridges, you learn to expect the unexpected.

He pulled himself upright, waving the plastic sheet away, revealing the Kenmore refrigerator box that served as his mattress. He appeared to be about forty years old. He needed a haircut and a shave. His feet landed on a pair of discarded automotive floor mats. I glanced around his setup. There was a five-gallon bucket off to the side, a pair of neatly arranged sneakers, a clean set of clothes, a jug of water, and a folded copy of *The Times-Picayune*. He cleared his throat and reached for a damp dishrag to clean the sleep from his eyes.

"Sorry to bug you," I said, "but I was wondering if you might know what happened to the men camped down by the concrete?"

"Yeah," he said, dragging the rag over his arms and hands, still a little hazy. "Teenagers driving by were shooting guns at them. They were probably looking for a safer place to live. Why do you ask?"

"Well, my editor spotted the camp from the road and thought it might make a good story."

"I guess it would have."

We talked about homelessness and my editor's idea for the story. I complimented him on his campsite.

"It's safer than others I've tried," he said. "Out of sight, close to the guardrails."

He looked me over and picked up the newspaper. "You're looking for a story?"

"Always." I smiled.

There was a short pause while he fingered the pages. "You ought to do a story about me."

I'd heard this line many times before, usually from folks with inflated egos or people just wanting to have their picture taken.

"And why would I want to do that?"

He looked me in the eye. "Because I've played in three Super Bowls."

I wasn't sure if I'd heard him right, but he had my attention.

The paper was folded out to the sports page. "Do you see this series y'all are doing?" He read the headline: "The Real Life: Surviving after the NFL."

"You ought to do a story about me," he said again.

"So, what's your name?" I said.

"Jackie Wallace," he said as he handed over a ragged ID card.

I nodded my head. The name meant nothing to me, but I didn't say so. I'd paid attention to football since I was old enough to sit in my dad's lap, but I wasn't the kind of fan who memorized rosters.

I scribbled a few notes into my notepad. I didn't know what to say. To be honest, I didn't believe him. We talked some more, I shot a few more frames, and then I thanked him for his time.

As I walked back to my car, I wasn't sure what had just happened. Had I heard him right? I checked my notebook. "Jackie Wallace." I clumsily dropped my gear into my hatchback. I didn't radio my editor. I didn't talk to anybody. I raced back to the building and bounded up the three flights of stairs. I squeezed the two rolls of exposed film in my hand and raced past the darkrooms and past the photo desk. I rushed straight for the sports department, where a couple of dozen reporters, editors, and interns were busy pounding out their daily beat assignments. I found the first editor who wasn't on the phone—Tim Ellerbee.

"Has anyone ever heard of a guy named Jackie Wallace?" I asked, louder than I'd intended. I was breathless.

Every head popped up like groundhogs from their dens. "Sure," Tim said, and he gave me a quick rundown. Others joined in, laying

out broad details of Jackie's career—that he'd been a star at St. Augustine High School and the University of Arizona, and then had gone to play professional ball with the Minnesota Vikings, the Baltimore Colts, and the Los Angeles Rams. He had helped his teams in two Super Bowls, not three, as Jackie originally said.

"But once he was released from the Rams," Tim said, "he dropped off the map. Nobody knows where he is now."

I was about to bust. "I think I found him. And you won't believe where."

By now, sportswriter Jimmy Smith—the writer who had written the NFL series in the paper that day—was by my side, hanging on to every detail. Tim and Jimmy were sharing glances.

"You think he's still there?" Jimmy asked.

"I sure hope so."

We talked on the way out to our separate cars.

"Are you sure that's what he said?"

"Yeah, Jackie Wallace." I showed him my notebook.

We sped back to the same spot near the weeds. I led us through the underbrush and past the shadows along the trail, and there he was, just as I'd left him, except now he was dressed and moving around. His T-shirt read: "On the Road of Life," and, then, in tiny letters, "you need training wheels."

Jackie wasn't at all surprised to see me again. I introduced Jimmy as the writer for the "Surviving after the NFL" series. As the two men talked, I noticed Jackie's impressive build, six foot three with lanky limbs and powerful thighs, strong and athletic. He moved deliberately but with quick reflexes. Jimmy and Jackie settled in for an extended interview while I circled for portraits with my longer lenses. Jackie answered every question we knew to ask. When he talked about his football career, his eyes danced. When he pondered his future, his brow dimpled between his eyes. When the conversation stalled, he was quick with a joke. His gap-toothed grin charmed.

He said he'd been out of football for ten years. He said he still wasn't sure why he got cut. "I had a good year," he said as he talked about his last season. He said he knew he'd lost a little speed, but as a cornerback, experience was more important than speed. He was still feeling healthy and productive. Then suddenly, his career was over. He'd tried to get on with other teams, he said, but nobody was interested in him.

He said he was homeless by choice. He'd tried living in the St. Thomas housing projects, but he'd grown tired of the violence there. He wanted to be alone, he said. I scoured the surroundings and backgrounds for details. Graffiti overhead read, "For birds only."

"Our society says you have to live in a house and wear Gucci shoes," he said. In an odd comparison, he quoted scripture and compared himself to Jesus: "Foxes have dens to live in, and birds have nests, but the Son of Man has no place even to lay his head." Then he added, "I have to do what I see fit, on my own terms."

Jimmy scribbled notes and flipped pages as fast as he could.

"So far, I've been lucky," Jackie said. "I haven't had to dig in garbage cans to find food, I know how to go two days without eating. I'm extremely fortunate. And extremely blessed."

Jimmy was satisfied. He could get everything else he needed from coaches, experts, and family, so he headed back to the office. I hung around for more pictures. I needed more time.

Almost everyone wears a mask when the cameras first come out. With enough time, the real person emerges. But with Jackie, there was no pretense. He was authentic from the first shot. He didn't preen or pose. He confessed his failures. He had nothing to hide.

I settled in and made myself comfortable, sitting cross-legged in the dirt, keeping a close eye out for anything that might make a photo. I watched for subtle moments that might reveal his character. I watched the changing light for any opportunity to photograph him in his environment. We talked until the traffic overhead softened. Long shadows crept across the steel until darkness finally compressed our space to a few square feet. I had to remind myself that I hadn't known this guy just a few hours before. Did he have a history of violence? Was he mentally stable? Years on the street had taught me to control these perfectly reasonable fears. I decided to trust this stranger. I had to. How else would I get him to trust me?

After five or six hours, when our conversation had finally grown stale, he gathered his gear like puzzle pieces—a short piece of garden hose, the five-gallon bucket, and some plastic bags. "It's laundry night," he said as he placed a set of clothes into the milk crate.

It was nearly 10:00 P.M. when we left his camp. I followed him through dark brush past closed businesses to a backstreet water faucet. There, he filled his bucket and dunked and scrubbed his shorts, shirts, and socks until the water ran clear. He bathed himself under the hose in much the same way, taking special care of his feet, which he had wrapped in plastic. Back at camp, he draped everything over a steel girder to dry in the summer air.

When he settled in for bed, when there were no more pictures to take, I headed home, where my wife, Nancy, was patiently holding dinner. My two sons had been in bed for hours.

THE NEXT DAY was the Fourth of July, hotter than the third. As was our custom, Nancy and I loaded the car with our two kids, a couple of side dishes, and my oversize American flag and drove to my home state of Mississippi to celebrate with our relatives. Thirty minutes north of the suburbs and levees, between Manchac and Ponchatoula, the land transforms seamlessly from haunting cypress swamps into the beautiful rolling hills of the Bible Belt. The fertile pastures dotted with dairy cattle and the "Welcome to Mississippi" billboard felt like it was written just for us. Seventeen miles past the state line and two hours north of New Orleans, we were home.

McComb and her twelve thousand citizens rest at the crossroad of Highways 98 and 51 in southwest Mississippi, not to be confused with the crossroad of legend in the northwest Delta, where bluesman Robert Johnson supposedly sold his soul to the devil. On the contrary, McComb was founded in 1872 on temperance and holiness, when Colonel Henry Simpson McComb, president of the New Orleans, Jackson and Great Northern Railroad Company, moved the repair shops from New Orleans to escape the city's gin-drenched atmosphere. Under Colonel McComb's request, a special legislative charter was written to ensure that there would never be an open saloon in the city limits of the new town. Within a few years, a timberman named Captain John J. White donated thousands of dollars to erect churches of all persuasions. I arrived eighty-four years after McComb did, in 1956.

The fifties and sixties were a daunting time in America, when blacks and whites renegotiated the social contract of decency and coexistence. In those days, white Mississippians put up a vicious fight and gave themselves a permanent black eye.

When I was a child, my mother taught me about fairness. She emphasized it with equal treatment among her three sons. I wondered why fairness didn't apply to our neighbors, too, especially the black folks who lived nearby. Why did they live so differently than we did? I would observe their house down the road—unpainted and decrepit and surrounded by scraggly trees. The siding peeled in sections, and the rusty tin roof seemed to be tacked in place. The front porch sagged where the small children darted in and out of a tattered screen door. I wondered why they didn't have what we had.

By comparison, our house was pretty and white and surrounded by oaks, full grass, and mounds of azaleas. Four columns framed our front porch. I had five acres of woods, tree houses, and a large playground on the side. My dad added a master bedroom, a second bath, and a carport and expanded the kitchen as our family grew.

When my family and I went to town, friends warned us about catching dreadful diseases if we played in the streams that drained Burglund, the black area across the tracks. Blacks in return knew to avoid white neighborhoods. Downtown, black men often showed deference to white women when they met on the sidewalk. Public businesses often had three restrooms, labeled "Men," "Women," and "Colored." As marching bands paraded downtown each year, I saw how the black dancers were mocked, ridiculed, and humiliated. Sometimes I joined in. "It was a different time," I could say all these years later, but that position is impossible to defend.

Like many towns across America, the division of blacks and

whites was by design. And in Mississippi since the days of Reconstruction, lawmakers used education and policy to keep blacks undereducated and poor. Between 1890 and 1960, Mississippi intentionally spent $25 billion less on educating black children than whites. In the first half of the twentieth century, the discrepancy was appalling. For every $9.88 spent for white instruction in 1939, $1 was spent on blacks. Governor James Vardaman (in office from 1904 to 1908) once said, "The only effect of Negro education is to spoil a good field hand and make an insolent cook." Poll taxes and literacy tests effectively suppressed the black vote at every turn, thus protecting the hierarchy. Erasing the ancient institutions of racism took time. But it was easier to change corrupt laws than corrupted minds.

As my family drove on to our destination, it was easy to see how times had changed in the twenty-five-plus years since the march on Selma and James Meredith's march through Mississippi. If you didn't know Mississippi before the sixties, you might not notice the progress. The separate water fountains are now gone, along with most of the Confederate flags. Blacks and whites work side by side in the businesses and relax and mingle together in the coffee shops and in most of the parks. Forced integration—as painful as it was—helped blacks and whites forge a new society. It also helped blacks attain a more equal education. By 1964, most black Mississippi adults could read and write, but fewer than 5 percent of the population held a high school diploma. By 1990, the high school graduation rate was 47 percent. By 2006, it had improved to 70 percent. Education and voting rights gave blacks a place at the table. Blacks have since held every political office in the state except governor. While education and integration made folks more comfortable with one another, many slights, slurs, and tensions remain. On the sidewalks and in the shopping malls, blacks and whites still pass one another with a cautious eye. There's still plenty of history to overcome. While most Mississippians would like to forget it, the state's national reputation remains focused on blacks and whites who lost their lives in pursuit of civil rights: James Chaney, Andrew Goodman, and Michael Schwerner in 1964; and Vernon Dahmer in 1966.

But despite the unforgiving history, we Mississippians aren't so different than the rest of America. People everywhere seek reasons to despise people who are different. We've just taken longer to reconcile our differences.

WE TYPICALLY CELEBRATED the Fourth of July at my aunt Betty and uncle Charles's cattle ranch in Bogue Chitto. His barbecue spread was spectacular, with more fresh steak, ribs, and hamburgers than we could possibly eat. My boys and their cousins yelled, "Marco Polo!" in the pool and rambled the pastures and woods until it was too dark to see. Before leaving for home, we'd set the self-timer on my camera and smile for the memories to come.

But this year, it was Nancy's uncle Buddy's turn to host the family cookout. So instead of driving to Bogue Chitto, we turned west at McComb on Highway 98 and drove another hour west to Port Gibson, a quaint town set just off the Mississippi River between Natchez and Vicksburg. The locals there still live in the shadow of 1863's Battle of Grand Gulf, where Yankee general Ulysses S. Grant landed troops and began his march to burn Jackson—later called Chimneyville—on his way to capture Vicksburg. Grant spared Port Gibson of the torch, saying the town was "too beautiful to burn." There was a strong sense of southern pride there, albeit shrouded forever in the pall of cannonballs and surrender.

During our feast, I fielded a lot of questions about the latest

news involving crime and scandal in New Orleans. I was asked about the stories my colleagues were doing and about recent projects I had taken up. Despite my usual penchant for talking about such things, I didn't mention Jackie Wallace to anyone that day. Maybe I was simply enjoying family conversations and the kids too much to bother, or maybe I was afraid of drawn-out conversations about addiction and race. Maybe, still, I wasn't sure who Jackie was. But as we stacked our dishes in the sink, I thought about his camp. I wondered what he was eating—*if* he was eating—and whether he was alone.

I drove back to Mid-City on Thursday morning, eager to get another day's worth of pictures. As I approached his camp for the second time, Jackie was just getting dressed. His laundry was dried stiff across the girder. He reached for a pair of tube socks and crushed them into softness before pulling them on. There was no one else around, and he seemed genuinely glad to see me. I told him about my holiday, about Uncle Buddy and a story he'd told about an old Jeep and a bobcat. Jackie said he thought he and Buddy would probably get along well.

"Today, I'm looking for a job," Jackie said. The announcement seemed to me like a masquerade designed for my camera, but I figured I'd play along. I watched and made pictures while he gathered water, coins, and his collection of documents into a nylon duffel, whose logo read, "*Gulf Coast Outfitters,*" a defunct outdoor clothing brand from the once-prestigious Maison Blanche department store. It seemed appropriate.

For a guy looking for minimum-wage work, he didn't look too shabby. His shorts were clean. His T-shirt showed no stains or tears. He had shaved, and his shoes looked new. At our first stop, a bakery, I waited outside on the sidewalk, hoping to make a picture by the plate-glass window with the HELP WANTED sign. He walked out a few minutes later carrying a muffin. "They're not hiring," he said, even though the sign in the window clearly said they were. It was the picture I was looking for.

Sixteen sweaty blocks later, we crossed Claiborne Avenue, where two empty streetcars waited for passengers. Jackie rummaged through the dirt but couldn't find an unused transfer ticket, so instead, we crossed over to the center of Palmer Park, where a stone monolith rose in honor of locals who had died in World War II. Four live oak trees shaded the cobblestone walkway ringing the monument. There, Jackie found a bench and settled in with a copy of *The Times-Picayune.*

It would have been a beautiful park if not for all the spent needles littered around clumps of sleeping vagrants. Parents who dared to bring their children here kept a sharp eye for trouble. It was getting harder to find safe zones in this city.

Jackie cut a different figure from the other men there. While they sprawled in the tall grass, Jackie sat erect and alert. He spread his pages across his lap and immersed himself in one story after another. I framed a picture with my telephoto lens, visually compressing Jackie's shadowed silhouette against a background of tourists boarding the streetcar. A couple of bells signaled the car's departure. From our spot, I could hear the steel wheels grumble and

creak across a switch in the tracks as the car headed toward downtown. A few sparks arced from the lightning rods that connected with the overhead power lines. For only 60 cents, Jackie could have ridden the entire length from here to Canal Street. In forty minutes, give or take, he could be hustling tourists in the French Quarter for cash. But Jackie showed no signs of being a hustler.

As he turned another page of the *Picayune,* an older woman ambled over and struck up a casual conversation. Her Sunday-pressed cotton dress and pearls seemed oddly out of place in this heat and park but, with a floppy straw hat, tennis shoes, and a shade umbrella, made a fitting adaptation of New Orleans casual. She handed him the latest edition of *The Watchtower,* the Jehovah's Witnesses' monthly magazine. A second woman soon joined them, prompting Jackie to offer them a seat. For an hour or more, the women leafed through verses of scripture, and at times, Jackie took the book and looked up scriptures of his own. When he didn't know what to say, he leaned back and picked his fingernails. Jackie wasn't converted that day, but neither was he bothered. He enjoyed the company.

Before long, my editors would be expecting pictures for the story that was set to publish the next day. Right about now, they were probably gathered around the conference table for their afternoon budget meeting, wrestling over long lists of story descriptions, concepts, and choices, considering a story about a homeless NFL player without the benefit of images. I'd enjoyed my day with Jackie, but I had a deadline. So, I walked alone back to my car, drove to the office, and lost myself in the darkroom.

By 5:00 P.M., I had developed seventeen rolls of film and selected eleven frames. Just before 6:00 P.M., I had eleven 8-by-10 prints, labeled and captioned. Kurt edited them down to four, which he gathered into a folder with two others he had pulled from the paper's morgue file: a posed action shot from Jackie's St. Aug days and a head-and-shoulders portrait of Jackie as a rookie in a Minnesota Vikings uniform.

In the final budget meeting, twenty or so editors and designers looked over items for front-page consideration. Four were chosen. The police superintendent Warren Woodfork was calling for a public outcry over the staggering murder rate: 145 dead in six months. He predicted that if nothing was done, the city could reach a new record of three hundred murders by the end of the year, far surpassing the 1989 body count of 251.

In a press conference earlier in the day, Woodfork had announced that 32 percent of the year's murders had occurred in housing projects: 50 percent of the murders concerned narcotics; 82 percent of the victims were black males, as were 87 percent of those charged in the killings. "Look who's killing who," he said.

"It's black males killing black males." The editors emphasized that quote in the layout.

In other news, the state senate had approved Governor Buddy Roemer's $8.6 million budget, and NATO had drafted a proposal to ease growing tensions over nuclear weapons. But by the end of the meeting, the editors all agreed: local hero Jackie Wallace, having been found living homeless under a bridge, would anchor the page.

"Mark it up. Let's go."

A few hours later, every element was in place. The pages were designed. Stories were edited, and photos were sized. The section fronts were delivered to the pressmen by 9:00 P.M. If everything stayed on schedule—plates burned and proofs approved—the presses would roll at 10:00 P.M., and 275,000 copies would be printed by morning. Four red lights on the ceiling glowed in confirmation when the mighty machines whirred. If I stood in the right spot on the third floor, I could feel the presses come to life.

Only two days earlier, Jackie Wallace had casually looked me in the eye and said, "You ought to do a story about me." In just a few more hours, he would be front-page news.

Long before sunrise, the papers were rolling out the bay doors and into the newspaper's big box trucks, which in time rendezvoused with individual carriers at designated warehouses across the region. Loyal readers, local sports fans, and curious vacationers across Louisiana and southern Mississippi picked up the newspapers from their driveways, from their porches, from racks in drugstores, gas stations, and street boxes. The headline read, "A new address under I-10 for ex-NFL pro," with a subhead, "Life after football: too soon, too hard." Jackie would need twenty-five cents to purchase and read the rest.

He pulled his copy from a box at a nearby Exxon station, using one quarter to snatch the entire bundle. By afternoon, he was flashing the broadsheet around Central City. He passed the Liberty Street house where he had been raised. He passed Cabbage Alley, where he had been swaddled as a baby. He walked to the Mississippi River, where his dad had earned a living on the wharfs. At Jackson Avenue and Tchoupitoulas Street, he saw a stranger reading a paper. "You know who that guy is? It's me."

After nearly eleven years out of the spotlight, Jackie Wallace reemerged as a celebrity.

CHAPTER TWO

Son of Liberty Street, Son of the South

1951–1969

The debauchery of the 1951 Carnival was now five weeks past—the season against which everything seems to be measured in the city. And now, the *good* Catholics reverentially soldiered through their last weeks of Lent. Around New Orleans, the verdant new leaves on the azaleas and crepe myrtles signaled a vibrant rebirth after a dreary winter.

And while few people noticed, Jackie Wallace was born at Charity Hospital in the days leading up to Palm Sunday and Good Friday. For Audrey, March 13, 1951, seemed like an auspicious day. The gawking eyes of her two older toddlers couldn't tear her attention away from her beautiful baby boy as he nestled against her breast. Roland Jr., three, and Louvinia, two, proudly doted on their little brother.

Despite the glorious season, Audrey and her husband, Roland Wallace, brought their son home to their two-room home in a working-class slum known as Cabbage Alley, one of the most depressed areas in New Orleans. For nine years now, the couple had worked hard to claw their way out of this place. But for now, it would have to do. As she cradled her boy, she promised him a life of unconditional love while she prayed to God for better days.

Audrey and Roland met during hard times, introduced on a blind date in the early days of World War II, only weeks before Japan sank four battleships to the bottom of Pearl Harbor—killing 2,400 Americans in the process. Amid the chaos of a nation mobilizing for war, they vowed their love in a simple ceremony on February 20, 1942, just before Roland shipped off to boot camp. Roland was twenty-one. Audrey was sixteen.

Audrey was a short, high-spirited woman with dark skin, big hips, an ample bosom, and short hair. Roland stood five foot nine with big forearms—a burly man who had migrated to New Orleans to find work as a longshoreman on the Mississippi River docks. He came from Donaldsonville, a small town seventy miles upriver, known for its large sugar plantations.

By 1955, the Wallace family had grown to eight, with six children in all: Roland Jr., Louvinia, Jackie, Donald, Dabney, and Margo—all under the age of eight. So, they felt like they'd won the lottery when they were approved for an apartment in a relatively new development on the edge of town. The St. Bernard Housing Project, as it was called, afforded the family a sampling of modern amenities and three bedrooms that would finally give them enough room to spread out.

JACKIE SHARED A bedroom with his three brothers while his two sisters shared the other. The children enjoyed their new home and especially the adventure of exploring the green-space play areas set aside throughout the project. Jackie adored his mother and would do anything to win her approving smile. So, when he romped with a group of friends into the empty lot across Hamburg Street for a simple game of Humpty Head—a local version of hide-and-seek—he didn't intend to be rebellious.

The cleared lots were staged with lumber for new construction, a virtual paradise for the children, who darted and laughed as they hid behind piles of sand and debris. Audrey had repeatedly warned him to stay on the housing project property, but Jackie tended to reach for what he shouldn't have—call it the golden ring or forbidden fruit. But judgment fell quickly when a rusty 16-penny nail pierced deep into Jackie's left foot and drove hard against a bone.

In a jolt, Jackie jerked his foot free of the board and fell to the ground. He tried to fight back tears as his friends gathered around, but the pain shot like lightning up his leg, and warm blood pooled in his sock. However much it hurt, he knew the throbbing pain would pale in comparison to the trouble that lay ahead. He'd never disobeyed his mama like this. With help from his friends, he limped home. Maybe she wouldn't notice.

When he slumped into the kitchen, he confessed that he'd hurt his foot, but he downplayed the pain. He found a spot on the couch and told her he wanted to stay home from his kindergarten classes that afternoon. But Audrey didn't buy it. "Get dressed and get your butt to school," she said, and tossed him his school uniform, a pair of freshly pressed khaki pants and a khaki shirt. A fake limp might lead to truancy, and Audrey didn't tolerate foolishness. Neither did the school staff, who put a heavy emphasis on their students' success—to make something of themselves. Jackie pulled himself together and hobbled to meet his friends on the corner of Milton Street, and together they walked under the watchful eyes of the housing project mothers. Across the avenue, the children passed the Phillips 66 gas station and entered into a neighborhood of small houses clad in blond brick or white clapboards. Jackie had always admired them as he walked by, but today he fought back the tears from the pain in his foot.

Two blocks later, Jackie turned left into Edward Phillips Elementary and entered his land of wonder. He adored his teacher, Miss Dillon, and her way of welcoming him through the class doorway with hugs and smiles. Each day, he breezed through *Fun with Dick and Jane* readers and workbooks of colors, shapes, and numbers. He formed his upper- and lowercase letters in a little brown alphabet notebook. A distinct dashed line marked the boundary between the two cases.

But today, Jackie struggled to sustain his spark, preoccupied by the throbbing that only worsened as the day wore on. The bacteria inside his shoe had been shoved into the puncture by the nail. Infection had already begun to form. He soldiered through his classes and then limped home, but soon, blood poisoning coursed through his veins.

As his pain intensified over the next two days, Audrey finally discovered her son's swollen and infected condition beneath his pants leg. In a panic, she bundled her son against the cold and rushed him to the bus stop. The twenty-minute ride downtown to Charity Hospital seemed like an eternity, each stop along the way like torture.

The receptionist hurried them to an emergency exam room that reeked of germ-killing alcohol. Jackie writhed from the pain as the nurses cut away his jeans. Though he'd never witnessed a dead body floating in the bayou, he imagined this was how a rotting leg would look.

Audrey sat in horror as the doctors delivered the news: the infection had spread to his entire leg beyond any hope of saving it.

With little ceremony, the nurses prepared for amputation. Over Audrey's hysterical protests, doctors explained that they were beyond trying to save the leg. They were fighting for his life. Guilt overwhelmed her. How could she have allowed this to happen? Then she questioned the doctor's wisdom, and Jackie's future. What chance would a crippled black kid have growing up in a time like this? How would he work? How would he survive? She looked at the doctor, fixed her eyes, and made her choice.

"No. Absolutely not."

In spite of the doctor's expertise and judgment, she refused. She and Jackie would take their chances. She asked for alternatives. The doctor had nothing else to offer.

"Then let it rot off," Audrey told the doctors. "And if it doesn't rot off, then let him die. I'd rather let him go than to see him live with no chance at all."

When further pleas from the doctor failed to persuade her, the staff wheeled the boy from the exam room and admitted him to the ward reserved for black patients. Beneath the white cotton sheets, his small body cut a frail and pitiful figure. The nurses pumped his body full of antibiotics after his body rejected doses of penicillin. Alternative treatments were deliberated and planned. The Charity staff did what they could—heroics, in Audrey's mind—as she held vigil for a miracle.

In the long weeks that followed, Audrey wept and prayed for healing and made sure that all the members of her church prayed, too. She believed God would guide the hands of the doctors and nurses. As the leg slowly improved, Audrey wept again with relief and gratitude. Her fervent prayers had been answered, and Jackie was finally released.

Though he had missed most of his kindergarten year in the hospital and recuperating at home, Audrey's dreams for her son's future slowly returned.

THE ST. BERNARD Project is gone today, bulldozed after the hellish nightmare of Hurricane Katrina, rebuilt and replaced in 2010 by the Columbia Parc apartments. The homes are wired for high-speed internet and outfitted with granite countertops, a small movie theater, walk-in closets, and a pool. The toddlers peering through the beautiful wrought iron security fencing turn cartwheels on a

coiffed carpet of centipede grass, a much safer environment than
when crack cocaine and violence emerged in the mid-eighties. At
that time, most people considered St. Bernard to be a no-go zone.
But it didn't begin that way. The concept for New Orleans housing
projects was conceived as a noble experiment.

Federal agencies made their first venture into the landlord
business—the first model for American public housing complexes—
in New Orleans. As more and more rural Americans migrated to
cities for jobs in the midst of the Great Depression (1929–1939),
they settled in among the city's slums. Planners in New Orleans
targeted these undesirable "back o' town" areas for redevelop-
ment. They called them "projects" because that's how they were
conceived—as collaborative enterprises with the goal of improving
society.

For the second largest of New Orleans' six project sites, planners targeted a rustic black village on the northern edge of the city
limits along the old Gentilly Ridge. There, just beyond the Fair
Grounds Race Course—past the collection of dairy and truck farms
beyond—an army of workers replaced shanties and outhouses with
1,460 garden apartments in 134 multifamily two- or three-floor
buildings. The complex covered eighteen city blocks, roughly seventy acres. Green spaces were professionally landscaped for socializing and play. Rents ranged from $8.25 to $22 a month based on
the tenant's income. Officials named the seventy-acre property St.
Bernard after the city avenue that terminated there. Residents called
it Polly Land. No one seems to remember why.

In the beginning, the New Orleans projects were wildly celebrated, and for the Wallaces, they represented a major step up: a
home with its own address: 3820 Hamburg Street, New Orleans,
Louisiana. Their home included a living room, kitchen, bathroom,
and three bedrooms. It came with an electric refrigerator, gas

range, and water heater, a built-in bathtub, combination sink-laundry tray, closet space, and a yard space to dry clothes. There were nurseries for working parents, supervised playgrounds, and civic activities for children and adults.

But even as his foot healed in 1957, Jackie could imagine bigger dreams as he peered through his bedroom window at the undeveloped private acreage beyond St. Bernard being slowly transformed into wood-framed houses with nice porches and private fenced yards. But future aspirations aside, the little man admired his father most, and they woke up long before daylight to sit and talk over the morning *Times-Picayune,* Roland's chicory coffee and shared buttered toast while they waited for the "boss man" to call with wharf and ship assignments. Roland made a respectable living the only way he could, with his strong back shouldering heavy banana stalks for United Fruit Company. It took him thirty minutes and a series of bus connections to reach the Erato Street wharfs, but he didn't mind the long commute. As a matter of fact, he enjoyed the bus rides. It gave him time alone to clear his head when life got complicated—like a man staring into a reflecting pool after a long, hard day.

He felt pride in his contribution to New Orleans. At that time, the Mississippi River and the port formed the backbone of the city's economy—a leading reason why it had grown to be the sixteenth-largest city in the country, with nearly six hundred thousand residents. He took even greater pride in his six children's progress in school. Each day he returned home by three or four to help with homework, as much as he was able. He emphasized his limited opportunities imposed by his second-grade education. He claimed that he couldn't read or write, which amused Jackie as he watched him linger over the newspaper and prepare the family's taxes each year. Roland tried to inspire his children beyond a life of manual labor. They would need an education and a clean police record if they wanted a "sit-down" job. If they wanted to shed the bonds of servanthood, they needed to become "respectable Negroes."

To that end, he enforced his house law the only way he knew how: with his belt. He had a soft touch with his punishment, never abusive, but his leather meant business. He administered justice swiftly and surely. But Audrey didn't suffer fools easily and would occasionally lose her temper in the heat of the moment, which caused her to fumble over her children's names. She bellowed, "You boy, get in here," when she targeted Jackie. Once, when Jackie had pushed her beyond all sanity, she hurled a lamp his way. His speedy reflexes saved his head, but Audrey made him pay for the broken lamp.

As much as one might reasonably expect for such a big family, the Wallaces kept a quiet, calm house. Their black-and-white television sat as the home's focal point and became a portal into the white middle-class world through shows like *My Three Sons* and

Father Knows Best and westerns like *Wagon Train* and *Rawhide*. At bedtime, Roland would bellow part of *Rawhide*'s theme song to hustle the kids along, "Head 'em up! Move 'em out!" The kids would scurry, giggling while teasing their dad with their own variation of the refrain, "Roland, Roland, Roland." But the television offered few opportunities for the black kids to see role models that mirrored their own lives. Viewers in the 1950s and even into the 1960s were hard-pressed to find black roles beyond slaves, servants, or the caricatures of Amos 'n Andy.

As Jackie grew, his injuries healed and his legs grew stronger. His uncommon speed naturally attracted him to athletics, and his intellect attracted him to reading. Roland encouraged his athletically minded boys to read the *Louisiana Weekly*, a black-owned New Orleans tabloid. He especially directed them to the sports columns written by Peter "Champ" Clark, a black journalist who built a pioneering career advocating for young black athletes at a time when others were quick to ignore their talents. Even better, Champ lived only a few blocks away from the Wallaces, just outside of St. Bernard. Roland told his boys to get noticed by Champ, in the hope that one day this connection would pay off.

Roland saw sports as a great way to keep his boys out of trouble, and not just from the petty silliness of swiping a few bottles of Barq's Root Beer from the delivery truck that came by once a week. Roland worried more about big-time crime, as well as the growing influence of some cousins who were known to be "gangsters, shoplifters, thugs, loan sharks, and enforcers," as Jackie later would remember them. His older cousin Rudolph Mills—probably the worst of them all—strutted the city with a Bersa Thunder .380 in his waistband. Rudy didn't play around. He went after big targets—the numbers runners like the Mafia boys in New York—and usually succeeded by his ability to push people around. Still, Rudy had a soft spot for his younger cousin and called him out when he spotted Jackie pocket a candy bar from the sweetshop. "Put it back," he told him. "You're better than that."

Big justice came for Rudy one afternoon while he was hanging out in the Wallace living room. Suddenly, the front room door burst open and federal agents swarmed the apartment, brandishing guns and screaming orders. Jackie squeezed out the door and ran for his mama, who had been visiting with neighbors across the courtyard. Together, they watched as agents led Rudy away in handcuffs. "It's all right," Rudy said to the wide-eyed Jackie. "It's all right." But after a routine trial, a federal court convicted Rudolph of heroin possession and sentenced him to ten to fifteen years at Angola State Penitentiary, as Jackie remembered.

Soon after, Jackie walked a narrow path as he watched troubled teens around him spiral from petty theft into more serious trouble. Some ruined their chances for honest work. Once jailed, no one would hire them. Without a job, they resorted back to crime. They were now caught in a cycle of cause and effect. For some, that one bad choice led to a permanent condition. Jail often made these perpetrators worse and conditioned them to become lifelong criminals.

The New Orleans police tried to nip crime at the youth level by keeping the black youth "in their place." The solution was partially devised into the system. When urban developers designed parts of New Orleans, new white enclaves surrounded the "back o' town" slums. The new subdivisions had deed covenants that explicitly forbade sales to black families, creating alternately black and white pockets.

At first, deed restrictions were created with zoning ordinances, just like commercial zoning and residential zoning, segregating land use by race. The Supreme Court ruled the practice unconstitutional in 1917. But New Orleans ignored the ruling and continued building them anyway.

The resulting neighborhoods resembled a black-and-white checkerboard pattern around the city. The boys of St. Bernard Project knew where their black square ended. They were free to wander a few blocks east to Paris Avenue among the higher-class black folks, and four blocks west through the middle-class neighborhoods to Bayou St. John. To the south, the railroad tracks marked the edge of the neighborhood for working-class whites. Police took great care to patrol Mirabeau Avenue to the north, to protect the rich, lily-white high class who lived there—the "Anglo Saxons," as Jackie called them. Cops used intimidation to enforce the boundaries, and the segregated children of St. Bernard lived a correspondingly segregated understanding of the city beyond these borders. Jackie rarely encountered white people except for occasional bus rides to Central City. Audrey repeatedly warned her boys against straying across the boundaries. The girls didn't seem to have the same problems. The police didn't see black girls as a threat when they wandered into white neighborhoods.

But regardless of police-enforced boundaries, Jackie kept a

rigid respect for the law. If his mama told him not to touch some-one else's pencil, he wouldn't touch it. That would be tantamount to stealing. He tried to please his mama wherever he went. He took her nickname for him, "You boy," as a sign of affection. And instead of describing her as sweet and doting, he thought of her as no-nonsense and fair, and he adored her for it. She covered for his mistakes and kept his secrets. And despite his deep respect for his dad, he interpreted his relationship with his mama as pure love. But most of all, he respected her for her abiding faith in God. Audrey reserved Sunday for a day of rest, socializing with friends and, above all else, worship at the Greater Mt. Rose Baptist Church in Central City. For her children, she insisted on regular attendance in Sunday school. As Jackie remembered, no one said no to Mama.

Audrey hustled her children—and occasionally Roland—all dressed in their Sunday best to the bus stop for the thirty-minute ride to Central City. Sunday school started at 9:00 A.M., followed by two-and-a-half-hour church services. They'd arrive home by 3:00 P.M. at the earliest. Although Jackie learned the basics in Sunday school, he appreciated lessons about the Ten Commandments and the love of God back on Hamburg Street, a few doors down the hall from his apartment. Each Tuesday, Miss Sally, a sweet, heavyset Creole woman, welcomed a throng of children to her living room and showered them with snacks and Bible stories. She reminded Jackie of a black Aunt Bee, the doting Mayberry matron he knew from TV. Miss Sally stamped Jackie's imagination with classic church hymns like "What a Friend We Have in Jesus" and spirituals like "Swing Low, Sweet Chariot" and "Jesus Loves Me."

Despite full doses of gospel choirs, sermons on hellfire, and those sweet lessons from Miss Sally, Jackie's faith remained simple and childlike. Jackie believed that Jesus loved him, not because the

Bible told him so but because his mama told him so. He neglected accepting Jesus as his personal savior; he didn't ask to be baptized, and Audrey didn't press him on it. She wanted his faith to be a personal conviction.

As Audrey reserved her day of rest for church, Roland reserved his for the NFL. In the late fifties and early sixties, as the pro games began drawing big ratings on TV, Roland suggested that the kids ride the bus home by themselves after Sunday school. He enjoyed having his boys around him while watching the Sunday games. He argued they were mostly bored, messy, and noisy during the long services, so Audrey bent the rules for those weeks of the year. The way he saw it, sports supplied a surrogate religion for keeping the boys out of trouble.

By the sixth grade, Jackie weighed ninety-nine pounds and had grown head and shoulders above the other boys, just one inch shy of six feet. He stood awkwardly and nearly a foot taller than his classmates, and he thought of himself as a Watusi, an African people stereotypically known for their impressive height. But his abnormal stature came in handy during pickup games on the fields and the courts at school, although his nagging nail-to-bone foot injury kept him on the sidelines for some of the courtyard games. Due to the injury, and the idle time he spent because of it, he developed a sweet shyness around his friends—reserved around the boys but ever bashful with the girls, a disposition he'd carry into his football career.

But football was still far from his mind. Jackie and his younger brother Donald, who seemed to be the more gifted athlete, loved baseball. And Foy Court, only a block away from Jackie's door, was their home field. The one-hundred-by-one-hundred-foot courtyard surrounded by three floors of brick apartments sparked Jackie's imagination. It felt like a miniature Yankee Stadium.

The kids taught themselves the rules and techniques of the game until St. Raymond Catholic Church organized a league for the children. For even more competition, the ten-year-olds hopped boxcars to the Ninth Ward for pickup games at Sampson Park. They kept those games a secret from Audrey.

Jackie's powerful arm made him a natural for third base, catcher, or left field, while Donald's pitching arm proved strong and accurate. Roland attended as many games as he could and offered his opinions around the dinner table. He wouldn't mention Jackie's three hits, only the one strikeout. He didn't mention Donald's no-hitter, but only asked why he didn't strike out everyone. The boys fed off the pressure for excellence, but even more than that, they were thankful for this attention.

The Wallace household took gratitude seriously, so when Thanksgiving Day came each year, they embraced it with great ceremony. Roland took charge of the turkey, Audrey baked the dressing, and the rest of the family pitched in where they could. Beginning at six years old, Jackie made the potato salad.

As they gathered around the bounty, Roland said grace, then poured each child an ounce of Mogen David wine, lifting his glass to announce a toast. "To the waist, to the taste," he said. No one knew what it meant, but it felt like gratitude. After the meal, the Detroit Lions played on TV. Jackie couldn't take his eyes off the game, even as others surrendered to naps.

A MONTH BEFORE Jackie's sixth birthday, civil rights leaders gathered at the New Zion Baptist Church in Central City, just a few blocks from the Greater Mt. Rose. There, 28-year-old Martin Luther King Jr. met with local civil rights leaders and formed the Southern Leadership Conference, which renamed itself the Southern Christian Leadership Conference later that year. The group elected King the group's first president. A new day for civil rights had dawned. When march organizers needed children to hold signs for the demonstrations, Audrey pushed Jackie to the front row, strategically positioned for the news cameras. The organizers loved it, and the news photographers ate it up. A few years later, and just across town, first-grader Ruby Bridges made history when she boldly walked through a screaming crowd of protesters into an all-white elementary school. In her six-year-old innocence, Ruby thought she had wandered into a wild Mardi Gras celebration.

Jackie watched in awe as the national movement took hold on television—the sit-ins, the marches on Washington, I Have a Dream, the Civil Rights Act. He couldn't believe the leader's boldness as they spoke about empowerment and self-determination in the face of racial struggle. These were dangerous times for a black man in the South. Even as a child, Jackie could sense that someone could die over these words. He could feel it.

Unlike Jackie in Central City, I was sheltered from the racial tensions that escalated year after year and as one event flowed into the next. James Meredith integrated Ole Miss in 1962. As a six-year-old, I didn't notice. In 1964, when a white family in town offered aid to voter-registration workers, racists threatening violence drove them from town. No one told me. Two years later, Meredith planned a lone march from Memphis to Jackson that he called his March Against Fear. A sniper shot him on the second day, near Hernando. I didn't hear a word about it.

I didn't know what civil rights meant, much less why Mom and Dad sat glued to the television set every time President Kennedy spoke. In the schoolyard, children called Kennedy a "nigger lover." The older boys chanted, "Two, four, six, eight—we don't want to integrate! Eight, six, four, two—send those niggers to LSU!" I understand now that my parents were trying to protect my innocence by shielding me from the harsh news. Because of that, I remember my little town as quiet and peaceful.

We pretended to be Mayberry, but the truth played out in the shadows of night. Between 1882 and 1968, there were 539 lynchings in Mississippi, far more than any other state in the union. The weeks between April and November 1964, when I was eight years old, were especially violent for McComb, with more black church bombings in Pike County than any other county across the South. I heard whispers through my bedroom door one night about violence in town, whispers of the editor and publisher of McComb's *Enterprise-Journal,* Oliver Emmerich, being pushed through a plate-glass window for his liberal stance on integration. Mom cried many nights over the tensions, even more when we woke to find a KKK poster randomly tacked to a tree in our front yard. It featured the face of a man, half black, half white. It read: "Don't be just half a man. Join the Klan." Mom and Dad were horrified and torn. I remember their dilemma. If they ripped it down, they'd surely invite the Klan's wrath. If they left it, neighbors would assume we were supporters. Worse yet, they may think we'd put it there. All I knew was that by the following morning the sign had been taken down.

That's not all I worried about. I was entering the age of accountability.

In the sixties, before southern pastors began emphasizing God's
amazing grace, many preachers relied on hellfire and brimstone to
inspire altar calls. The sermons terrified me into cold-sweat night-
mares of stars falling from the sky and gaping gashes in the ground
swallowing me whole. But even so, my innate shyness kept me
from responding to the call of salvation and baptism. And much
like Audrey, my mother didn't push me on it. Week after week of
inaction turned into years of anxiety and guilt over my unforgiven
sins. I sincerely feared the fires of hell.

My day of reckoning came one Sunday while sitting with my
preteen friends among the front pews. The preacher wrapped up
his sermon and offered his usual invitation. We all stood to sing a
familiar hymn:

Oh, do not let the Word depart, and close thine eyes against
  the light;
Poor sinner harden not your heart, be saved, oh, tonight.

Tomorrow's sun may never rise, to bless thy long-deluded sight;
This is the time, oh, then be wise. Be saved, oh, tonight.

As the sweet, four-part harmony prodded me, the double doors
in the rear of our small building abruptly swung open. I felt the air
suck from the sanctuary. Every head turned, except mine. I froze,
locked with dread. Wild eyes darted all around. Mouths gaped.
The song leader held his composure as we continued to sing, but
the cadence had lost its rhythm. The preacher's son, standing beside me, whispered, "Do you see who just walked in?" I nodded
yes—a lie—but I already knew. The Rapture had begun, and I
had been found waiting and without hope. I wanted to pray, but

I had waited too long. Jesus had returned to judge the world. And he had chosen the McComb Church of Christ to make his first appearance.

Despite this stunning turn of events, closing words were spoken anyway, which were met with a deep, booming voice from the back pew that bellowed, "AMEN!" I shrunk in fear and almost cried. Another booming "AMEN!" followed the benediction. Finally, after an eternal pause, I turned to face my maker. And there he stood in all his majesty at the end of the pew in the back row: a black man.

The man, a traveler with his family, had assumed that our services started at eleven like most other churches across the South. The congregation mingled and spoke politely, stunned by his audacity. I just thanked God the man wasn't Jesus.

As I grew older, I believed that these attitudes and reactions about race wouldn't last forever. I saw them as lingering inheritances from another era—a worn-out legacy of fear and mistrust. I knew that the good people of my hometown far outweighed the few who stirred up trouble that led to violence.

I grew to measure a man by his callused hands and his charitable heart and distrust a man filled with bitterness and shallow hatred. I grew to appreciate holiness and moral obligation as I listened to my preacher's sermons. They taught me that God's blessings came with moral obligation and heavy responsibilities.

I learned my most indelible lessons of charity, compassion, and honesty directly from my parents and their parents. I watched my father's faith grow through his distaste for hypocrisy. He was known for his quiet generosity as he offered shelter to hapless and penniless travelers. I watched my mother as she discovered her spiritual gift for hospitality. She visited and comforted the sick more than anyone I knew. And my grandfather was called "honest to his own hurt" after he discovered a blemish on a calf that he'd already sold. I was surrounded and raised by good people.

I carried those noble lessons with me as I grew older. We all know we aren't perfect, but we all know we could be better.

But my sheltered upbringing isolated me from a changing world. The news stories I saw on television about Vietnam, Woodstock, Martin Luther King Jr., and urban poverty seemed to be happening in another dimension. And as the civil rights movement churned across the South, the ground shifted beneath our feet. I still had a lot to learn.

By the time I turned thirteen, I had still never heard of a housing project.

ROLAND WALLACE'S HARD work and steady pay raises at his job on the wharf eventually disqualified the family from subsidized housing, and their St. Bernard apartment, so he found a rental house in Central City close to Audrey's church. The move came in 1964 at the height of the segregation movement, as whites fled to the suburbs, leaving new real estate opportunities for blacks. But Central City had been historically black, settled by emancipated Protestants and non-Creoles moving from rural areas. Whereas the St. Bernard Project had unwittingly isolated the family ethnically, the new neighborhood felt more culturally open and engaged.

Jackie saw New Orleans culture first in Central City, mostly from his Liberty Street stoop, where bands of black men costumed as Mardi Gras Indians roamed neighborhoods with wild shouts and rhythmic taunts. An adoring entourage surrounded the Big Chief as he strutted in his prodigious outfit, hand stitched from a four-week paycheck's worth of beads, sequins, rhinestones, and ostrich plumes. A trailing Flag Boy waved the squad's emblem on a fanciful staff of feathers. The Spy Boy—whimsically conceived yet menacingly commissioned—prowled ahead of the group, scouting for competing "tribes" to either avoid or challenge in a duel of Big Chief finery. He saw it on Fat Tuesday when, as a twelve-year-old, he and a friend wandered down to Shakespeare Park at Washington Avenue to watch krewes as they prepared to board their floats. Red tractors attached to papier-mâché figures lined up beneath hundred-year-old oaks and behind more than three hundred years of tradition. Black-faced Zulus chomping giant plastic cigars hurled hand-painted coconuts and trinkets at the gathering mamas, daddies, and their babies. As the ludicrous, whimsical, beautiful machines lurched forward, the crowd surged in, with arms flailing and with screams that fell just short of heaven.

As Jackie leapt for the prized coconuts and dodged others, his friend offered him a bottle of rum. He swigged a mouthful with little thought—a rude awakening for a preteen. Unlike the yearly toast of Mogen David wine at Thanksgiving, this drink burned his throat, tripped his head, and wobbled his legs. He held it together as he staggered through his morning.

The rite of passage didn't lead to trouble—at least not yet.

Jackie's new home at South Liberty Street, at the corner of Terpsichore (pronounced locally as TERP-sick-core), offered much more style and grace than the brick monoliths of the St. Bernard Project. But what it offered in form, it took back in function. The classic New Orleans shotgun double is fundamentally a duplex with two one-room-wide apartments with a common wall separating the two. The Wallace family rented the right side.

The front wood facade featured one door and one window, mirrored on the neighbor's side. A gabled roofline added a small but elegant overhang to protect the two concrete stoops from the New Orleans rain. Since a shotgun house has no hallways, one room led directly into another. The whole apartment measured 884 square feet, about the same size and dimensions of a standard railroad box-car. Twelve-foot ceilings offered the false impression of space.

The family of eight felt cramped. Two of the boys, Roland Jr. and Dabney, made their bed in the front living room. Mama and Dad took the second room. Donald, Jackie, Louvinia, and Margo packed into the third room, with the boys sharing one double bed and the girls another. The beds left barely enough room to squeeze past into the kitchen.

From the living room window, Jackie could see the downtown city's lights that glittered just over the Greater Mt. Rose Baptist Church three blocks away. But these days, the church captured less and less of Jackie's imagination, his attention drawn instead eight blocks upriver, as New Orleans directions go, to Shakespeare Park and its five open acres of grass. Immediately behind the playground stood Carter G. Woodson Junior High School and his new social center.

There, Jackie found new friends and fell for his first girlfriend, Wanda White. He caught her attention by saving the side of her head from a flying coconut. How many young loves start like that?

Jackie often wondered. The two became a couple in the classroom, in the school yard, after school, and after ball games. However, Wanda's mother didn't approve of the relationship at all and tried to push them apart, telling him, "You're nothing but a black, nappy-headed nigger from the project." He'd never thought of himself as inferior, but now the words left him stunned and speechless. For the first time, he began to piece together his dad's heritage in Donaldsonville and its connection to antebellum plantations. When he thought about the implications, he pushed the probable links to slavery deep down into his gut. If it were true, he didn't want to know. He took Roland's advice and focused instead on his future. He filtered out the distractions, like a horse fitted with blinders. His daddy taught him to forget about the past. He saw it as a form of hatred and as the last thing he needed in his life.

His fears of the past caused him to rebel against his own culture. He cast a skeptical eye on the second lines and the whooping Indians. He came to think of gumbo, fried chicken, and chitlins as mere slave food. He cringed when people told him what he should do with his life, suggestions ranging from dancing to playing music and singing to the tourists to working as a longshoreman. Instead, the words of Martin Luther King Jr. inspired him to see America as a land of opportunities despite its racist past. He looked past all the negative stereotypes in his life and locked on to King's dream. From then on, he imagined open doors everywhere he looked. And when he found a real one, he stepped through it. He saw his greatest opportunity in baseball.

Baseball lit a competitive drive in Jackie's mind. He pounded his ball into his glove as he walked the broken sidewalks to Shakespeare Park. There he studied his stance at the plate and focused on his swing. He smiled as he watched his hits fly farther and farther. He learned to love the smell of his well-oiled leather glove and the feel of the ball's seams across the tips of his fingers. He longed for more time with the neighborhood leagues as they formed teams with real rosters, dugouts, and uniforms. Steady workouts added muscles to his lanky limbs, adding speed and accuracy to his throws. And he loved the attention and instruction he received from his coaches and teachers—especially Winston Burns.

Coach Burns was a growing legend in New Orleans. A handsome black man with a tight mustache, the forty-year-old veteran of World War II and the Korean conflict would eventually be decorated with the Congressional Gold Medal. He joined Woodson as a physical education teacher in the early sixties and served as the school's disciplinarian. Winston's background made him perfectly suited for the task of keeping the rough boys in line—a nightmare for most teachers. He gave the boys "the look" that made them feel ashamed for not putting their best foot forward. Students rewarded Coach Burns with a respect bordering on reverence. His knack for recognizing talent, spirit, heart, and dedication identified something special in Jackie. Champ Clark, the sports columnist who'd watched Jackie and Donald since St. Bernard, saw the same spark on the baseball diamond. As the boys' stats grew more impressive, Champ began dropping the Wallace brothers' names into his sports columns.

One afternoon, Woodson principal Harold Boucree called Jackie aside as he walked down the hallway. "I need to talk with you," he said as he shooed Jackie's friends along. "Have you ever thought about St. Aug?" Boucree knew how to steer the school's best prospects into the best schools. His question suggested more than a passing thought. Boucree had recommended Jackie for an invitation from the school. For Jackie, it represented the chance of a lifetime.

Josephite priests founded St. Augustine Catholic High School in 1951 specifically for the education of young black Catholic men. In the mere fourteen years since its inception, the school had blossomed into an academic juggernaut. A story in the January 1, 1965, issue of *Time* magazine called it a "separate and superior" school. This invitation represented a chance to both get a first-class education and become a better human being. The invitation came with a tuition waiver, which could be considered a golden ticket to academic success.

St. Aug had a growing reputation for athletic excellence, too. Under a new, young football coach, Eddie Flint, the Purple Knights had won three state championships and one district championship in the past four years in the all-black LIALO League (Louisiana Interscholastic Athletic and Literary Organization). In 1966, segregation rules still didn't allow the black schools to compete against the whites.

As Jackie weighed his decision, close friends and even some family members cloaked their jealousy with ridicule and mockery. They called him a Tommy for trying to be like educated white folks. Others called him a faggot for attending an all-boys school. Jackie couldn't understand why wanting to be smart made him a target. He was like a crab trying to crawl free of the basket, he said, and the other crabs kept trying to pull him back in.

Jackie finished ninth grade at Woodson and entered St. Aug at the end of summer as a sophomore. He said goodbye to many of his old friends, some of whom he'd never relate to again. In a natural, end-of-summer split, Wanda White left for Cohen High. Donald also received an offer from St. Aug, but he decided on Booker T. Washington High instead, which many considered to be an "authentic black" school. There, Donald's interest in education waned as his reputation as a pitcher grew. Many considered him to be the best in all New Orleans.

St. Aug's campus felt small compared to its growing influence in the city, sandwiched between Law and Hope Streets along London Avenue. The two-story building with two wings and a parking lot took up every available square foot of space. After class, the baseball players walked to nearby Hardin Park.

The practice field had no outfield fence for home runs, no yard lines for the football team or goalposts for the kickers. Nothing but dirt and grass. Teammates recognized Jackie from the league play and introduced themselves. "Oh, you're Donald's brother," they'd say. Jackie would hold out his hand and say with a huge smile, "Yeah, I'm Jackiewallace," all one word, no space or breath. He made friends easily and learned to hit the fastball and the curve. He learned the secrets of speed—to lift his knees and pump his arms. He also joined the basketball team. Before long, Otis Washington, the junior varsity football coach, took note of the six-three, 170-pound sophomore. It was hard not to.

"You ever play football?" Coach Washington asked one day.

"No," Jackie answered without apology. He'd always enjoyed the touch games on the playground but didn't like hitting people, and he especially didn't like being hit.

Washington didn't listen, or if he did, Jackie's answer didn't register. "Yeah, you're gonna play football," and he escorted Jackie to the equipment lockers behind the school and shoved a uniform at him. "Try that on."

Jackie stripped down in the open walkway (the school didn't have a gymnasium or a locker room at the time) and, for the first time in his life, tugged on the snug-fitting pants and pads. He lifted the shoulder pads over his head and shifted them around for a fit. He couldn't find the adjustment straps because he had put them on backward. Washington laughed and rotated them around until they dropped into position. Washington sized a helmet for him and helped him stretch jersey number 10 over the pads. Chuckling at the awkward mess standing before him, he said, "We're going to make a quarterback out of you!" Jackie had no way of comprehending the magnitude of the moment. Like a small boat idling in the shallows, Jackie had been nudged into the cascading currents of his New Orleans destiny.

By the end of Jackie's tenth-grade season in 1966, Coach Washington had made good on his promise to make a quarterback out of him. He was tall and quick and could escape the pocket when he needed to. He could sprint for big gains and could roll out and throw across his body with ease. During the year-end football banquet, coaches honored Jackie as junior varsity back of the year.

As a junior, Jackie could hit a Coke case with a football from fifty yards—no sweat. Varsity coach Eddie Flint saw great potential in this young recruit. He watched as he threaded a swinging tire with a tight spiral like a dart. Jackie studied the playbook with uncommon comprehension. He carried a calm and collected temperament. His teammate Dale Brock described him as a gentle giant, "a big teddy bear," always looking out for others. No one ever remembered seeing him angry or upset, a rarity in the arena of high-stakes, testosterone-fueled competition. His execution still looked a bit raw, but his demeanor, talent, and size made him the perfect backup to quarterback Floyd Sandle.

The 1967 campaign opened with great promise. The Purple Knights had racked up a 26–0 record in the previous two and a half years and were eager to build on their previous dominance. But in the season opener, Booker T. Washington of Lake Charles shocked the Knights with a 30–27 lead with only seconds remaining on the clock. In a strategic gamble, Flint decided to test Jackie's arm. On his first-ever snap on a varsity field, Jackie threw a strike into the end zone for a touchdown. Pandemonium erupted until

players and fans noticed the penalty flag. A holding penalty nulli-
fied the touchdown and the win. The streak had ended, but Jackie's
career had just begun. Three games later, in his first start, Jackie
threw for two touchdowns and ran for another for an easy 28–0
win. The next two games would make Louisiana sports history and
help shape Jackie's young life. But first, a little background.

DURING ST. AUG's dominating run, sports fans, black and white,
whispered that the Purple Knights had a great football program—
at least by the standards of the all-black league. St. Aug knew it, too.
Everyone knew that white powerhouses dominated the gridiron.
Only by facing Jesuit, Holy Cross, Redemptorist, Rummel, De La
Salle, and St. Aloysius could anyone accurately gauge St. Aug's
talent.

No one wanted to prove St. Aug's fitness more than Flint and
the school's principal, Father Grant.

But when St. Aug applied to join the Louisiana High School
Athletic Association in August 1964 and again in '65, their ap-
plications were denied. The all-white LHSAA locked and barred
the admission process against them. Though the school met all
the league's requirements, the LHSAA voted 185 to 112 against
St. Aug. The public generally understood that the association had
rejected the application strictly over race.

St. Aug eventually filed suit against the league and ultimately
won in court. The ruling read, "The evidence amply supports the
inference that St. Augustine was denied membership on racial
grounds. No other reasonable inference is supported by the record
and no other explanation is offered to us." St. Aug essentially wiped
out prep school sports segregation in Louisiana.

The ruling came halfway through Jackie's junior season.

Coach Flint scrambled to rearrange and upgrade his schedule, starting with St. Aloysius on October 13, 1967, at City Park's Tad Gormley Stadium, confident St. Aug would dominate the Catholic League. Nearly ten thousand fans were expected, but twice that number piled in for the show. "Purple Power" banners hung from the tiers as the Knights trampled the Crusaders 26–7. A news article the next day included a short but revealing line: "There were no incidents."

The next two games brought sellout crowds, 26,500 for a 24,500-capacity stadium to see St. Aug lose two close games against Holy Cross, 29–21, and Jesuit, 13–6. As the Knights prepared for Redemptorist, LHSAA Commissioner T. H. "Muddy" Waters stepped in and declared that forty-five St. Aug athletes, including nineteen members of the football team, were academically ineligible for athletic competition mainly based on St. Aug's use of *Time* magazine—an unapproved textbook—in teaching a civics course. He fined the school $100 and forced a forfeiture of the three games in which the offending athletes had played, including their historic win over St. Aloysius. This all came on the heels of civil rights leaders being jailed and black churches being bombed across the South. Riots were breaking out in nearby Bogalusa, Malcolm X had been assassinated, and the Klan and the Black Panthers were growing in influence across the South. School board members feared for their political futures, and parents feared for their children's safety.

The decision devastated the team. Star athletes, some competing for college scholarships, were sent to the bleachers. Now, the team needed Jackie—who had dodged the ax since he hadn't taken the civics course—as junior varsity players filled the vacant slots. Sophomore fullback Burton Burns, a friend of Jackie's and Winston Burns's son, shored up the decimated backfield.

With most of the team's power gone, the Purple Knights lost the rest of the season's games. Still, Jackie put up impressive numbers, throwing to junior wide receiver Ronald Arceneaux. A bulging press presence took notice of the team's accomplishments. Even with a final 3–7 season, the team had pulled off one of the most significant triumphs by integrating the white-only league. Although tensions remained, they had carried the hopes and dreams of the black community into battle and had won.

IN THE CLASSROOM, the sixteen-year-old excelled in his academic work. After school, his social life blossomed as well. Most of the brotherhood of students introduced their classmates to their sisters, who attended the all-girls St. Mary's across town. Parents hosted plenty of parties and dances throughout the year to bring them together. The "waistline parties" were especially popular, where the hosts measured the kids' waists at the door to determine their cost of admission. Thirty-two cents for a thirty-two-inch waist for all the food they could eat. The big boys didn't seem to mind—they got their money's worth.

Still inherently shy, Jackie used silly jokes to break the ice with the girls, who demurred and giggled and were generally overwhelmed by the attention from the handsome young quarterback. But despite the adulation, he kept his relationships casual, until his friend Eric Forest set him up on a blind, double date with Kate Sondra Smith. She was cute and intelligent. She and Jackie became regulars at St. Mary's family house parties, where they danced to Gladys Knight, the Temptations, and Aretha Franklin's "R.E.S.P.E.C.T."

Jackie and Eric would strut around in the same sharp clothes they wore to school, khaki pants, nice shoes, and occasionally a tie, a requirement for school. They mimicked James Brown's slick spins and dramatic knee drops with adolescent awkwardness.

Even though Jackie dabbled with underage drinking, which

was a natural, semi-endorsed part of the New Orleans culture, he didn't care much for alcohol. Even when his buddies sneaked in liquor and smoked weed, often offering him a drag, he'd wave them off casually; he enjoyed dancing with Kate more than getting high with the boys.

Roland and Audrey enjoyed watching the young couple's relationship blossom. But as Wanda White's mother before, Kate's mother, being "a bourgeois lady," dredged up Jackie's housing-project past to her daughter. But now, Jackie's St. Aug credentials raised his stock—proof of his hard work to better himself and his future.

Nineteen sixty-eight also proved to be a pivotal year for the nation. While the world heralded Mahalia Jackson and Louis Armstrong as shining ambassadors of New Orleans, the United States raced against the Soviets to land the first man on the moon. The North Vietnamese Communists launched the Tet Offensive, prompting Walter Cronkite to declare the Vietnam War effort "mired in stalemate." Antiwar protesters took to the streets on the heels of previous years' race riots. On April 3, amid the mounting social unrest, Martin Luther King Jr. preached before a group of striking sanitation workers in Memphis. He said, "Like anybody, I would like to live a long life—longevity has its place. But I'm not concerned about that now . . . I've seen the Promised Land. I may not get there with you."

On April 4, 1968, while Jackie and his classmates concentrated on their studies, the news broke that Martin Luther King Jr. had been shot and killed on the balcony of the Lorraine Motel in Memphis. The next day, Jackie and his classmates walked out of class in protest. The Josephite priests, concerned about violent clashes and riots breaking out across the country, sat the boys down and prepared them for the coming days. "As you walk the streets, police officers will stop you and question you just to see what was going on," they told them. "Here's what you have to say: 'I attend St. Augustine High

School. Whatever you want me to do, sir, I will do it.' Wear your black shirts. Make your statement. But remember, St. Aug men are expected to be jewels of the community. Don't tarnish the jewel."

As a result of the LHSAA commissioner's ruling the year before, St. Aug played the 1968 season on academic probation. As Jackie stepped into the starting quarterback role, he took responsibility for directing the inexperienced players. He scolded receivers who ran poor routes and linemen, many of them young, who missed their blocks.

Around the league, St. Aug still carried the reputation of a football powerhouse. But inside the huddle, Jackie remembers eleven scared kids. Times were tense. They were still the only black school in the association, and the white schools stacked their odds by passing around their St. Aug scouting reports and game plans. Refs called a biased game. Instead of first and ten, Jackie accepted that every series started with first and twenty-five. Jackie also understood that the white players with Jesuit and De La Salle were the forerunners of the city's power structure. The battle extended far beyond football.

Still, Jackie dominated the headlines and tally sheets, completing 78 out of 167 attempts with only 7 interceptions through October 24. In a highly touted homecoming game at City Park's stadium, Jackie threw for 227 yards, and Burton Burns, the promising young sophomore, ran for two late touchdowns in a disappointing 21–19 loss. The next week, Jackie threw for 180 yards and ran for 184 more. Although the young and mostly inexperienced team finished the season with three wins, five losses, and two ties, Jackie led the league with 103 completions.

Jackie graduated St. Aug with honors and was eager to celebrate his success. On his last day of school, as Jackie and Eric Forest caught the bus for home, something inside Jackie's brain clicked, a feeling he described as a random, spontaneous burst of destiny. "To hell with it, Eric," he said. "Let's go get some Old Forester and get drunk."

EVEN WITH HIS spectacular season behind him, there were no scholarship offers from Southeastern Conference schools. There were no calls or letters from LSU, eighty miles away. Surely, they'd been watching. But the silence didn't surprise anyone. The SEC had never recruited a black player until the University of Kentucky signed Nathaniel Northington in 1967. Neither LSU nor Alabama had a black football player on their teams until 1971. Before that, black players left the South in droves. The SEC began their decades-long domination of the NCAA once they claimed their local black athletes.

But schools across the nation were beginning to recognize the black talent coming from New Orleans, including USC, Oklahoma, and Nebraska. Notre Dame actively recruited Jackie as their next-generation quarterback. Coach Otis Washington advised Jackie to also keep his eye on the University of Arizona, who had just recently picked up several black players from New Orleans. But the only thing Jackie had ever heard about Tucson was the shootout at the O.K. Corral. Wasn't Tucson somewhere near Tombstone?

To help him expedite his decision, Notre Dame invited him to their campus in South Bend, Indiana, and sent a plane ticket so he could spend time with Coach Ara Parseghian and Notre Dame's two quarterbacks, Terry Hanratty and Joe Theismann. The opportunity excited him. He'd never been on a plane before. In fact, he'd never traveled outside the city.

Jackie packed a large suitcase and called Kate before leaving for the airport. He told her he'd miss her but that he wouldn't be gone long. When he arrived in Chicago, he got confused trying to navigate O'Hare Airport. His sponsor, Notre Dame shooting guard Austin Carr, finally found him waiting in the wrong terminal. On the two-hour drive from Chicago to South Bend, Carr pulled out three one-hundred-dollar bills from his pocket and handed them to the wide-eyed youngster. His spending money—his first payoff, as Jackie remembered. The offer caught Jackie by surprise, but then he spoke his mind: "If you're giving me three, how much did they give to you?" Austin smiled and drove on. "You're going to do all right here," he said. "Just fine."

Upon his return to Liberty Street, Jackie found a scholarship offer from Arizona. He put it aside for the moment and handed the $300 to his dad, who looked at the cash and said, "Boy, you're going to one of those colleges. I don't know which one, but you're going to one of them." Three hundred dollars represented more money than Roland made in a week, and Jackie had "earned" it simply by showing up.

Audrey couldn't have cared less about the cash or the colleges, and she resisted the outside appeals for her son's attention. Why couldn't he just stay close to home like Roland Jr. and Louvinia—or maybe attend other historically black colleges nearby, like Grambling or Mississippi Valley State? She couldn't imagine him being so far away. Kate didn't make Jackie's decision any easier. She threatened to break up with him if he left the state. Roland, as he was wont to do, advised his son. In matters of love, he told him, whatever divides you will always divide you. Cut the tie, and never look back.

Ultimately, the coddling from Audrey and the pressure from Kate made him want to leave even more. In New Orleans, Jackie could imagine only three opportunities for a black man: a job in the service industry, athletics, or working for the white man. St. Aug had opened him up to a new world, one he was keen on embracing.

There was a crucial detail that made Jackie's decision easier. Notre Dame admitted only male students. After four years at St. Aug, Jackie was tired of that. He found the national interconference letter of intent for Arizona, signed it, and sent it back.

CHAPTER THREE

The Wildcat

1969–1973

Jackie knew that Texas was big, but he was surprised at *how* big as he gawked from the windows of the Greyhound bus carrying him west from Louisiana. It was 1,410 miles from downtown New Orleans to downtown Tucson. Across the Lone Star State, the landscape took its time transforming from piney woods to barren sands and burnt orange sunsets. As Jackie crossed New Mexico and into Arizona, he saw the same iconic cactus he remembered from *Wagon Train,* tall and erect as if drawn for a cartoon. The dry air made his skin tingle. He had been raised below sea level on reclaimed swampland. Now the elevation took his breath away. Framed by mountains, Tucson appeared to him to have been built around the university campus—more specifically, around Arizona Stadium.

Since he'd always been good with numbers, he declared a major in mathematics with an accounting minor. When he stepped into his first classroom, his calculus professor assumed he was confused and lost. "Mr. Wallace, are you sure you're in the right class?"

"Yes, sir."

"You're from Louisiana?"

"Yes, sir."

"What about all the remedial courses you need to get in here?"

"You mean trigonometry, algebra?"

"Yes, sir. You should take those first. Otherwise, I'm not sure you'll be able to stay up with the class."

"Try me," he said, confident and eager to prove his pedigree.

Jackie's placement test, taken a few days later, sufficiently impressed the professor. "This is not what most people from Louisiana do," he said.

Jackie smiled. "That may be true," he said, "but I'm from St. Aug."

His intellect aside, Jackie found it intimidating to interact with the white students. Southern culture had taught him to shift his eyes away from white women and that talking to them could lead to a beating, or worse. So, naturally, Jackie looked away when Andrea Weinberg walked into English class. The pretty, blond co-ed from Shawnee Mission, Kansas, scanned the room for an empty seat and spotted one next to Jackie. Hoping to make a new friend, she approached.

"Excuse me, is there anyone sitting next to you?" she said, trying to be polite. Jackie felt the blood rush to his face and turned his head toward the wall. She rephrased her question and tried again. "Excuse me, sir, is there anyone sitting here?" Jackie's eyes shifted again, this time to the floor. His fingers tensed along the edge of the desktop. He talked to himself under his breath: "Just take the seat—just sit down and shut up." He couldn't understand why she was provoking him.

This time, Andrea cut loose. "Look, you black-assed nigger, I'm talking to you. Is anybody sitting here?" Much like Jackie's last day of high school, something clicked inside his brain. He leapt to his feet and partially knocked his desk into the wall. His books and papers scattered across the floor. Andrea held her ground without a flinch and pushed a hand into his chest. "Before you hit me," she warned, "I asked you two times nicely. I just called you what you *expected* to hear."

This time she softened her voice so he'd know he wasn't in the South anymore—and smiled.

"Is it OK if I sit by you?"

He opened his mouth to speak, but his words failed him. He'd never talked to a Caucasian girl as an equal. He smiled and awkwardly held out his hand. "Hi, I'm Jackiewallace." He realized that he was no longer in New Orleans and that he'd found his first white friend.

HIS TEAMMATES HAILED from foreign-sounding lands like San Francisco, Sacramento, and Oakland. Seventeen out of Arizona's twenty-one out-of-state recruits were from Southern California. But he and Caesar Pittman, a punt returner from New Orleans' Booker T. Washington, were the mysterious ones. In the dorms at night, they were peppered with questions about their exotic state. Do you know how to make a roux? Jambalaya? Do you know any Cajuns? Do you fish in the bayous? What's a krewe? What's a flambeau? Jackie didn't care for this kind of attention. He didn't come to Arizona to be a poster boy for Louisiana. He wanted to learn about Arizona. He wanted to learn about everything.

On the Arizona practice field, Jackie had a lot to prove if he wanted to keep his scholarship. In 1969, NCAA freshmen were prohibited from playing with the varsity team, so he had to earn his stripes on a freshman team on an abbreviated schedule. His main job was to adjust to college sports so he'd be ready for his sophomore season.

Nineteen sixty-nine was also thirty-five-year-old-coach Bob Weber's debut season. After three years assisting and coordinating at other schools, he was finally getting his chance to coach at the senior college level. The Wildcats were now his team, complete with a roster full of eager faces and a backfield flush with quarterbacks. He didn't need another quarterback, especially a black one, so he introduced Jackie to defensive back coach Fred Glick, a former all-pro safety with the Houston Oilers. Jackie offered no resistance. He didn't care how Weber used him as long as he kept his scholarship.

Jackie easily adapted under Glick. Instead of throwing tight spirals, he learned to catch them. Instead of sprinting for the open field, he learned to rush into the action. He maneuvered across pass routes and read the quarterback's eyes. He practiced his backpedal by walking backward across campus and running backward upstairs, building his speed to match the fastest wide receivers on the field. He learned how to catch with his hands instead of his chest. He learned to form-run to decrease his drag, lowering his time to 4.5 seconds in the forty-yard dash. Further, Glick taught him how to play bump-and-run against receivers and how to lead his tackles with his shoulder pads or the crown of his helmet. He taught the basics of the day: hit them hard, wrap up, and keep driving. "It was as simple as that," Jackie said. Most importantly, Jackie began to trust his coaches.

MR. HEARN, ON the other hand, didn't trust anyone. He didn't even like giving out his first name. For good or ill, his career in Air Force intelligence taught him suspicion, and his new job with the FBI didn't change that. He especially distrusted boys around his pretty, college freshman co-ed daughter, Jacqueline. To mitigate "problems" from boys, he insisted that she dress in long skirts, saddle oxfords, and no makeup, especially when she worked around the jocks in her campus job as a hospitality hostess.

Jacqueline, who was black, met Jackie her first semester, when a friend introduced them. "Jackie, have you met Jackie?" She looked at him and instantly saw someone special. He wasn't muscular or boastful like the other players, but tall, thin, and sweet. He sported a tight Afro and dressed in a casual college style—slacks and penny loafers.

He took her hand and smiled, "Hello, beautiful."

Thanks to her dad's strict rules, no one had ever talked to her like that. Although Jackie had meant it in a friendly, flirty way, she was captivated and thought it might lead to something more.

But the two quickly developed a brother-sister relationship. They'd tell friends that they were twins—"Jackie and Jackie"— and that their mother liked the name so much she had used it twice. He always greeted her with a peck on the cheek. And because he was a true gentleman, even Mr. Hearn approved. If guys cursed around her, Jackie would remind them that they were in the presence of a lady. She thought of him as an angel. He alternately charmed and deflected her compliments. Jacqueline even teased Jackie that one day they'd get married, but he'd put her off with a joke and a smile. "No, siblings can't do that."

Jackie's white friend, Andrea Weinberg, had a sibling-like relationship with Jackie as well. She came from a rich Kansas family but carried herself with an honest, easy way that Jackie liked. Andrea was attracted by his intellect. They'd often turn heads when they went out together—a black man with a white Jewish woman—so they preferred to socialize in groups. And because Jacqueline's parents were so strict, the two women never met.

Jackie also enjoyed his time alone. On weekends, when most freshmen enjoyed keg parties and social mixers, he explored the desert with a tent and camped alone in the mountains. There, he built a small fire and warmed a portion of "Mad Dog" 20/20 fortified wine in a cowboy-style tin cup for the last, serene salute to the fading light. He felt peace in his new home.

SPRING IN TUCSON meant wildflowers and rattlesnakes in the desert, short pants and sandals on the campus, and the annual football showcase, the Wildcats' Red and White Spring Game. Coach Weber had slogged through a disappointing 3–7 season in 1969 and was now counting on his incoming class to breathe new hope into the team. In the Red and White Game, Jackie didn't disappoint his coaches, the fans, or the sportswriters. He covered his receivers well and returned an interception for a ninety-yard touchdown. The *Tucson Daily Citizen* predicted that he'd be a key man on defense. With his ego properly stoked, Jackie counted the days until he could prove himself in a regular-season game.

ON SATURDAY MORNING, September 19, 1970, Jackie twitched excitedly as the team bus drove onto the University of Michigan campus in Ann Arbor. But Jackie wasn't as impressed as he thought he'd be as the famed Michigan Stadium came into view. From a distance, the "Big House" didn't look so big. The low-slung profile reminded him of his 26,000-seat high school stadium back home. But up close, and inside, he realized he'd misjudged the size. And when he walked out on the Michigan Stadium field before 80,386 rabid Wolverine fans, he suddenly learned how small he felt in the largest college-owned football stadium in the country. He'd never attended a big-time college football game before. And now, he was about to start at safety for Arizona. During warm-ups, he tested his footing on the Tartan Turf, the latest and finest variation of artificial grass. He wore special shoes, with smaller cleats for a better grip. He'd flown here on a chartered jet. He looked around and savored the moment.

The television announcer called his name for the national audience as he trotted onto the field in his white jersey, emblazoned with a red 25, white pants, blue trim, and a cherry-red helmet. He could barely contain his nerves. He knew his mom and dad, his siblings, and all his friends from New Orleans and Tucson would be watching. He thought back to his tense moments on the field at St. Aug, when he kept his cool by telling a joke in the huddle or by simply remembering that football was only a game. But here, when the crowd roared and the Michigan band played "The Victors" fight song, he realized that he'd been kidding himself. Football was big business.

No one expected much from the Wildcats that day. Michigan, a twenty-two-point favorite, was ranked eighth in the nation. Most sports fans still thought of Arizona as basketball country. The Wildcats were hoping to change that.

The game began as expected, with Michigan scoring in their second and third possessions. But the scrappy Wildcats fought back with a pair of field goals. Then Arizona's defense shocked even themselves by holding the Wolverines scoreless for two and a half quarters. The offense added another field goal. With only three minutes left in the game, Michigan led by only one point, 10–9. As seconds ticked down, Michigan flexed their pedigree and scored twice to put the game away, 20–9. But even in defeat, the headline read: "Cats Win Respect in Loss to Michigan."

Back in Arizona, Coach Weber made some adjustments. Caesar Pittman's blazing speed—9.6 in the one-hundred-yard dash—had proved to be a great asset against Michigan when he returned a kickoff forty-six yards early in the game. As a result, Weber moved him to running back, giving Jackie a chance to handle punt return duties, something he'd never tried before. At first, he misjudged the high ones. Others slipped through his hands. But as he practiced, he discovered on his own how to flex his fingers to create a softer touch on the ball. He figured that if he held his right hand higher to stop the spiral force and if he used his left hand to stop the momentum, he could control the catch. It worked. He practiced his new strategy until his muscle memory kicked in. He coordinated with his gunner blockers on fair-catch decisions. With their better perspective on the coverage, they yelled "Mardi Gras" for a fair catch or "New Orleans" for a return. After the catch, he focused on the moment when a defender transitioned into tackling mode. One juke to the left or to the right, and he was off to the races. Practice made perfect. Perfect turned into reflex.

After Michigan, the Wildcats entered their home opener with lofty expectations. Nearly thirty-nine thousand fans piled into the forty-thousand-capacity stadium—a new record—to watch the Wildcats eke out a 30–29 win against San Jose State—a "tragic comedy of errors," one writer said. But late in the third quarter, Jackie used his new technique to field his first punt. Forty-four yards later, he'd scored his first college touchdown.

The Wildcats extended their winning streak on mediocre performances against mediocre opponents. But as a defensive back, Jackie's tackles grew more aggressive. His pass coverage grew more refined. His punt returns brought the fans to their feet and often left them dancing in the aisles. After week five, the Wildcats had clawed their way to a 3–2 record. But their biggest opponent lay ahead—a group of high-flying, highly rated Falcons from Colorado Springs: Air Force.

In October 1970, Air Force was ranked seventh in the nation—and undefeated—and marked the Wildcats' second top-ten opponent in six weeks.

Once again, the Wildcats rose to the level of their competition. They dominated on both offense and defense and built a 20–7 lead against the heavily favored Falcons. With only 9:02 left in the game, the Wildcats forced Air Force to punt to Jackie. But the ball seemed to drop straight down on him, and he lost his angle. The tip ricocheted off his elbow, and Air Force recovered on Arizona's 13-yard line and scored a few plays later. On their next possession, Air Force scored again but missed the extra point, which left the game tied. With time winding down, Air Force again drove downfield for a potential game-winning field goal attempt. Eager to make up for his earlier fumbled punt, Jackie dove with full extension as he tried for a block. He missed, but the kick sailed wide as Jackie rolled into the kicker, causing a roughing-the-kicker penalty that gave the Falcons a second chance from twenty yards out. This time, the kick sailed true, giving Air Force a 23–20 victory.

The team was nothing short of devastated. One coach cried. Jackie sat alone on a locker-room bench, speechless. In two plays, he alone had blown the game. The press howled. The fans slumped out of the stadium. In a screaming rage, Weber threatened to take his scholarship away.

A few days later, when the Tucson Towncats boosters club met for their weekly luncheon to review the game film, they were disappointed to find that the final seconds of the game had been snipped off the film. It had been cut because the coaches couldn't bear to watch it.

Jackie lost his starting position, along with several other sophomores, but the move helped him realize that he'd grown a little cocky. Maybe he didn't know as much as he thought. After two more losses, Weber rearranged his roster again and started ten sophomores for the last two games of the season. Jackie got another chance to prove himself—this time, with his ego checked. They won the next game but lost their finale to ninth-ranked Arizona State to close their season with a disappointing 4–6 record. But the team and their fans were buoyed in knowing they'd lost to three top-ten teams by a total of only 18 points.

Still, 1970 was a breakout year for Jackie. He made headlines and built a fan base. His stock rose. Girls swooned. Men idolized him.

AWAY FROM SPORTS, Jackie looked for opportunities to explore new interests. Many of Jackie's black friends and teammates were interested in the black Muslim movement on campus, formally known as the Nation of Islam. Local organizers invited Jackie, maybe even pressured him, to attend their house parties. Because of his connection with sports, he may have been targeted as a valuable recruit. Jackie saw no harm in learning more, so he tagged along.

At the meetings, he expected to hear inspirational messages of self-determination and empowerment but instead felt bombarded with radical dissent, conflict, and militarism. He learned that a decade before, the FBI had described the group as "an especially anti-American and violent cult." And while the speakers laid out their message with passion and enthusiasm, Jackie heard bitterness, and it turned him off.

They preached that a black man shouldn't worship a white Jesus. The speakers' logic followed that if the Chinese followed Buddha, who looked Chinese, and if white men worshipped a white Christ, then a Negro should worship a Negro god, which meant Muhammad. If Jackie wanted to be accepted into the group, they said, he'd have to fully denounce Christianity. The group demanded a clear choice.

Organizers held up Muhammad Ali—who joined the Nation of Islam in 1964—as Jackie's example. He, like Ali, could use his notoriety as an athlete to fight for justice. But Jackie had seen what "they" did to Martin Luther King Jr., Malcolm X, and others. Were they calling him to be a martyr?

He told the Muslims that he'd think about it, an honest response that he didn't intend to be dismissive. He pored over the Bible and the Koran and tried his best to understand both. But the more he studied and the more meetings he attended, the more confused he became. The Nation of Islam's teachings ran counter to everything he'd been taught in New Orleans, in church, at home, and in the civil rights movement. King taught unity. His parents taught unity. Christianity taught unity. He believed that everybody, regardless of race, had value.

The more Jackie pondered the Muslim teachings, the more his Baptist roots beckoned him. He looked forward to Sunday services, when he could find a soothing reminder of family, home, and a dependable diet of the Baptist Gospel. Old Testament sermons reminded him of his parents' favorite movie, *The Ten Commandments*. Jackie was inspired by Charlton Heston's portrayal of Moses's words: "Let my people go!" He enjoyed the sermons of faith and forgiveness and the old-time spirituals like "Swing Low, Sweet Chariot," which transported his mind back to Miss Sally's living room. Besides the reliable sermons, church socials were a great place to meet new friends, and he didn't feel guilty about mixing spiritual business with pleasure. After services one Sunday, one young woman caught his eye. Like so many times before, he introduced himself with an outstretched hand and a broad smile.

"Hi, I'm Jackie—"

"Wallace," she said. "I know who you are. Hi, I'm Mary Hall."

Mary Janet Hall, to be precise—a university student who grew up in Tucson. She was built like a "Big Ten girl" as Jackie described her: five feet eight inches with "thick hips and big legs," just the way he liked them—not petite and frail like SEC girls. She had a light complexion, a little darker than "red bone" but nothing near "chocolate." They started dating almost immediately. His friend Andrea approved.

As their relationship grew, Jackie shared his conflicted views about religion. Mary thought he needed to take a long, hard look at his spiritual priorities—and to take his love for God more seriously. Maybe she saw how he had used church as a social club, or worse yet, as a ruse to meet girls. Maybe he needed to turn his problems and his life over to Jesus. She challenged him to commit.

Jackie's Nation of Islam friends also pressed for a commitment. But Jackie believed their teachings to be nothing more than a reverse of southern discrimination. Sure, he could see a power imbalance, but he couldn't imagine that more hatred and division could solve anything. If he followed the separatist concept, Jackie figured that he would "leave a multicultural country of assholes, to live in a singular-cultural country of assholes." Andrea reminded him that people came in all colors, and each had its share of assholes. Instead of fighting against the system, Jackie simply wanted a God of unity.

His decision didn't sit well with the Muslims, which made him worry about his personal safety. He thought about how Malcolm X and Martin Luther King Jr. had both died violently before turning forty. Friends told him he was overreacting, but he couldn't ignore the physical stomachaches this paranoia caused. He woke up in a cold sweat. He worried that he might disappear in the middle of the night.

With Mary's encouragement, he decided to make some changes in his life. He approached his pastor and asked to be baptized. He prayed the best way he knew how: "OK, God, I want to do whatever You want me to do. Let me be in Your corner, and I'll be all right." As he prayed, he suddenly felt release. As he rose from his baptism, he felt protected.

THE 1971 FOOTBALL season started with a bang. After two convincing wins, the Western Athletic Conference named Jackie their defensive player of the week. He also broke a conference record three weeks later with a ninety-four-yard punt return against UCLA, a conference record. But Weber's new offense was already sputtering, and the team fell to 3–4. Jackie was one of the team's few bright spots, which prompted one writer to suggest that the Wildcats should forgo trying to move the ball with their anemic offense. Just punt the ball on first down and wait for the opponents to punt to Jackie. He was their only chance to score! By now, Jackie was one of the conference's most exciting performers, averaging 16.1 yards per punt return, with three touchdowns on twenty-eight tries. Though the team finished with a disappointing 5–6 season, Jackie broke five school records, intercepted three passes in one game (twice), finished second in the nation with eleven interceptions, and returned punts for 510 yards and three touchdowns. He was named an AP All-American honorable mention.

But with his junior football season over and the semester finished, he had no interest in going home for Christmas. Nothing interested him except for Mary, so he invited her to spend the Christmas break in his dorm room. By the end of February, she broke the news. She was pregnant.

The couple planned their wedding as a simple ceremony in Mary's living room for March 4, 1972. Mary was nineteen. Jackie was nine days short of his twenty-first birthday.

Before the ceremony, Jackie and his best man, Barry Dean, a wide receiver from Pasadena, sat in the small fenced-in backyard. They pretended to be men while they sipped Jack Daniel's from paper cups and talked about life's curveballs. "You know, Jackie," Barry said, "we could jump this fence right now." They looked at each other and chuckled. "You know I couldn't do that to Mary," he said. "I can't do that to that woman. Come on." Jackie realized that he'd have to grow up—and quickly—and learn to take on new responsibilities. The time had come to step up as a man.

Once everyone had gathered in the living room, the minister unfolded his Bible and nodded to begin. Jackie blushed as Mary stepped out in her nicest dress and they joined hands. He slipped a ring on her finger and sealed the vow with a kiss. Mary's family, including her mother, two brothers, and her stepdad, were there, but Roland and Audrey sent their congratulations over the phone. They couldn't afford a bus ticket. But they wanted him to know how proud and happy they were for him.

Jackie didn't tell them about the baby.

The couple spent the night at a nice hotel in old Tucson and enjoyed a couple of days together. After a short stay in Mary's childhood bedroom, the young newlyweds moved into a house of their own. In 1971, Arizona scholarships allowed for free room and board and a $15 monthly stipend for pocket money. But for a star like Jackie—in the years before the NCAA clamped down hard on recruiting violations and under-the-table payments—there were other monies available. "Let's just put it this way," Jackie said. "I got a house. We didn't ask questions and all the rest of that. I just showed up and signed the papers. All the money was taken care of."

Other benefits followed. Many shop owners told him his money was no good in their establishments. Jackie could pick out items at no charge. He took a part-time job at H. Cook's Sporting Goods Store that paid much more than minimum wage. Power brokers arranged for a secretarial job for Mary, and suddenly she was making good money, too.

Before long, women vying for Jackie's affection started grousing about the nature of his marriage. They didn't believe Mary was pregnant at all. Jackie was destined for the NFL, and everybody knew it, so naturally, Mary had to be a gold digger. Jackie defended her honor. Mary wasn't that devious. He didn't ask for proof. He didn't need any proof. He trusted her. He loved her. But after only a month of marriage, she lost the baby.

Friends offered their support, but the jealous women kept piling on the pressure, encouraging him to file for divorce. He didn't believe the gossip, or he didn't want to believe it. He didn't know anymore. But as he focused on himself, he fell for the caustic talk. Eventually the mean-spirited whispers and comments took their toll. Jackie began withdrawing from his young bride, which was probably the worst thing he could have done. But as the young couple drifted emotionally and physically apart, Jackie says he never cheated on her. He just became hard to live with. As quickly as the marriage had come together, it began to break apart.

With such a chaotic summer, practices for the upcoming season made him increasingly more distant. He found it hard to concentrate in either place. Pressures began to build, and he didn't know how he would handle it.

Earlier in the year, just before Jackie's wedding, sports information director Frank Soltys began a massive public relations campaign to tout Jackie's credentials for All-American honors. He mailed five hundred pieces of propaganda to organizations, writers, editors, and coaches of influence. As the Wildcats' season ramped up in the fall, Soltys's efforts paid off. *Playboy* magazine named Jackie to their 1972 preseason All-American Team. Arizona fans were ecstatic. If they couldn't have a winning team, at least they could have a star.

Jackie and twenty-four other honorees from across the country

flew to Chicago to celebrate at Hugh Hefner's famed Playboy Mansion. There, the honorees met Hefner, danced with the *Playboy* Bunnies, and drank until they passed out, according to Jackie. The next morning, most of them battled massive hangovers and stumbled through the 9:00 A.M. photo shoot. He remembered it as one of the best parties he'd ever attended.

After the magazine published the photograph, Arizona saw enrollment from the Midwest and the New York area jump by over two thousand students. In his growing arrogance and with no evidence to draw from, Jackie gave himself all the credit for this surge. And due to this self-confidence, practice suddenly seemed easier. His running seemed faster as the accolades poured in. It seemed like everybody wanted his autograph.

The team criticism from 1971 continued, and fans looked to their newly anointed star to carry the load.

By late October, the team had dropped to 3–4 while Jackie collected his third conference defensive player of the week award.

But even with this newest honor, he knew his performance didn't live up to his past two seasons. Fans had come to expect "a touchdown or two," from their All-American, but the magic seemed to be gone. Maybe the hype had gone to his head. Maybe the pressures of being a husband or the whispers about the baby had left him distracted. But the repercussions of another losing season were clear. The time ticked faster on Coach Weber's clock, and the entire locker room felt the pressure to not just perform but to win.

On November 18, 1972, Jackie felt he needed to be aggressive against the Wyoming Cowboys. But his approach backfired. After the game, Wyoming quarterback Steve Cockerham boasted that they'd planned on Jackie's aggressive play. "We not only knew it, we depended on it. And it worked for us," he bragged. "We counted on him coming up fast to stop plays and we used that knowledge to toss two touchdown passes over his head."

After the game, a writer asked Coach Weber if he'd put his house up for sale yet. Weber couldn't find the humor in it and said so. The next Saturday, the Wildcats lost to rival Arizona State to close their season 4–7. Jackie felt guilty for not doing more and apologized to his coaches for letting the team down. He blamed himself for not being all he should be.

Weber resigned the next day.

As time and again before, Jackie handled his disappointments and defeat with uncommon grace. He looked for the good in everything. His teammates and friends loved him for it. And usually, good things followed. Any remorse Jackie felt for the season quickly melted away as the Associated Press picked him as a third-team All-American; United Press International named him a second-team pick; and *Sporting News* and *Time* magazine gave him first-team All-American honors.

On December 30, 1972, he turned in a brilliant performance

in the East-West Shrine Bowl in San Francisco, intercepting two passes and deflecting at least three more. He won the Most Valuable Defensive Player award. He followed with a fine showing at the Senior Bowl in Alabama with an interception and a fumble recovery. There was only one pass caught over him in the two games. He returned to Tucson a happy man.

On a picture-perfect Tuesday afternoon, January 30, 1973, Jackie finished his shift at the sporting goods store by helping a customer with a pair of ski boots. The store manager had been listening to the radio while working in his office. He walked out with a smile and said, "Jackie, you've just been drafted by the Minnesota Vikings—eighth pick, second round." Jackie broke into a grin. In 1973, the NFL draft wasn't the glamorous Radio City Music Hall affair it later became, with watch parties, expensive suits, hordes of cameras, and red carpets. Instead, it was a simple and unsophisticated meeting in a New York hotel conference room. Before 1970, player selections were tallied on a chalkboard. The first personalized jersey presentation didn't arrive until 1976, the first live broadcast in 1980.

To Jackie, his selection meant he had a real job.

Jackie glanced around the surrounding shelves and grabbed a heavy ski parka, took the customer's boots, and pulled them on his own feet. While the manager grabbed his camera, Jackie wrapped the parka hood around his face and smiled. "I'm going to Minnesota," he said, beaming as the camera flash popped. "Maybe the newspaper will be interested in this photo," someone said, and they all laughed. Jackie completed the sale, finished his shift, and headed home to Mary. "I guess we're going to Minnesota," he said, and without champagne, without ceremony, went to bed—and to sleep.

Back in New Orleans, things were moving along well enough without him. Roland Jr. earned his master's degree in education, and Louvinia moved into a doctorate program in education. Donald gave up on school but found a job as the first black streetcar driver in the city. Friends in Tucson, including Jacqueline and Andrea, hated to see Jackie leave Arizona, but they promised to keep in touch. Besides, he'd be back in the off-season. Every month or so he and Audrey would talk on the phone. Frequent cards and letters were much cheaper than expensive long-distance charges. She missed him sorely, but she felt pride in raising an independent son. A week after the draft, the Vikings flew Jackie and Mary to Minneapolis for a round of publicity events.

"We were all so sure he was going to have a wonderful life," his friend Jacqueline said.

CHAPTER FOUR

The Headhunter

1973–1979

Frigid winds that blew through the seams of the Minneapolis jetway caught Jackie and Mary off guard. They'd forgotten their heavy coats for their trip to meet coaches and the media. Jackie had bragged about loving the snow and had posed for that picture inside the store he worked, but he'd never been to Minnesota in February.

Head coach Bud Grant had drafted for speed and did well with his first three picks: running back Chuck Foreman, Jackie, and wide receiver Jim Lash. But before they could step on the field, contracts had to be settled.

In 1973, most players entering the NFL signed three-year deals, plus a small signing bonus. Most understood that they didn't have much of a choice. Once players were drafted into the league, the NFL controlled their right to work. Because the draft locked Jackie with the Vikings, and because free agency didn't exist at the time, he became their exclusive property.

Jackie lined up agent Arthur Morse to negotiate the details. In a rare move for the day, Morse advised Jackie to hold out for guaranteed money—a decision that rankled Bud Grant and his chief negotiator, general manager Jim Finks, who lived by Gil Brandt's (of the Cowboys) philosophy: We're the rancher, and you're the cattle. Ranchers can always get more cattle.

While the businessmen went to war over the details, Jackie and Mary returned home to Tucson to work on their marriage. Until training camp in July, Jackie worked on finishing his college degree.

When camp opened, Chuck Foreman and Jim Lash were suited up and ready to compete for their positions. But with no settled contract, Jackie was a no-show. But one day later, the two parties inked a deal: a $25,000 signing bonus on a $27,500 *guaranteed* salary—the equivalent of $304,047 in 2019 dollars. Not bad for a twenty-two-year-old, but nothing compared to today's multimillion-dollar contracts. With a guarantee, Jackie could easily assume the thirty-year mortgage on the house in Tucson. All things seemed to be moving in a positive direction.

Jackie and Jim Lash shared an apartment near the training facility while Chuck lived a few doors down the hall. As the disco craze swept the nation, the trio soon discovered that they had more in common than just football as they lit up the Minneapolis dance clubs dressed in stylish *Super Fly* outfits—big lapels and big-soled shoes. Even in the glitzy clubs, surrounded by adoring women, Chuck remembered Jackie as a loyal, one-woman man, "a good ol' country boy" who constantly talked about his family.

Bud Grant didn't like being manipulated by his players, and Jackie's contract negotiation left him bitter. He was a "show me" kind of guy who built his teams around seasoned veterans and believed rookies had to wait in line. Ironically, Chuck Foreman and Jim Lash were two of the rare exceptions to the rookie rule. Despite a plethora of running backs, it was clear that Chuck was the best of the group, with his signature spin move. Jackie, on the other hand, had a bevy of high-performing veterans ahead of him. The season before, twenty-nine-year-old Bobby Bryant had intercepted four passes. Twenty-six-year-old Nate Wright was on his way to a thirty-four-interception career. Paul Krause was an All-Pro who finished his career with eighty-one interceptions.

Jackie's first pro effort started with a thud in a preseason game against the Pittsburgh Steelers and their erratic fourth-year quarterback, Terry Bradshaw. Jackie's pass coverage was adequate, but on his first punt return, he and Bobby Bryant confused their signals and collided over a fair catch. Jackie caught all the blame for the turnover since Bryant ended the game with two interceptions and a ninety-three-yard touchdown return. By the end of the preseason, Grant moved Jackie to the taxi squad. If needed for a game, he could be activated in seventy-two hours.

By mid-season, Jackie joked that he could outrun the older backs backward, but it didn't matter. For the most part, the Purple People Eaters were doing just fine without him—in dominating fashion. The Vikings finished 1973 with a 12–2 record. When Chuck was named Offensive Rookie of the Year and selected to play in the Pro Bowl, Jackie celebrated without a hint of jealousy. He continued to help his teammates prepare for the playoffs, until a painful swelling in his elbow and shoulder sent him to the hospital, where doctors diagnosed him with arthritis. The team advanced through the postseason without him, all the way to Super Bowl VIII in Houston, Texas, where they were summarily crushed by the Miami Dolphins under the weight of Miami's bruising fullback, Larry Csonka.

Meanwhile, a thousand miles away, the Vikings' second-round draft pick, former All-American star Jackie Wallace, watched from his living room couch in Tucson. He swore that next season, he'd be in the starting lineup. Next year, people would know his name.

JACKIE'S FIRST SEASON had been hard on Mary. Unlike college ball, pro football consumed all his time. From July through the playoffs, there were no visits and no weeks off. Bye weeks weren't added until 1990, so there was no time for Mary. Besides, she couldn't understand what made football players so special. The constant adulation from the women in public worked on her nerves. She mocked them in singsong fashion: "How are you doing, Jackie?" "You're looking good, Jackie." "I saw you on TV, Jackie." She felt like he encouraged the interactions wherever he went. "Who do you think you are?" she'd ask him. It seemed as if people believed he was beyond human, and she wondered why he didn't pay her the same kind of attention.

So, it came as no surprise when on his first week back to Minneapolis, divorce papers were waiting with the rest of the mail. "Until death do we part" had lasted just over two years. Jacqueline Hearn called when she learned the news. He sounded depressed, she remembered years later. She thought it was a shame, married so young, so fast, and now divorced so young, so fast. On the phone, Jackie said he just didn't want to talk about it, but he thought back to his junior high days and his father's advice on women. "Cut the tie, and never look back." He dutifully signed the surrender and gave her the house. He never returned to Tucson.

Jackie contacted a New Orleans banker, an ardent Minnesota Vikings fan who had called him earlier about houses being built in New Orleans East. In short order, Jackie signed papers on a nice ranch house on Rockton Circle for $497 a month, principal and interest—no down payment, no points, no closing costs. And before the end of the year, Audrey called with a house she'd found on elegant Fontainebleau Drive. He told her he'd take care of it and handled the deal in the same way, except his parents would try to assume the mortgage payments in time.

On July 1, 1974, days before training camp was set to begin, the NFL Players Association disrupted the preseason by calling for a strike, focused mostly over a player's right to switch teams after their contracts expired. Picketers cried, "No Freedom, No Football." Owners scoffed at the notion, saying such changes would lead to anarchy.

On the first day of camp, Jackie Wallace and Larry Smiley were the only players to cross the pickets. Jackie believed in the players' cause. He'd fought over the same issues in his own contract negotiations. But he couldn't afford to make more trouble with Coach Grant. The NFLPA's bitter strike ended forty-one days later, with none of the association's demands met.

Jackie's hard work in the preseason paid off. In the fifth and final preseason game against San Diego, he intercepted his first pass and made the active roster. All he needed was a break. It came in the season opener against Green Bay. While Jackie paced patiently on the sidelines, seventh-year cornerback Bobby Bryant went for a tackle and broke his forearm. "Go in, Wallace!" Grant yelled. Jackie suddenly had a shot at some serious playing time. Under NFL irrevocable waiver rules, the injury benched Bobby for the season.

Three weeks later, against the Cowboys, Jackie got a taste of his old glory days as he high-stepped into the end zone with a blocked field goal return. Even though the refs ruled the play dead before he ever touched the ball, he felt the roar of the crowd. During the game, Jackie also pounded the receivers with added anger. Something primal came out of him—maybe the result of an off year or the frustration of his divorce. At one point, Coach Grant told

him to dial it back. He'd never seen him so aggressive. Too much could get Jackie hurt. And more importantly, too much could also get him burned on the long ball. His eagerness for the big play—a hangover from his Arizona days—left him vulnerable. Coaches picked up on these small quirks and developed strategies to exploit them. Quarterbacks watched for opportunities. But by mid-October, Jackie made his first interception against Dan Pastorini, a play that brought his confidence back. Back home in New Orleans, some fans dubbed him "The Headhunter."

The Vikings ended their season with a 10–4 record, with the defense allowing only twenty-one touchdowns in fourteen games, the fewest in the league. The defensive backs benefited from the dominant pressure applied by the front four, and the entire defense allowed only eight touchdown passes, the fewest in the NFL. As the Vikings breezed into the postseason, newspaper articles focused on the Vikings' obvious weak link: the erratic, overeager "second-year man" Jackie Wallace. "Minnesota Defense Must Stop Bombs," read one headline. The story read, "In three of the Vikings' four losses, the winning points were either scored or set up by long passes caught over Wallace's outstretched arms." Jackie admitted that when he got burned, it came at the worst time and that he didn't blame quarterbacks for going after him, especially considering that Nate Wright played on the other corner with six interceptions on the year. But he tempered his opinion of his season. "For the most part, I think I've had a pretty solid season."

Going into the playoffs, two things bugged Jackie most: he hadn't scored any touchdowns, and he had only one interception, the fewest of all the Vikings defensive backs. "I made the big plays in college," he told an AP reporter, "and I'll make them as a pro. And soon. Maybe sooner than anyone thinks."

He was true to his word.

During the Vikings' Conference Championship against the Los Angeles Rams, Jackie stunned everyone as he pulled off what some considered the team's biggest play of the season. With the Vikings leading 7–3 in the fourth quarter and the Rams threatening from the Vikings' 7-yard line, James Harris rolled out of a collapsing pocket and threw to Pat Curran as he sprinted across the back of the end zone. Jackie read Harris's eyes perfectly from the goal line and tipped the ball directly into the hands of linebacker Wally Hilgenberg, who quickly downed it for a touchback. The dramatic play led to the eighty-yard drive that clinched the game. The victory sent the Vikings to the Super Bowl to face the Pittsburgh Steelers.

As if fate were writing the script, the game would be played January 12, 1975, in New Orleans.

Louisiana and the NFL had envisioned Super Bowl IX to be the christening event for the glorious new Superdome—the largest and most spectacular domed stadium in the world. But the mice and men failed to build in enough buffer time to account for deadline overruns, so the game had to be moved to the archaic, 1920s-era Tulane Stadium.

Local sports personalities welcomed Jackie home to New Orleans, as did *The Times-Picayune*. "I'm in an ideal situation," he told the newspaper. "There are added pressures . . . to be sure. But, there's something about playing before relatives and friends which make a man perform better." Champ Clark touted Jackie's St. Aug roots and his All-American pedigree in a front-page story (with a photograph) in the *Louisiana Weekly*.

Jackie's coaches trusted him to roam his Central City haunts with his friend Chuck Foreman in tow. Jackie's baby sister Margo, now nineteen, had placed a large banner in the front yard of Roland and Audrey's Fontainebleau house that read: "Jackie Wallace—cornerback—Minnesota Vikings." Chuck enjoyed getting to know Jackie's New Orleans. Having grown up in the Maryland/DC area, he had never eaten raccoon before and hasn't since. But he never denied that it tasted good. Before leaving, Jackie left his parents a block of game tickets. It would be Audrey's and Roland's first time to see him play since St. Aug.

Oddsmakers favored the Steelers by three points. Although the Purple People Eaters were playing great football, many felt as though they were outmatched. The Steelers were a young team, loaded with talent like Franco Harris, Joe Greene, Jack Ham, Jack Lambert, speedster wide receivers Lynn Swann and John Stallworth. Defensive back Mel Blount was so cocky, he bragged that he wished his team could face a tougher opponent. If the Steelers had a weak link, the media said, it had to be twenty-six-year-old Terry Bradshaw, who had been booed in Pittsburgh for five long years. The press howled all week that he was too dumb for the position. NBC commentators warned that the Vikings' chances depended on how well the rookie, Jackie Wallace, played against the Steelers' wide receivers. They repeated the popular verbiage and called him "mistake prone."

The morning of the January 12 game dawned cold and wet. A strong north wind swirled through the old stadium and made it feel much colder than forty-six degrees. The rain stopped just before kickoff but left the artificial turf slick. Almost eighty-one thousand fans huddled into their seats. Since the game was completely sold out, the NFL suspended the local blackout, which meant the fans who couldn't get tickets, or who couldn't afford the $20 ticket price, would now be able to see the game at home. NBC play-by-play announcer Curt Gowdy and color commentators Al De-Rogatis and "Dandy" Don Meredith prepared their audiences for the unfolding drama. A fan's banner read, "Minnesota Iron against Pittsburgh Steel," and their regular seasons were nearly identical, 10–4 and 10–3–1, respectfully. Each was eager to prove their superiority. Jackie said in his interview with *The Times-Picayune* that he didn't care about the margin of victory: "Everything's cool as long as there was a 'W' behind the Vikings' name after the game." By kickoff, all the talk became irrelevant.

From the outset, the Steelers flexed their muscle with a seemingly inappropriate level of confidence. But while their powerful running game drove deep into Vikings territory on their first two drives, they failed to score on either. Like so many quarterbacks before him, Bradshaw identified Jackie as the weak link and went to work on him when Pittsburgh was driving during the Steelers' last possession of the first quarter. From the 16-yard line, Bradshaw spotted Frank Lewis as he broke behind Jackie and fired a strike to the left front corner of the end zone. But Jackie recovered and tipped the ball away to save the touchdown. In subsequent possessions, Bradshaw targeted him repeatedly on short underneath patterns and long balls over the top. But Jackie responded again and again, earning respect from the fans and the announcing crew. Jackie was playing the greatest game of his life in the biggest game of his life. As one announcer said, Bradshaw realized that the weak link he had counted on simply didn't exist.

After both offensive units failed to produce points, Pittsburgh's "Steel Curtain" defense pinned Fran Tarkenton in his own end zone for a safety with 7:34 left in the half. From there the Steelers dominated by holding the Vikings running attack to only seventeen yards. But the Vikings defense kept pace. With 8:46 left in the fourth quarter, the Steelers led 9–6.

With such little time left, Bradshaw went on the attack. From his own 42, on third and two, he fired thirty yards downfield over strong safety Jeff Wright to a leaping Larry Brown. Jackie sped across the field to help out. At midfield, he plowed his shoulder into Brown's chest and flung him to the ground. In the violent collision, Jackie wormed his fingers between the ball and Brown's chest and yanked the ball loose. The football seemed to levitate as Brown's rear hit the ground. Linebacker Jeff Siemon dove for the ball as it tumbled away. "Minnesota has it!" Gowdy shouted. Jackie ecstatically ran with his teammates toward the jubilant Minnesota bench. "That's Wallace," Don Meredith said as he watched the television replay. "That guy's played a good ball game."

As the Vikings celebrated, the head linesman rushed over and ruled that Brown had been down by contact before the fumble—a referee's choice call in the days before instant reply. Pittsburgh kept the ball. Meredith took note as the crowd howled in protest: "And here in New Orleans, they have a way of stopping ball games when they don't like those decisions." But Bradshaw wisely took a hurried snap to end the discussion. The Steelers capped the next nine plays with a touchdown pass to Brown. It would be the last score of the game. Steelers: 16, Vikings: 6.

Meredith called Jackie's hit on Brown a critical "if and but" play that could have provided the Vikings a crucial turn of momentum and a legitimate chance to win. But it wasn't. Viking fans agonized over their third Super Bowl loss—their second in a row. In Pittsburgh, 224 fans were arrested as they celebrated the Steelers' first NFL championship in their forty-two-year history.

In the locker room, Bud Grant complained that the official who overruled Brown's fumble made the call from across the field. AP writer Austin Wilson said the television replay indicated Grant's complaints were valid. It was the most talked-about play of the game.

Joe Greene sympathized with the Vikings' players: "To lose in this game has got to be the lowest feeling you can get." But Jackie had no regrets about his own performance. Lynn Swann and John Stallworth, Pittsburgh's star receivers, had been neutralized, catching only two passes for twenty-four yards. Some even said that if the Vikings had won, Jackie might have been named the MVP instead of Franco Harris. Those were the words Jackie would remember.

A few weeks after the game, the mother of Wanda White, Jackie's junior high girlfriend, ran into him at a party and rushed to apologize for her "nappy-headed nigger" insult in 1965. Jackie deflected with kindness. He didn't hold grudges. Instead, he'd used her words through the years for inspiration in the classroom. They'd echoed in his head as he pounded out long practice runs. They'd raised his ambitions. Her words had cut him deeply, but now he could see that they'd made him a better man.

JACKIE HAD NO reason to return to Arizona during the off-season. Now, with his professional reputation polished, he settled into his home in New Orleans East. After the divorce, he'd asked Mary for only three things: two wicker chairs and a Mustang he'd bought with his signing bonus. He dispatched a buddy to load and ship them to New Orleans.

There, Jackie suddenly became a hot item on the motivational speaker's circuit. Champ Clark recommended him to give the keynote speech for the annual NAACP fund-raising banquet. While he sat at the dais eating his chicken dinner, the chapter's president struck up an especially fresh conversation.

"You're cute," she said.

"I'm your speaker," Jackie demurred, though he rarely discouraged a pretty girl's attention.

"I don't care," she said. "I'm Dyan French Cole."

Within days, they were dating. Within a few months, Dyan had moved in. He enjoyed having a woman's companionship again.

Dyan was a bold, feisty community activist—six years Jackie's senior—who wore long dreadlocks and big glasses and her passion for social justice like a sword. People on the streets knew her as "Mama D."

Dyan's political affiliations and Jackie's newfound star status made their home a natural party spot for the city's power brokers: council members, police chief Joe Giarrusso, future mayor Ernest "Dutch" Morial, and Judge Israel Augustine, to name a few. She introduced him to President Jimmy Carter at campaign events and brought him to Saks Fifth Avenue and Lord & Taylor on New York shopping trips, where she'd send expensive gifts to girlfriends back home.

Jackie couldn't wait to get back to Minneapolis for training camp and his teammates. His Super Bowl performance had given him the emotional boost he needed to elevate his performance. But even with the greatest game of his brief career behind him, Bud Grant still resented Jackie's drawn-out contract negotiations, or maybe he'd grown wary of his tendency for big-play mistakes, or possibly both.

For whatever reason, during camp, Grant moved him to waivers to make room for defensive back Joe Blahak from Houston, perhaps thinking no one would claim his on-again, off-again cornerback. Meanwhile, head coach Ted Marchibroda of the Baltimore Colts had other ideas. After his administrative assistant screened Jackie in a telephone interview, coaches added his name to the strips arranged on a magnetic whiteboard. Next to Jackie's name, they added a black dot to identify his race.

THE MOVE TO Baltimore thrilled Jackie. It felt small-town southern to him. He liked that everyone seemed to know everybody. "Smaltimore," as some locals called it, felt a bit like New Orleans with her centuries-old architecture, her port, and her shadows of bold history. The stanzas of "The Star-Spangled Banner" seem to waft along with the salty air.

And even though the team was reeling from a disastrous 2–12 season, Jackie knew he was joining a long line of alumni greats with names like Johnny Unitas, Y. A. Tittle, Art Donovan, Lenny Moore, and Bubba Smith. With that kind of legacy, Colts fans had tasted high-end football and were hungry for more. Marchibroda wanted to rebuild the team on youth and excitement, centered around twenty-four-year-old quarterback Bert Jones (the Ruston Rifle from LSU) and twenty-six-year-old running back Lydell Mitchell. Jackie, at twenty-four years old, fit perfectly into their plans.

Jackie loved Marchibroda's inspirational attitude. He famously asked his players and staff, "What have you done today that will help the Colts win?" He included everyone, from his quarterbacks to his secretaries, remembered Maureen Kilcullen, who managed Marchibroda's office. It was infectious.

Jackie's personality fit right in. He and Maureen became great friends as they teased and joked among the office staff. Together, they ribbed a twenty-three-year-old intern named Bill, who consistently missed deadlines for sending out game films to upcoming opponents. Maureen called him "Billy" because he hated the name so much, and Jackie tagged him for the team donut runs. But each week, Maureen dutifully put his mail in the slot labeled "Bill Belichick."

Marchibroda gelled the team around a fun atmosphere. Linebacker Joe Ehrmann coined a new motto: "A team that parties together and plays together wins together." "We did all that," remembered Maureen. But the winning didn't come immediately or easily.

After a 1–4 start, Marchibroda made key changes, and the Colts erupted into a nine-game winning streak. The locker room exploded around a new slogan, "Shake and Bake," coined by wide receiver Glenn Doughty, and the media dubbed the season "The Miracle on 33rd Street." Jackie caught fire in the headlines at free safety, winning multiple game MVP honors and setting a team record by running back two interceptions for touchdowns. After a dramatic 10–7 overtime win against the powerhouse Miami Dolphins in the fog, the fans stormed the field with a religious fervor. Among them, a twenty-one-year-old drunk named John helped drag down the goal posts while his best friend ripped up the wooden sideline bench for souvenirs. He screamed and howled as he helped carry the post toward the exits but disappeared into the crowd as the police moved in. It was the greatest thing he'd never been a part of, he said years later. After eight wins in a row, the Colts were headed to the playoffs.

Jackie rode his new wave of popularity into a community media blitz as a guest on radio talk shows and in personal appearances where he donated televisions to children of single moms. He mostly enjoyed the quiet, discreet visits with poor families during Thanksgiving, when he cooked holiday meals. He rode the public bus or walked to Memorial Stadium on Sundays so he could cavort with his fans on game day. He handed out free tickets and signed autographs all along the way. The mayor of Baltimore presented him with the Baltimore's Best award for his altruistic contributions to the city.

But despite a miraculous 10–4 regular season, Terry Bradshaw and the Pittsburgh Steelers beat them soundly in the first round of playoffs in Pittsburgh, 28–10. The Steelers continued their march to their second consecutive Super Bowl victory.

Instead of heading back to New Orleans for the off-season, Jackie signed on with the Colts' speaker's bureau, which allowed him to stay in Baltimore and earn off-season cash. For school children, Jackie reworked motivational lessons from *Schoolhouse Rock!*'s "Conjunction Junction," *H. R. Pufnstuf*, and *Winnie the Pooh*. For graduation ceremonies, he personalized the lines of Nikki Giovanni's "Word Poem (Perhaps Worth Considering)." In prisons, he brought his street cred to demonstrate hope for the fallen. For fans at local Colts Corrals, he wore a number 12 Jets jersey (Joe Namath's number) to the podium, then ripped it off and playfully tossed it on a fired grill to the raucous howl of the crowd. Mama D visited Baltimore frequently and encouraged him to unchain himself from his homeboy mentality. Traveling and exploring, she said, was the secret to enlightenment. Baltimore gave them that opportunity. Together they visited the must-sees of freedom: Mount Rushmore, Gettysburg, and, of course, Baltimore's Fort McHenry. The steps of Washington's Lincoln Memorial, where King had shared his dream, left him speechless. A new patriotism swept over him.

Nineteen seventy-six marked the bicentennial year for America, sparking an explosion of patriotic fervor and nostalgia. The U.S. Mint pressed commemorative quarters, cities sponsored elaborate firework displays, an international fleet of fourteen tall-masted ships paraded in ports along the Eastern Seaboard. Red, white, and blue paint coated every conceivable surface from mailboxes to train locomotives. People wanted to celebrate. The contentious era of the Vietnam War, Watergate, and the civil rights movement had come to a close. Jackie felt a new surge of optimism spreading across America. But then again, Jackie saw optimism no matter which direction he looked.

The '76 NFL season opened appropriately with the Baltimore Colts visiting the colonial New England Patriots. But even with minutemen shouldering muskets along the sideline, the Colts dominated 27–13, setting the tone for the team's second-chance season, their chance to prove that '75 wasn't a fluke. As they plowed through their schedule, they made winning look easy, outscoring their opponents 417–246. When the dust settled, Jackie led the team with five interceptions and seventy-four unassisted tackles, and the Colts had clinched their division with an 11–3 season. On December 19, 1976, the Colts once again faced the Steelers in the divisional playoff grudge match, this time in Baltimore.

Marchibroda adamantly relied on the belief that his high-octane inspiration could overcome any obstacle—but the Steelers extinguished the fire before the Colts knew what hit them. On the third play from scrimmage, Terry Bradshaw took the snap at his own 24-yard line, glanced quickly to the left to sucker defenders, and then heaved a seventy-six-yard bomb to Frank Lewis as he streaked deep down the right side of the field. When the ball dropped perfectly over Lewis's shoulder, a blue-and-white number 20 trailed desperately by three yards. Jackie never caught up, and neither did the Colts. One of most dynamic collections of talent in the NFL couldn't overcome that initial shock. The Steelers destroyed the Colts, 40–14.

Ten minutes after the game ended, a man ran into the locker room shouting that a plane had crashed into the stadium. Defensive back Bruce Laird was in the shower at the time and cursed the guy for telling such a sick joke after the trauma the team had just experienced. But it turned out that a deranged pilot had tried to land his Piper Cherokee on the field as a stunt but ended up nose down in the upper deck of one of the end zones instead. Remarkably, no one had been seriously injured, not even the pilot.

In typical fashion, Jackie found humor and a positive spin for the reporters. He said that he'd known that the plane was going to crash, so he let Frank beat him on the out-and-up pattern. If it hadn't been for his first-quarter blunder and the lopsided score, the stadium would have still been rocking, and more people would have gotten killed. "I saved all those lives," he said.

Despite his positive and humorous spin, the media and Jackie's teammates branded him as the scapegoat. The next morning in *The Times-Picayune*, a large photo showed Jackie desperately chasing Frank Lewis on the fateful catch. The headline on the caption read, "SO LONG, JACKIE."

When he returned for training camp, the locker room felt cold and bitter. After he got beat for a touchdown in an exhibition game, defensive coordinator Maxie Baughan let him have it. Jackie screamed back that it was only a single play, nothing more, but the die was already cast. Baughan had signed Lyle Blackwood and, for the remainder of the season, started him at free safety. On September 7, 1977, the Colts announced Jackie's release.

Jackie's diehard fans heard the news before the presses rolled. When he returned to the training camp hotel, one of his NAACP friends was waiting in the lobby, looking heartbroken, furious, and ready to mobilize. "You do too much for the community," she said. She was ready to fight the Colts the only way she knew how—with petitions and public protests. Jackie calmed her by saying, "It will be OK. I'll find a spot somewhere."

In a matter of weeks, he suited up as a Ram.

That season, Lyle Blackwood, who had replaced Jackie in the Colts' backfield, led the NFL with ten interceptions.

JACKIE WASN'T SURE if he'd fit into the West Coast atmosphere of Los Angeles. He rented and settled into a small hotel room on the Pacific Coast Highway—humble accommodations by Tinseltown standards—but by now, he'd learned to live one month at a time in the "Not for Long" league. He settled his gear in his new locker labeled "20—Wallace," right next to a locker labeled "12—Namath," his old nemesis from the AFC East. Such are the ironies in the NFL.

If the Rams had hoped to excite the L.A. fans with Broadway Joe's celebrity, they caught him a little late. Namath hit Sunset Boulevard nursing bad knees and a beat-up body. After an encouraging 2–1 start, the Bears intercepted Namath four times in a loss to Chicago on *Monday Night Football*. Pat Haden took the field as Namath took a seat on the bench. But until his retirement at the end of the season, Joe instilled life into every party. Jackie felt sorry for Joe. And being a bit starstruck, he told Joe that he would have given him his knees to see him play again.

With a wingman like Joe, Jackie learned to rub elbows with many of his Hollywood idols. Suzanne Somers, Cheryl Ladd, George Peppard, and countless other Hollywood stars frequented the sidelines and the locker room. In one ego-boosting chance encounter, NFL legend Jim Brown recognized Jackie on the streets. Later they shared talks about spiritual matters and the proper place that football should play in your life. "Life is about doing the better things to help my fellow man," Jackie remembers him saying. He told him, "Football will not get you into heaven. Learn to think of bigger things to do with your life. Football isn't your shining star."

The metaphor stuck as Jackie watched Namath hobble around. He noticed the aging stars of Beverly Hills and the tarnished stars on Hollywood's Walk of Fame. He pictured his own fading star— his life beyond football—and it scared him. In 1977, he had played in ten games, but he hadn't started in any of them. The Rams finished their season 10–4, a good year. But Jackie intercepted only one pass, and it worried him.

After a wet, sloppy divisional playoff loss against Minnesota, team owner Carroll Rosenbloom ran out of patience with Chuck Knox. The coach resigned before Rosenbloom could fire him. By the end of August 1978, Jackie was out of a job, too. Back in New Orleans, he sat with no team, no prospects, and no phone calls. He considered making a career change—possibly teaching math at St. Aug. But just when he felt most worthless to the world, Rams defensive back Eddie Brown and punt returner Billy Waddy went down with injuries. Jackie flew back to L.A. the next day and began to prepare for game three against Dallas.

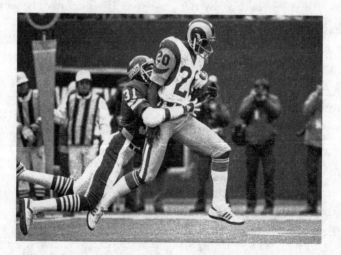

Jackie's teammates gave him a new nickname—Touché Turtle, after a popular Hanna-Barbera cartoon character—that suggested that he'd lost a step. But Jackie explained to the media that he wasn't slow—he was deliberate, he lulled his defenders to sleep. But at twenty-seven, he found it more difficult to cover the speedy receivers, who suddenly seemed younger and stronger. The bruises and sores seemed to require longer recovery times. In the fourth game of the season, he tried to tackle Houston's Earl Campbell and got his head wedged between his "big thunder thighs," as he called them. He blacked out for a moment, and then, once back in the huddle, told his defensive linemen to stop him next time. He wouldn't be making that kind of tackle again.

He dedicated his attention to his punt returns, and at season's end, he was named to the *Pro Football Weekly* All-Conference first team and led the NFC with 11.9 yards per punt return and the NFL with 52 returns and 618 punt-return yards, which remains the Rams' team record to this day. He was back on top.

The Rams finished the season 12–4 and headed to the playoffs again, beating the Vikings 34–10 in the first round, only to be humiliated a week later by the Cowboys, 28–0, falling one game short of their first Super Bowl ever.

For now, he ignored Jim Brown's advice about looking beyond football. Football defined him. He spent his off-season doing jobs that would improve his physical conditioning, slinging garbage cans into the back of New Orleans sanitation trucks and hauling cargo along with the longshoremen on the docks. He added a strict regimen of running along the Interstate-10 service road every day. He knew he had to work hard to win out over the twenty-two-, twenty-three-, and twenty-four-year-olds competing for his roster spot. He wanted to show up at training camp in the best shape of his life.

Back at training camp for the 1979 season, his friend, Rams kicker Frank Corral, watched Jackie fidget on the sidelines, game after game, as he wrangled for playing time, growing more anxious and agitated as he waited. Frank thought he saw subtle signs of depression as Jackie spent much of his free time alone. In an effort to draw him out, Frank often invited Jackie to casual hangouts after practice and even to his house for late-night dinners. But Jackie seemed to have lost interest.

When the Rams announced their final fifty-six-man roster, they listed twelve defensive backs. Jackie Wallace didn't make the cut. The younger set had won out, and punt return duty went to Eddie Brown. As Jackie packed his gear for a lonely trip back home, Frank tried to lift his spirits. "It's a numbers game," he told him. But this time, the cut felt deeper. This time, it felt final.

In late November, after the twelfth game of the season, the phone finally rang again. It was the Rams saying they needed a nickelback.

There were only four games left in the season, and the Rams were 6–6, but Jackie's optimism rebounded. This could be his chance to turn some heads. So he packed his car again and drove back to L.A. A week later, he was in uniform again and earned a game ball against the Minnesota Vikings. But he didn't get nearly the playing time he'd been promised in the phone call. He spent too much time watching from the wings.

By season's end, the Rams had clawed their way into the playoffs with only nine wins, a feat that had never been accomplished before. In the playoffs, the Rams surprised everyone with a revenge upset over the Cowboys. Then they beat Tampa Bay to earn a berth to the Super Bowl. The media attacked. Most pundits, even many of the team's own fans, felt as though the Rams' season was a fluke. *Sports Illustrated* called the NFC Championship Game "a game for losers, played by losers." But even so, the Rams had legitimately earned their first trip to the big game. Jackie saw it as one more personal opportunity to beat the odds. He could see his big moment of redemption coming, in sunny Pasadena.

Once again, he would have to face Terry Bradshaw and the Steelers.

CHAPTER FIVE

The Crash of Icarus

1980–1990

Following the victory over the Buccaneers, the Rams' locker room danced on a cloud of disbelief. Some called it a miracle.

It had been a remarkable yet turbulent year for the franchise. In April, the team's owner, Carroll Rosenbloom, drowned while swimming in the ocean in Florida. Amid great public dissension, his wife, Georgia Frontiere, a former entertainer and socialite, inherited 70 percent ownership in the team, becoming the NFL's first active woman owner. The other 30 percent went to Carroll's five children. The *Los Angeles Times* wrote that Ms. Frontiere was a "colorful and controversial eccentric," who "loved music, embraced astrology, wrote poetry." Others said she was unfit to run a pro football team.

Jackie kept his opinions about ownership and the coach's management to himself. At the moment, he could not have cared less. With whoops and screams, Jackie and his teammates celebrated their chance to compete for the biggest prize in sports. He'd spent twelve games of the season on waivers, but now he was headed to his second Super Bowl. He felt a comeback performance on the way.

Never before had a 9–7 team advanced to the big game, much less to face down the 12–4 defending champions. The Rams arrived under the leadership of backup quarterback Vince Ferragamo after starter Pat Haden broke his finger in week ten. Sportswriters mocked the Rams for believing they belonged on the same field with the Steelers, who were making their fourth Super Bowl appearance in the last six seasons. Any optimism that existed in the Rams' clubhouse had to be manufactured by the coaches and the players. If they had any advantage at all, it was that they slept in their own beds the night before. Pasadena's Rose Bowl was just five miles from downtown Los Angeles.

On January 20, 1980, Jackie and his teammates took the field in gold pants and white jerseys with blue numbers, surrounded by 103,985 spectators, the largest crowd to ever attend a Super Bowl up to that point. The natural turf felt a bit sloppy from rains earlier in the week, but the supercharged crowd roared as the Rams' cheerleaders trotted on the field with glittery pompoms—a stark comparison to the Steelers fans, who waved their "terrible towels" in bold anticipation of a trouncing. On the sideline, Jackie stood at attention with his cheeks smeared with eye black to absorb the glare of the afternoon sun as members of the military unfurled a giant American flag at midfield. Cheryl Ladd sang the national anthem, dedicated to the fifty-two American hostages being held in Iran.

Despite expectations of a blowout, the Rams brought their best fight from the opening whistle. Their offense dominated the first quarter, stunning everyone by scoring the only touchdown of the period to answer Pittsburgh's earlier field goal to end the quarter 7–3. Jackie watched patiently on the sideline for the long-yardage situations that he'd practiced for and coverage opportunities on special teams. On kicks and punts, he controlled his primary assignment, turning runners upfield on the right edge, but he couldn't penetrate beyond the blockers to make the tackle. Time and again, he was muscled to the ground.

Despite the Steelers' power and swagger, the Rams stood their ground. With nothing to lose, Rams' head coach Ray Malavasi abandoned his typical conservative running game for an all-out passing attack, only to fall short of the end zone time and again. Frank Corral added points with two field goals.

Jackie made brief appearances covering the deep middle but made no impact as Bradshaw threw short and cautious passes to his running backs, mostly in deference to an inspired Rams pass rush. By halftime, to everyone's surprise, the Rams controlled the game, 13–10. The local fans, who had scoffed at their team through their unlikely regular season, suddenly turned into true believers. Terry Bradshaw and the Steelers left the field looking disheveled and confused while Jackie and the Rams bounced into the locker room looking forward to a big second half.

As the Rams took the field in the third quarter, the defensive coaches altered the lineup in a way that diminished Jackie's influence in the game. They reassigned the nickelback position to Eddie Brown—the position that Jackie had practiced for all week. The decision left Jackie dumbfounded and angry as he waited, mostly useless on the sideline.

With less than three minutes elapsed in the third quarter, Bradshaw tested the new defensive configuration and connected on a forty-seven-yard pass to Lynn Swann for a quick touchdown, just over the outstretched fingertips of Nolan Cromwell with Pat Thomas pursuing. It was Bradshaw's first long-ball attempt of the day. In Jackie's mind, Bradshaw threw deep because he knew he wasn't there.

The Rams answered Bradshaw's bomb with a touchdown drive of their own (missing the extra point), tilting the score back

again, Rams: 19. Steelers: 17. On a Rams' punt coverage downfield, Jackie made his first tackle of the day.

As the sunlight faded on the San Gabriel Mountains, Bradshaw
went to work on Brown. From his own 27-yard line, third and long,
Bradshaw unloaded downfield to Stallworth. At first, Stallworth
thought he'd been overthrown and turned to run with all his might.
The ball fell perfectly beyond the outstretched arm of cornerback
Rod Perry for a seventy-three-yard touchdown. Eddie Brown, who
was responsible for the deep middle, was supposed to be helping
Perry on the deep ball, but for some unknown reason, he let Stallworth streak past. Jackie knew that he would have played the coverage properly. He seethed from the sideline as he watched Stallworth
celebrate the touchdown with Bradshaw. The Steelers had taken the
lead, 24–19.

The Rams fought back, but on the Steelers' subsequent third-
and-long (another nickel defense situation), Bradshaw again called
for the big play, this time throwing forty-five yards downfield to
Stallworth, who caught the ball over the wrong shoulder in full
stride. Four plays and an interference call later, Franco Harris sealed
the game with a one-yard touchdown run. The Steelers led, 30–19.
Two pivotal plays (leading to two touchdowns) had been thrown
over Jackie's reassigned position.

As Bradshaw leapt and hugged his way to the sidelines, Jackie's
competitive fire raged. He screamed and swore words his mother
would have been ashamed of.

For the fourth extra point of the game, Jackie tried in vain to
block the kick. As he watched the final one minute and fifty-two
seconds tick off the clock, he made the loss personal and exploded
in frustration. He could have stopped Bradshaw. He could have shut
down Stallworth. He was the only back tall enough or fast enough.
He figured that he'd been benched in the second half because of

his performance-sensitive contract. He cursed everyone in sight as his team slumped off the field. He believed the coaches had played Eddie to save a few bucks, and it had cost them the Super Bowl.

Photographers and reporters surrounded Bradshaw and followed the jubilant Steelers into the locker room. There, on live TV, Commissioner Pete Rozelle awarded the Lombardi Trophy to team owner Art Rooney Sr. "We'll have to stop meeting like this," joked Rozelle as he handed the trophy to Rooney for the fourth time.

Another live camera crew broadcast from the Rams' locker room, which was full of commotion and confusion as players and coaches shouted and pointed fingers. The team's new owner, Georgia Frontiere, and a group of executives filtered in to congratulate the team for its valiant effort. But their timing couldn't have been worse. Jackie's hopes for a comeback had been dashed. His pride had been crushed. With live cameras rolling, Jackie—fueled with bitterness and anger—screamed his analysis of the loss. "Nobody wants to pay nobody no f—ing money." He then dropped his pants, showed his rear, and screamed, "Y'all can kiss my ass!"

Frontiere didn't see it. Most of the live television audience didn't notice the spontaneous, out-of-focus antics in the darkened background. But some of Frontiere's people saw it—"yes-men," as Jackie called them. They made a note of the outburst.

FINISHING SECOND PLACE in the biggest sports spectacle on earth can be especially hard on an athlete. It's impossible for a defeated player to slink off quietly into the night as if nothing has happened. To make matters worse, Jackie's nonperformance and his bitter tirade left him with the ugly sting of disgrace. The next day, he turned in his gear and emptied his rented hotel room for his long, lonely drive back home.

Nineteen hundred miles of interstate highway gave him plenty of time to process his year. He wandered into a deep funk as he drove into the endless sky of the desert. He glanced only briefly as he passed through Tucson, within two miles of the University of Arizona stadium. He stared at the mountains where he used to camp when he was so young and ambitious. He remembered the first time he'd seen cactus as an eighteen-year-old as he traced his route back to Louisiana. As he pulled into his driveway in New Orleans East, he tried to recollect his self-esteem.

From his couch, with Dyan at his side, Jackie tried to make sense of his life and his future in the NFL. Three months later, in April, he grew concerned when the Rams drafted two-time All-American defensive back Johnnie Johnson out of Texas. But he didn't see the fine print in the transaction section of the newspaper that quietly listed his waiver from the Rams. So when he drove back to California to training camp in July, the coaches were surprised to see him. "You didn't know you were waived?" one asked. "We sent you a letter." He stood frozen in the doorway, flat-footed.

He should have seen it coming. But there is something in the mind of an eternal optimist that obscures obvious facts. He'd sat out twelve games of the '79 season, and he hadn't played much when he'd finally been re-signed. His Super Bowl ring had arrived unceremoniously in the mail. He had ignored all the clues. Even standing in the doorway at the training facility, he couldn't fathom that his career with the Rams had come to an end. As he looked around, he noticed that Johnnie Johnson was dressing out in jersey number 20.

Jackie tried in earnest to cover his crushed ego with a brave face. "Look, it'll be all right," he told everyone. "I'll find something. I'll see what's going on." He pointed his car north on Interstate 5 and drove six hours to San Francisco and wrangled a tryout with the 49ers. He tried his best to impress coaches as he covered second-year wide receiver Dwight Clark, "like I was going out of style," he remembered. Coaches said they were impressed and that they'd be in touch if someone got hurt. Jackie was twenty-nine.

Jackie drove back to New Orleans to reframe his attitude. Maybe he could relive another "Local Boy Does Good" chapter of his life with the New Orleans Saints, who had finished the 1979 season with an 8–8 record, just behind the Rams in the NFC West division. With his knowledge about the Rams' inner workings and their defensive schemes, he could help the Saints capture their first winning season ever and maybe even get into the playoffs. Who knew—maybe he could help the Saints earn their way to the Super Bowl! He thrilled at the prospect of being ". . . in that number when the Saints go marching in." Considering how much New Orleans loved their football team, the city would go absolutely crazy. As he fantasized, he realized that the NFL had scheduled the next Super Bowl for the Louisiana Superdome.

Champ Clark arranged a Saints tryout, but defensive backs coach Lance Van Zandt told him flat out that he wasn't good enough. Jackie was floored. Just two years before, he'd led the NFL in punt returns. And now he wasn't good enough to play for perennial losers like the Saints?

Dyan tried using her political connections in Cleveland, but the Browns weren't interested either. Meanwhile, Jackie attempted to connect with Bill Belichick, who was now a special teams coach with the New York Giants. Jackie figured that at the very least, Belichick would remember his name from their days together with the Colts. But there was no response.

Jackie doggedly persisted, desperately exploiting every connection he could find to get back into the game. Dyan was more pragmatic. She told him to let it go. She tried to convince him that he'd had a good run. "How many people get the chance to do what you've done?" she reasoned. The average NFL career lasts four and a half years. (The Players Association says three, the NFL says six.) Most people never get near a field. Jackie had already beaten the odds with seven seasons. But it didn't matter how hard Dyan reasoned; Jackie didn't want to hear it.

He sat through the fall schedule on his couch and fumed at the TV, confident he could outplay everyone on the screen. People he'd never heard of were playing *his* position, making *his* money. He analyzed each pass and every reception. He criticized every mistake on every punt return.

He dissolved into a puddle of self-pity and wondered why no one from the NFL had called to offer transitional counseling. He'd been put out to pasture. No, even a pasture would have been honorable. He'd been shoveled off to the dump.

He sat and focused on the spectacular losses of his life, starting with high school. He had excelled at St. Aug in the middle of integration strife, but he'd never finished with a winning season. Arizona was the same. With all his glory, glamour, and honors, his Wildcats had never finished better than 5–6.

In seven years in the NFL, he'd helped his teams get to three Super Bowls, and they'd lost all three, even Super Bowl IX, where he'd turned in the best performance of his life. He tallied his life among the losers—a victim filled with regret and sour grapes, a mentality that Roland and Audrey had preached so hard against. He questioned God and prayed the prayer of the defeated. "Why would You do this to me?" he demanded of God. "Where were You when I needed You? I've trusted You and You let me down. Why would You lead him to touch the hem of glory and then leave me so short?"

Depression consumed him.

To make matters worse, his mother, Audrey, had recently been diagnosed with lung cancer.

Jackie and Dyan's relationship soured as their conversations turned into arguments. Each morning as she left for work, Jackie would lay in the bed, despondent and depressed. "You've got to do something," she pleaded. "You need to get on with your life. Let me hook you up. You can always have a good job, a permanent job. Forget about football."

She tried every idea she knew to transition him back to the real world. He, in turn, interpreted her offers to help as criticism, not acts of love. He resented her for her suggestions. His entire identity had been built around football. He couldn't imagine living without it. For eleven years—as a college and pro athlete—he'd grown accustomed to being a commodity, bought, sold, packaged, and managed. He was told when to wake up, when to go to bed, when to get on the bus, when to get off the bus, when to eat, and what to eat. He'd lived with purpose, drive, status, camaraderie, and a constant parade of fans. Suddenly, with no transition, his structured and meaningful life had vanished.

As he sunk deeper into his couch, he mulled over money. He had planned for a ten-year career to set his financial life right. Along with his own mortgage, he had been carrying his parents' monthly note ever since Roland had been laid off from the docks. Jackie also had lingering troubles with the IRS after failing to pay taxes on his signing bonus in Minneapolis and failing to claim mortgage exemptions on the house in Tucson. On top of that, he'd never saved any money.

In his seven years with the NFL, he had earned an estimated $435,000, including incentives, bonuses for playoff games, and two Super Bowl appearances. His top pro salary had been $45,000. Because of his taxi squad year, only six of his seven years had been vested for his retirement fund. He believed three more years in the NFL would have allowed him to pay off both mortgages and the

IRS while leaving some cash in the bank. But now, with no salary, he fell behind on mortgage payments.

In a last-ditch effort, he drove to Florida to try out for the upstart Jacksonville Bulls of the newly formed United States Football League, a league that counted Donald Trump among its team owners. Jackie didn't care what team or which league he played for. He just needed cash. He ran coverage routes and filled out forms, then waited in the team's hotel for further instructions. After two days, the hotel manager notified him that the Bulls were no longer paying for his room. So he packed up his suitcase and drove home. He never heard from the team again.

He still felt as vital as ever, but it seemed that the episode in the Rose Bowl locker room had left a long trail. He brooded in darkened rooms and stared at a phone that never rang.

One night, after another argument with Dyan, Jackie finally snapped. He stormed through the house collecting every stitch of her clothes he could find and hurled them into the front yard and screamed for the whole neighborhood to hear: "Get out of *my* house! Later that night, he walked two blocks to the K&B drugstore, bought a big bottle of cheap wine, went home, and got drunk.

FOR MONTHS, AND with Dyan gone, Jackie sulked and slowly deteriorated, not unlike his bank account. He drank in the morning and at night. When his gas and power were cut off, he drank in the dark. After six months of nonpayment on his house, his banker offered to work out a new mortgage plan to help him avoid losing it. Jackie told him to come and take it. He was done. When the repo men arrived, he took his few remaining possessions and moved from family to friends, from friends to family, finally landing with a Melancon cousin who earned cash by cooking and selling crack cocaine. Jackie earned his keep by cooking the meals, cleaning,

and standing lookout. Cheap wine kept him satisfied as he continued to wallow in self-pity. If there was any consolation, it was that
he had no interest in the product his cousin was offering.

Jackie finally found camaraderie and emotional support among
other former NFL players who were living in the city, among them
former Saints Pro Bowl running back Tony Baker. Tony's wife,
Bernadette, ran a local beauty salon. Jackie enjoyed dropping by
for friendly visits from time to time. One day, Bernadette tried her
hand at matchmaking. She could tell Jackie needed a break.

"Jackie, I know you're looking for a girlfriend," Jackie remembered her saying. "I've got Gail coming in for an appointment this
afternoon."

"Who's Gail?" Jackie said.

"She's a customer from Kenner."

"Oh, Lord, a country girl." Jackie laughed, teasing about the
New Orleans suburb's edge-of-the-swamp geography. His imagination compared this hayseed exaggeration with Dyan, who was
politically connected, worldly, and dynamic. He realized what a
fool he'd been for losing her.

But Bernadette encouraged him to hang around and meet
Gail. She promised that he wouldn't be disappointed. When she
walked in, Jackie couldn't believe his eyes. He later remembered
her sashaying through the door like Reese Witherspoon's character
in *Legally Blonde*. She was the most beautiful, elegant woman he'd
ever seen, like "Lola Falana and Gladys Knight mixed together,"
he remembered. As they got to know each other, Jackie discovered
her inner beauty. They bonded on an emotional and spiritual level.
Their budding relationship brought Jackie's spirit back to life.

Gail worked as a payroll clerk at ODECO, an offshore drill-
ing company headquartered in New Orleans. At her first opportunity, she arranged for a job interview for Jackie, which went very

well. Soon he was bringing home a paycheck that was "damn near" equal to his NFL salary. He worked seven days on and seven days off in twelve-hour shifts as a Class B gauger on a production platform in the Gulf of Mexico. Jackie and Gail found an apartment together in Harahan, and he gave her full control of his paycheck. He had no desire to own anything. He felt healthy, strong, and productive again.

He only wished he could say the same for his mother. In the fall of 1982, Audrey's lung cancer turned aggressive. Before long, her shortness of breath had deteriorated so badly that doctors confined her under an oxygen tent. Roland took her decline the hardest. The two had virtually grown up together as best friends. But once he accepted that she was in her last days, he vowed to stay by her bedside until the bitter end. Many of the children thought she'd receive better care in a nursing home, but Roland promised to honor her last wish: to be able to die in her own home.

Jackie dutifully catered to her requests, too, and fetched her cigarettes whenever she asked. "When Mama told me to do something, I did it, no matter how much it hurt," he remembered.

On Friday, October 29, 1982, Roland took a short bus ride to clear his head. When he returned, Audrey had died. Roland never forgave himself for leaving the house.

Jackie got the news while working offshore. He caught the next available helicopter home. When he walked into his parents' house, his baby sister Margo met him at the door with harsh accusations and blame over the cigarettes. "You killed Mama!" she screamed, berating her brother without mercy. Jackie had no response. He knew Margo was mourning in her own way, and while he refused to shoulder the blame, he took the rebuke personally.

At the funeral, many of Jackie's old friends dropped by, including his grade school girlfriends, who came out of respect for the family. Jackie stood back and stared at the casket. Memories rushed in: church services, pressed school uniforms, hospital vigils, hugs, kisses, and Thanksgiving feasts. His mother's hand had shaped him. Her love had sustained him through all of his trials. Gail snuggled at his side as he wept. Sisters and brothers reached into the casket to touch the cold body, but Jackie couldn't find the strength to do so. Donald leaned into the casket and kissed his mother goodbye.

When the last prayer was prayed and the last amen dismissed the graveside service, Jackie drove Gail back to their home in Harahan. After dropping her off, he drove away, promising to return soon. He said that he needed some time alone.

He drove aimlessly toward New Orleans, past the New Orleans Saints training facility in Metairie. He intentionally bypassed his mama's cemetery on Airline Highway. By now the young men would be rearranging flowers and tossing dirt onto the casket. He merged onto the I-10—passing and yielding with people driving into the city for a good-time-Friday night. Downtown, Jackie ignored the exits for Central City and swung north past the Superdome. Memories and regrets clouded his vision as the exit ramps blurred past and disappeared one after another. Before he knew it, he'd barreled past Elysian Fields and turned toward his cousin's place in the east where he'd lived before meeting Gail. He raced like a disoriented child scrambling for a place to hide. He wheeled into a parking space and banged on the apartment door. Just as he expected—and hoped—he found his cousin in the kitchen cooking up a fresh batch of crack cocaine. Jackie walked in and announced his intention. He wanted an escape more potent than a big bottle of wine. After a prolonged and heated debate over the dangers of addiction, Jackie demanded the rock. He found a comfortable spot and lit up a pipe, drew in the toxic smoke, closed his eyes, and waited.

The tiny rock crackled in the glass tube as it burned. Initially, Jackie was repelled by the taste some have described as burning rubber, which indicates poor quality. But nonetheless, he took another draw. He didn't feel anything at first, but the drug quickly absorbed into his bloodstream and rushed to his brain. After several minutes, he floated in a sea of pure love—and then, a rush of euphoria, as he described it. For a few minutes, he forgot about the emptiness. But the soothing effect evaporated almost as quickly as the smoke. He was left feeling anxious and agitated, with a powerful craving for another hit.

Jackie had cash from his job. He had time. He had a convenient supplier. And now, with a second rock in his hands, he had the makings of an addiction.

FOR OVER A year, Jackie held his fragile secret from Gail. At first, she had no idea, but she grew concerned and then suspicious when his mood gradually darkened and his paycheck deposits dwindled. For $10, Jackie could get a piece of crack the size of a square of gum and break it off in smaller rocks to smoke. If he smoked it all, he could get high for an hour or more. While he smoked, he learned to watch the black oil that traced up through the tube with each drag. By letting the oil cool to a sludge, it would harden into a resin. Now each drag intensified, the effect more potent. Before long, his pipe looked like a tootsie roll from the collected resin. Better-quality crack delivered a more immediate effect. The purest rocks left a sanitized taste in his mouth, which filled him blissfully until his wallet ran dry.

Slowly, his new habit chipped away his daily motivation. He still understood the impulse for a normal, responsible life, but he lacked the vigor now to pursue it. For a while, he succeeded in this flimsy masquerade until one morning, he missed the helicopter shuttle for his offshore shift. When his ODECO supervisor called to check on him, he offered an excuse like a child missing a homework assignment. Since his bosses liked him so much, and because he was doing such a good job, the excuse bought him time. But when Gail confronted him about it, he confessed to his trail of deceit. Gail had zero tolerance for drug use and told him so, but she also sympathized—as Dyan had—with the source of his pain. She tried to coach him through his loss with love. "We have a good life going," she reminded him. "Hold on. We'll get help."

But Jackie didn't see the need. He thought he could handle it on his own. The next time he missed the helicopter, he failed to call in with an excuse. He also failed to pick up his paycheck. When Gail saw that he'd missed the money, she realized the depth of the problem.

By then, the drugs had become his priority. He'd crossed a threshold to a single, critical choice. Gail made her choice, too. "To hell with this," Jackie remembered her saying. She hadn't signed up to be a babysitter to an addict. She kicked him out.

Jackie returned to his cousin until he also grew tired of him. From there, Jackie made his way back to the streets of Central City without a precise intention. He walked past his old house on Liberty Street and wandered into Shakespeare Park, where he'd learned to hit a curveball twenty years before. There, without a solitary possession to his name, he slept alone. Weeks turned into months as he struggled to afford his habit. In "dibs and dabs" he scrounged just enough for another lick. He tended ovens at the Turnbull Cone Baking Company and stretched dough to make Melba toast. His supervisor at Melba praised his work, loved his personality, and offered him a supervisor role. But on a Friday, Jackie asked for a $50 advance on his pay for "extra expenses." They never saw him again.

As his crack binges grew worse, he clamored for easier cash. He forgot everything his parents had taught him. As his body screamed for more and more drugs, he obliged. When he felt desperate, he returned to his dad to ask for money. But Roland had no sympathy for an addict. It sickened him to see his son this way. Roland believed in hard work and self-reliance, not pity and indulging a sloth. "I help all my children if they ask," he said, but he felt that Jackie had pushed his family's help too far. He pointed to Jackie's siblings, who were all doing well with good jobs and living responsible lives.

Roland's rejection left Jackie feeling as though he'd been expelled from his family. The checks and balances he'd always relied on from his parents now felt like harsh judgment, especially from Roland. "My family does nothing but point a finger at me and scold me," he said at the time, realizing full well how far he'd crashed from glory to the gutter. "I don't want my family to be ashamed or embarrassed by this," he said. "They have nothing to be ashamed about."

He found work as a convenience store clerk uptown and shared rent on a house on Martin Luther King Jr. Boulevard in Central City. On July 5, 1984, police entered the house where he was staying and arrested him on charges of issuing $1,050 in worthless checks, a felony. Serving a short sentence in Orleans Parish Prison did little to quell Jackie's addiction or his need for cash.

From time to time, he walked from downtown to the New Orleans East—a three-hour journey—to the home of his younger brother Dabney, who was an engineer with the U.S. Army Corps of Engineers. Dabney felt pity for his brother, whom he'd always admired. On his home office desk, he still displayed a picture of Jackie in his Vikings uniform.

To help out, Dabney hid a key to the back door so Jackie could help himself to a sandwich, a shower, and an occasional nap. In the summer of 1986, when Jackie had the house to himself, he rummaged through Dabney's desk drawer until he found a bundle of old checks, and cashed one for $100 at a business just blocks from St. Aug. It seemed too easy, so he tried it again. On his third attempt, the store manager locked the door behind him and called the bank. When Dabney arrived, he stood in the doorway dumbfounded.

"I never would have thought it was you," he stammered.

"Just lock my ass up," Jackie finally said. "That's what I need."

After pleading guilty and serving another stint in lockup, he moved in with a cousin in the St. Thomas housing projects. Two years later, in 1987, he was arrested and convicted for simple burglary and aggravated assault.

In 1989, he spent nine months in Orleans Parish Prison on theft charges. On his arrest records, he listed himself as a trash collector, a pizza deliverer, or unemployed. Roland and all his relatives heard the stories, but they couldn't find him on the streets. He'd found a quiet place to hide under the Pontchartrain Expressway at Carrollton Avenue.

There, he'd dragged an old, rusty box spring that he'd found in the weeds against the bridge supports and overlaid the bed with enough cardboard to form a crude mattress. He'd found a clear sheet of plastic to serve as a blanket. He scrounged up a pair of old automotive floor mats to cushion his bare feet.

And on the morning of July 3, 1990, Jackie picked up a copy of *The Times-Picayune* and opened it to the sports page. He read the top headline, "The Real Life: Surviving after the NFL," the final installment of a three-part series about former NFL players transitioning out of football. The story, written by Jimmy Smith, chronicled Jackie's old teammate, Baltimore Colts defensive tackle Joe Ehrmann, and his reincarnation to an ordained minister. As Jackie read the story, he wondered if someone might be interested in doing a newspaper piece about him.

But instead of indulging such a fantasy, he carefully folded the paper and put it away. He undressed, lay down, and pulled up the plastic around his chest. He closed his eyes and dreamed.

And that's where I found him.

CHAPTER SIX

Twelve Long Steps

1990–1991

It was Friday, July 6, 1990, and Burton Burns, the assistant football coach at St. Aug, felt drained as he stepped out his front door to collect the morning paper. Summers are more oppressive in New Orleans than in other cities across the South—not that it has to be a competition, but here, the marsh-saturated heat feels like it presses a body to the ground.

It had been a short holiday week, and Burton looked forward to a quiet weekend. Outside his door, he paused for a moment to survey his New Orleans East neighborhood and liked what he saw, except for the grass, which desperately needed mowing. As he turned to walk inside, he pulled the folded edition from its plastic wrapping and felt his knees go weak. He scanned the headline again, looking closer at the picture and then the photo's caption for confirmation. Jackie Wallace. His former high school teammate. His mentor. His hero.

This picture of his half-naked derelict friend "sleeping in a plastic bag" sickened him. The last time he'd seen his old friend was in a Colts uniform, in Lincoln, Nebraska, on the field before a preseason game in 1976. It was Jackie who had helped Burns earn his nickname, "Big Stony," after New Orleans Saints linebacker Steve Stonebreaker, for his bruising running style, tough as nails just like his father, Winston, before him—Winston Burns, who had shepherded Jackie at Woodson Junior High.

To Burton, Jackie was the pride of Louisiana, setting the world on fire. He was the last guy he would have expected to see homeless.

Burton Burns was one of the first black players to be recruited by Division I programs in the South. Even the governor of Louisi-

A new address under the I-10 for ex-NFL pro

Jackie Wallace: Fumbled life after football

Jackie Wallace sleeps on a cardboard mattress in his home beneath a freeway overpass

Life after football: too soon, too hard

See related story, C-5

Story by JIMMY SMITH
Staff writer
Photos by TED JACKSON
Staff photographer

Last month, Jackie Wallace decided to break free from the shackles of the drug-infested St. Thomas housing project and search for another place to live.

During a seven-year National Football League career with the Minnesota Vikings, Baltimore Colts and Los Angeles Rams, Wallace became accustomed to staying in fine hotels, preferring to live in hostelries during the regular season while returning to his New Orleans home in the off-season.

Today, Jackie Wallace is one of the city's homeless. You can find his home next to a westbound entrance ramp of Interstate 10 at the Carrollton Avenue interchange, not far from the flashing Baumer Foods-Crystal Preserves neon sign that provides light on dark summer nights.

"Not too many people know I'm here now," Wallace said. "It's nice and comfortable; within walking distance of everywhere I want to go."

Wallace shows off the dwelling with a long sweep of his arm. There's graffiti on the concrete pilings supporting the maze of freeway overpasses.

Underneath the guardrail near a hole, above where Wallace sleeps, someone, perhaps the spot's previous occupant, has spray-painted: For Rent Birds Only.

Long pieces of cardboard and two discarded automobile floormats provide the flooring next to Wallace's bed. It's an iron bed frame he found laying in the weeds surrounding the interstate, now covered by a makeshift cardboard mattress. A balled-up yellow windbreaker in a plastic bag serves as a pillow.

A large piece of clear, heavy plastic protects Wallace from New Orleans' night air.

See WALLACE, A-5

Wallace hangs his wash out to dry on a roadway railing. 'I am homeless by choice,' he said.

ana at the time, John McKeithen, tried to convince him to sign with LSU, but Burton decided on powerhouse Nebraska. He wanted to play with the best. But his dreams of playing professional ball ended when he injured his knee in his sophomore year at Nebraska. He landed an assistant coaching position with the Cornhuskers. It was there, during warmups for a preseason Vikings game, that he had last seen Jackie.

When Burton saw the headlines, he was an offensive coordinator at St. Aug—a mere waystation before landing his dream job in 2007 at the University of Alabama, coaching running backs under Nick Saban. There, he molded the university's two Heisman Trophy winners, Mark Ingram and Derrick Henry.

But in 1990, these lofty ambitions were far from Burton's mind. As soon as he hit campus on Friday morning, Father Matthew O'Rourke, the school's president, called him into his office for a special assignment. O'Rourke had already gathered several men together, and he wanted Burton to head up the rescue mission. The newspaper was spread open on O'Rourke's desk; no one had to ask what the mission was for.

Burton had always been known as a bruising, hard-nosed player on the field, but off it he was known for his compassionate, honest friendships, which made him the perfect recruit. "We're not going to let a St. Aug alumnus sleep under a bridge," O'Rourke told him.

Before noon, Burns, and coach Tony Diagas, along with two of Jackie's high school teammates, Keith Pete and Dale Brock, had all found their way to Mid-City. They had no idea what they were getting into. They watched one another's backs as they surveyed the strewn trash and the homeless men in the distance. They weren't accustomed to rummaging around the interstate underworld. And they were even less confident that they could find Jackie at all. The shadow of the expressway, overgrown, wild, and dangerous, presented a lot of area to cover. But O'Rourke, an efficient and determined man, expected results.

The men found the search to be more direct than they realized. The story on the front page included this detail: "You can find his home next to a westbound entrance ramp of Interstate 10 at the Carrollton Avenue interchange, not far from the flashing Baumer Foods–Crystal Preserves neon sign that provides light on dark summer nights." They first spotted him from across the tracks, asleep just as I had found him three days before. They glanced around nervously at the filth and piles of rotting clothes nearby. But Jackie's site still looked neat and orderly, almost serene. Still, they were shocked to see their old friend in such an environment. They feared that he had totally changed from the guy they once knew.

They woke him gently by calling his name.

Jackie opened his eyes and recognized them immediately. "Hey, what's going on," he said. "What are you doing here?"

The reunion was a bit surreal, as Burton remembers it, as if they were all just walking into a coffee shop, or a group of old friends passing through the neighborhood with Jackie sitting on a porch swing. He cracked a few jokes, perhaps to offset his own discomfort.

A few minutes later, the conversation turned to business. "What can we do for you, Jackie?" Burton said. "Father O'Rourke sent us. He wants you to come home. He wants you back at the school."

And then came the call to action: "What do you want to do, Jackie?"

Jackie couldn't say that he was fine. He couldn't tell a joke to disarm the moment.

The day before, during our long walk along Carrollton Avenue to Palmer Park, Jackie had told me why he'd decided to share his story with me. He said he wanted to help others avoid his fate. He had never actually considered that the story might help him.

Jackie sat like the disgraced former champion that he was, a pitiful figure before fellow warriors. His brothers had stepped up. His team had finally returned. There was nothing else to do but to get up and go. He had nothing to pack.

"I want help," he said.

THE MEN DROVE Jackie back to St. Aug and into the welcoming embrace of Father O'Rourke. Jackie shamefully admitted that he didn't feel worthy of their love, but the men prepared a dinner and celebrated his return. As the story spread across the country via the wire services, friends called to offer solutions and aid. Former Arizona teammates offered shelter and employment. The story broke the heart of Ray Clarke, a fellow defensive back who now served as president of the Urban League of Tucson, who offered to do whatever was necessary. He meant it, too. While he admitted that Jackie's situation was not unique—that many talented kids aren't prepared for what comes after their athletic careers are over—he personally offered Jackie a one-way plane ticket to Tucson, assuming Jackie was willing to leave his hometown.

But Father O'Rourke had other ideas. He wasn't about to let Jackie slip from the school's fraternal bond so easily. "Once you're a Purple Knight, you are part of a family," he'd preached, and now he stood ready to defend the school's founding principles. That night, Jackie slept in a spare bedroom in Father O'Rourke's own residence—the "Priest's house," as the students called it. And in keeping with the school's motto and philosophy, *Gratia Est Vita* ("Grace Is Life"), the brothers gave him a new set of clothes.

Father O'Rourke took a holistic approach to his job and to his students. He wanted the boys to succeed in life as opposed to just in the classroom. From the moment he first saw Jackie's picture in the newspaper, he'd planned the next step. Another Josephite, Father Joseph Verrett (also a St. Aug alumnus) had a spiritual calling for addiction rehab and had just recently left the school two years earlier to run a state-funded drug rehab facility in Baltimore called Tuerk House. Housed in a renovated hospital site, the facility offered seventy-five beds for an inpatient drug and alcohol treatment program, designed for people with no health insurance. About 95 percent of the clientele came from below the poverty line, 65 percent was jobless, and 74 percent was homeless. Jackie matched the profile as if it had been designed for him. Better yet, the program had a reputation for lasting results.

On Monday morning over breakfast, O'Rourke handed Burton two plane tickets and asked him to prepare Jackie for their ride to the airport. He instructed Burton to keep Jackie at his side until he personally handed him off to Father Verrett.

The men's conversation on the way to the airport and through the terminal was relaxed and casual, just like two old friends talking about good times. But as they boarded the plane, Jackie's mood suddenly turned somber. For the first time since the two had met on a dusty practice field, Jackie grew remorseful. Burton tried to shrug it off, but Jackie kept trying to apologize for the trouble he was putting everyone through, for his addictions and for not living up to the St. Aug standard. "I'm so sorry," he said. Jackie fought to hold back his tears.

"No need to apologize to me," Burton told him. He could see that Jackie was serious about changing things.

As the plane sped down the runway and lifted, a calm came over Jackie. He promised himself he was going to make things right—to start fresh with his friends, his family, and with God. As the aircraft banked north, he watched the elegant crescent arc of the Mississippi River and the New Orleans skyline slowly drift from view. He leaned back in his seat and reflected on his glory days.

It was the first time he had been on a plane in over ten years.

ON MONDAY MORNING, back in the newsroom, I collected a dozen copies of Jackie's front-page story and stacked them under my desk for my portfolio. Within days, sources told Jimmy that St. Aug had moved Jackie into an undisclosed drug rehabilitation center in the East. I had never been happier with a story's outcome in all my professional years.

Jackie's rescue reminded me why I got into this business—to tell stories and unleash the awesome transformational power of photography. The impact of my photos and Jimmy's story quickly became apparent. Before the story broke, only two teams, the Denver Broncos and the Houston Oilers, had programs to help players adjust to life in the real world. But now, within weeks of publication, the NFL had hired a former player, John Wooten, as director of a players' program that helped athletes with finances, college degree completion, and the adjustment to life after football.

I returned to my daily life of photo assignments, church life, and family vacations while Jackie waged a brutal war inside his own body and mind. Crack is one of the most addictive substances, and it doesn't let go without a vicious fight, but I didn't know much about that, not yet. In my mind, he was all but cured.

NOT BREAKING FATHER O'ROURKE's promise, Burton Burns escorted Jackie off the plane in Baltimore and into the open arms of Joe Verrett, who immediately drove them to Tuerk House. After intake and formalities, staffers led Jackie upstairs and locked him behind alarmed doors just like everyone else. No one knew of his

NFL history, nor did Jackie boast of it. Patients were more invested in their own detox and recovery than any fading accolades. Any talk of past glory would've fallen on deaf ears.

But Dr. Joe (as everyone called Verrett) envisioned a bright future for his new patient from New Orleans.

Over his eight years of addiction, Jackie had built up a tolerance for crack, which had pushed him to use more and more to achieve the same psychotic effect. Without it, his body went into a semishock condition, with bouts of depression, aggression, fatigue, delusion, anxiety, insomnia, paranoia, agitation, and suicidal thoughts, all disrupted by constant cravings for another hit. His body screamed for more. For most patients, the most intense symptoms persist for a week or more.

During Jackie's binges, the cocaine constricted his blood vessels, raised his blood pressure, and stressed his heart. This on-again, off-again cycle of abuse elevated his chances of an aneurism and heart attack. But unlike other addictions, detoxing the body of crack doesn't usually require specialized treatment beyond blood pressure monitoring. As long as crack isn't present, the body will slowly adjust back to normal. But detoxing the mind is another matter altogether. The cravings preoccupied his mind like a little house of horrors. His desire to escape reality had now become a habit and a pattern of behavior. Walking away from the drug was much easier than walking away from the lifestyle. Crack addicted his mind much more than it addicted his body.

According to his counselors, full mental rehabilitation required total surrender and humility. Jackie needed a broken spirit—what many addicts call "hitting rock bottom." But just because Jackie had been living under a bridge didn't mean that he had been broken. Even though he had readily agreed to come to Baltimore, only Jackie and God truly knew his heart.

At first, somewhat atypically, Jackie just wanted to sleep. His body felt like a car that had run out of gas—or, more precisely, like he'd been smashed up against a wall. At every opportunity, he fell limply into bed. But sleep-ins weren't allowed at Tuerk. Each morning started early with a healthy breakfast to help him replenish the nutrition that the crack had sapped from his system.

In the first days, paranoia clouded his mind. The chaplains compared it to the Old Testament proverb "The wicked flee though no one pursues." But as his mind slowly cleared and his strength returned, Jackie discovered a renewed security in the structured environment. The organized programs minimized his stress and uncertainty. The compassionate staff gave him comfort. As his strength returned, so did his willingness to open up and participate.

Tuerk House literature described the recovery process this way: "Diabetics need insulin, heart patients with clogged arteries undergo bypass surgery and a chronic alcoholic or addict—absent a miracle—needs a clean bed in a safe environment in which to begin the long road back to a life worth living." For Jackie, that seemed to be enough. Tuerk House's program lasted twenty-eight days. The days began at 6:00 A.M. and ended at 10:00 P.M.

Tuerk House was formed in 1970 with "five beds in a derelict rowhouse" in a rough area of Baltimore. Just two years before, on June 30, 1968, public drunkenness in Maryland was considered a crime. On the next day, Maryland officially made it, by law, a medical issue. The Baltimore *Evening Sun* headline read: "Drunkenness Becomes Health Issue in Maryland Starting July 1." As the pioneering Baltimore alcoholism researcher Dr. Max Weisman once explained, "Drinking . . . is not the cause of alcoholism, no more than eating sugar is the cause of diabetes." He and the clinic's namesake, Isadore Tuerk, believed that alcoholism is a disease rather than a moral failing. Tuerk was one of the first psychiatrists in the nation to recognize that truth.

Father Joseph Verrett, formerly of St. Aug High School, took

over the program in July 1988, just as it was teetering on the edge
of financial collapse. His leadership proved crucial to the program's
survival. In 1990, the revitalized program had just relocated to a
freshly renovated, three-story hospital structure in West Baltimore.

Verrett was armed with a doctorate in clinical psychology, and
his success was attributed to his no-nonsense style. Most people
were afraid of him. "He was grumpy, wore really thick glasses, and
it was hard to see his eyes," wrote journalist Rafael Alvarez, a his-
torian for the facility. "He chain-smoked, walked fast, and didn't
really talk to anyone other than tell them what to do." He didn't
believe in coddling addicts. He didn't allow them to wallow in self-
pity. Even his closest friends described Dr. Joe as a "tough old bird
from the Crescent City."

Patients lived under lockdown and were prohibited any com-
munication with the outside world—no telephone or letters. The
windows were blocked to discourage patients from living outside
their recovery. The view of the rough neighborhood surrounding
the facility might, as Verrett believed, trigger a memory of "good
times." Even in detox, addicts can sometimes forget how bad the
life was, he said. Some people live in that image.

Jackie's space was a renovated hospital room, furnished with
two iron beds set on casters, the kind a child of the 1940s would
smash his knee against, as one former patient described it. The
walls were bare. A small hutch held a few changes of clothes, toilet-
ries, and a small collection of books. The bathroom was industrial,
like it belonged at a gas station, except that it had a tub. Chairs
lined the long corridor. A slip of paper taped to the laundry door
reminded clients of the weekday laundry service. A black-and-
white photograph of Isadore Tuerk watched it all from above the
mid-century subway-tile wainscot.

On a strict schedule, a staffer would call out, "Bus stop," which prompted Jackie and the others to line up and march downstairs to the cafeteria for one-hour meetings, five times a day, for discussions and lectures. Hand-painted wall murals encouraged them. On one, a hand reached out with a skeleton key. On another, the hand of God reached down with the Serenity Prayer: "God, grant me the serenity to accept the things I cannot change . . . the courage to change the things I can . . . and the wisdom to know the difference." Finally, on the wall closest to the podium, unclasped hands released a butterfly.

During these sessions, Jackie learned how the human body physically responds to crack and alcohol. The presentations didn't spare any gruesome details, as photos, videos, and illustrations showed abused internal organs and stiffened veins and arteries.

Each evening, guest speakers presented graphic personal testimonies of abuse, violence, seizures, cardiac arrest, and tales from beyond death—much worse than anything Jackie had experienced.

Meetings were no less dire. Counselors asked each addict to look to the person seated to their right, and then look to their left. "One of you will not make it," the patients were told. Their chance of success was a slim 30 percent. The numbers didn't lie.

Whenever someone lost control of their cravings or demonstrated outbursts of disrespect, clinicians moved them to the center of the circle so everyone could speak their mind and offer suggestions on how they should change. The offender had to remain silent, with no defense.

The program forbade fraternization between the male and female addicts. During mealtimes and combined sessions, the women sat in the front of the room and the men in the rear to help the clients reestablish self-restraint. Anyone caught passing notes or whispering across the divide would be dismissed from the program. To some, it felt like grade school. For others, prison.

Jackie understood the point of the rules and tried to make the most of his time.

Church services were offered every Sunday. There, Jackie tried to reconcile his addiction with his faith. He missed the innocent child in St. Bernard who had learned to trust and obey at the feet of Miss Sally. He wondered if God still had a plan for his life. He wondered if a disease qualified as a sin.

By early August, Jackie completed his twenty-eight days and had transferred to Weisman House, an artfully sculpted but physically run-down halfway house on Maryland Avenue, an easy mile-and-a-half walk from the old Memorial Stadium site where he'd played some of his most glorious games.

The twenty-seven-bed, all-male facility looked like a vagrant's hideout—three derelict row houses repurposed into one facility. The unlevel, squeaky floorboards shifted beneath his feet as a staffer escorted him to his room. The high ceilings and vintage moldings felt familiar, vaguely like his shotgun house in Central City, but little else felt like home. The wood paneling peeled away in sheets from the wall. In some places, holes showed straight through the hardwood flooring to the rooms below.

He introduced himself to his new roommate in his typical way: "Jackiewallace" with an extended hand. The greeting received only a dull stare this time. Embarrassed by his forwardness, he averted his eyes to the items that completed the room's setting: two twin beds, two small closets, and two side tables. The bathroom downstairs needed an overhaul. Someone warned him not to lean against the sink—a casualty of an earlier conflict.

Only staff members could answer knocks on the front door. They were usually visitors or new clients, who were led past a rickety staircase through the door to the living room. There, a set of bay windows added a vintage elegance to the otherwise drab appearance. An old rug anchored the room's donated furniture, a table splayed with literature and a "pissy" old fabric couch with broken springs that left one's rear end sitting far below one's knees.

During breaks between daily chores, the house echoed with the occasional clacking of billiard balls and the foul-mouthed accusations to card cheats. A cloud of cigarette smoke hovered throughout the house, especially in the basement, where the addicts gathered for regular AA and NA meetings. There, the ceilings hung so low, even medium-size clients had to bow down to clear their heads. The room held about sixty chairs for meetings three or four times a day, open to anyone who wanted to attend. The "Early Birds" met at 6:45 A.M. and drew addicts from across the city.

The program restricted Jackie's movements for the first ten days. After that, he earned short outings, which gave him limited freedom for four to six hours. His destination had to be approved and verified. Off-campus visits with girlfriends were forbidden, and any and all violations would immediately lead to loss of the privilege. Serious or repeat violations resulted in permanent discharge. When he returned home, staff searched him for contraband and tested his urine for drug use. Weekend passes, available only for family visits, also had to be earned. But Jackie had no place to be, no family to visit, and no friend who knew he was there, so he mostly remained on the property.

During twice-a-week visits with counselors at Wyman Park Recovery Center, less than a mile north of Weisman, Jackie learned one of the fundamentals of staying sober: to "call a friend in recovery instead of an acquaintance on the corner."

For nine months, Jackie stayed clean and out of trouble. He found peace in the mandatory, repetitive chores that kept his mind focused and his time productive. One morning, while he mopped the floors by the staircase, he peered into the living room at a pair of especially nice legs. They belonged to Deborah Williams. She worked nearby as a secretary and volunteered to help Weisman and Tuerk organize special events throughout the year. That morning, she had come to Weisman to drop off a handful of flyers to promote the upcoming Christmas party at the Hyatt Hotel. She also carried a bundle of clothes for her brother, Jackie's roommate. While she waited in the living room, sunk deeply into the sofa, she failed to notice the man with the mop.

After a few days, Jackie connected the name and number printed at the bottom on the party flyers with the nice legs in the living room. He picked up the phone and gave her a call. Intrigued, but cautious about dating an addict, she invited Jackie to join her for the Christmas party, which was sponsored, approved, and chaperoned by Weisman.

Deborah was a tall, big-boned woman with a sparkling smile and a generous heart. Friends knew her for her fine cooking and her faithful, spirit-filled love for God. She described herself as a flower child of the sixties who believed that anything God touched was good—that everything was beautiful. She said that she'd specifically prayed for a man like Jackie to come into her life, and now here he was, warts and all. Despite her serious concerns, she prayed, "Lord, if I pass up this opportunity . . . he might be just what I'm looking for." Sincere prayer, she thought, could lead down interesting paths.

During the party a few days later, Jackie acted the gentleman—pulling out her chair and opening doors. When the party photographer ran out of film, Jackie volunteered to leave the party to buy more so that they could have a photo together. *Who does that?* she remembered thinking.

Jackie continued to live at Weisman for nine months, until May

1991, when he moved into his own apartment. Now that Jackie was able to move about and date freely, Deborah invited him to her apartment. They talked for hours, until his eyes grew tired and he fell asleep with his head in her lap. She thought it was endearing.

With the help of Deborah's cooking, his weight returned to normal. His health improved, and he felt responsible again. And with Deborah's encouragement, Jackie reached into the deeper tenets of the Alcoholics Anonymous' twelve-step program. He devoted the major parts of the "Big Book" (the first 164 pages) to memory and recited many of them word for word.

Under the "How It Works" chapter, the authors of the AA book bragged that addicts who follow the path "thoroughly" rarely fail. Easier said than done. The book, however, emphasizes spiritual progress over spiritual perfection. As long as Jackie showed up, as long as he made progress, he had a fighting chance.

In the pages of the book, the twelve steps read as a road map for what had worked for others.

Summarized, they helped Jackie admit that he had lost control of his life and that he needed to humbly rely on God to restore him. He needed to confess the "exact nature" of his wrongs to himself and others, make a list of persons he had harmed, and be willing to make amends to everyone he could—when appropriate. He needed to make a "searching and fearless moral inventory" of himself and promptly admit whenever he was wrong. He needed to develop a personal relationship with God through prayer, study, and meditation. And as a result of adhering to the steps, he should try to share his spiritual awakening with other addicts.

Jackie found the steps liberating.

With the encouragement, and insistence of Father Verrett, he finished the remaining twenty hours of his college degree at the University of Baltimore. His sister Louvinia, who was now teaching in the Orleans Parish schools, wanted him to return to New Orleans to coach and teach. But Verrett encouraged him to pursue a degree in social work to put his helpful spirit to work, and Jackie agreed. He felt like he was working his way back into society. And now, he believed he might be in love. Crack started to feel like a fading memory.

In September 1991, nearly fifteen months after I found Jackie under the bridge, Jimmy Smith wrote an update for *The Times-Picayune* about Jackie's recovery. In an interview, Louvinia told Jimmy that she was optimistic about Jackie's future, but she cut him no slack. "It took him 38 years to get where he was," she said. "He chose to be in the situation he was in. He just needed some help to get out of it. Right now, it's all up to Jackie."

CHAPTER SEVEN

Do You Believe in Miracles?

1991–1995

The glorious yellow pennant fluttered from the mainmast of the *Pride of Baltimore II,* a topsail schooner docked in the city's Inner Harbor. The eighteen-foot-long cloth snagged for a moment in the rigging but finally snapped free in the crosswind. The breeze that ushered in from the sea felt good on Jackie's face as he and two friends walked the docks to clear his head.

As they passed South Calvert Street, the scent of fresh-baked pastries drew them inside a small bakery. Jackie's hand-me-down clothes didn't fit in with the well-heeled office workers waiting in line, and a woman waiting at the back noticed. She thought this man looked disheveled, a bit suspicious, and . . . dare she say, vaguely familiar? Sweat drenched his shirt.

Though he'd been sober for over a year, he'd been fighting off a strong urge to use over the last few days. The two men beside him, his wingmen from Weisman, assured him they'd help get him through it. When he turned with his bag of bagels and coffee, the woman stepped out of line.

"Excuse me. Do I know you?" she sheepishly asked. As she

probed his hollow eyes, he assured her that she'd made a mistake and walked away. But she followed from a distance until it finally hit her. She approached again.

"Jackie?" she said, and stuck out her hand. He nodded his head slightly and apologized, saying that drugs had blown that part of his memory. That he had been so honest surprised even him.

"I'm Maureen, Ted Marchibroda's assistant, from the Colts."

Jackie broke into a grin at the chance meeting and engulfed her in a hug. It had been nearly fourteen years since they'd last talked, since they'd helped create some of the greatest football excitement since Johnny Unitas. Quickly, they recalled teammates and old stories. Then Jackie summarized his condition for her—how far he'd traveled and how far he'd come. They traded phone numbers and promised to schedule a lunch—the kind of conversation that typically leads to nothing but a smile and a lost scrap of paper. But a few days later, he called to thank her for being the spark he needed that dark day. Her hug had given him a lift.

They kept their promise and met for lunches over the coming weeks. "You're not on 'athletic scholarship' anymore," she told him. "College and the NFL are over. You have to dig deep and face life for yourself."

"Athletic scholarship" soon became their running joke, as well as his new mantra. She reminded him that he had a whole family of teammates in Baltimore. "Mo," as the veterans now called her, had become the glue that bonded the Colts family together. She invited him to be a part of the city's "Give Baltimore the Ball" promotion, which sought to bring an NFL expansion team to Baltimore. The city had been without an NFL team since 1983, when Robert Irsay sneaked his team out of Baltimore to Indianapolis in the dead of night.

On a Thursday night, August 27, 1992, Jackie joined the group of former Colts players who stood on the sidelines to watch the New Orleans Saints and the Miami Dolphins play an exhibition game at Memorial Stadium. The stadium of legend had not seen NFL football action in nine years. The roar of the crowd made Jackie feel as though he'd been welcomed home.

Jackie and Deborah's relationship continued to evolve and mature. Even though he still struggled with his cravings, he managed to be responsible. He accepted a job at Weisman, where he monitored the continuing rehabilitation programs. He enjoyed the responsibility, but he hoped that he could land a different job soon. As Jackie proved his trustworthiness, he and Deborah began to imagine a life together. He pictured a little house in the suburbs with the picket fence, just like the one he'd dreamed about from his St. Bernard bedroom window. He liked the idea of settling down in Baltimore.

As his sobriety took hold, he connected with the Early Birds, the AA/NA group that met at 6:45 A.M., every weekday in the Weisman basement. Jackie always arrived early, sometimes brewing the coffee and setting up tables. He had fashioned himself a leader and often accepted opportunities to give his personal testimony. He impressed everyone by reciting long passages without ever opening the "Big Book," which had now become his manual for life.

The meetings gave him dignity and purpose. Before long, administrators trusted him with more official tasks, signing verification documents for the "court slippers," the addicts ordered into the program by law. Jackie got to know the judges—and they got to know him—as he testified for an addict's compliance. The responsibility felt good.

IN THE DECADE of the 1990s, advertising and high subscription numbers kept newspaper coffers flush with cash. In turn, editors

spent lavishly on journalism. As a result, I began traveling exten-
sively for international assignments, first to Haiti and Cuba, then
to Germany, Saudi Arabia, Kuwait, and the Persian Gulf during
Desert Storm. My career had accelerated.

But one of the biggest days of my career came late in 1992.
As I sat writing photo captions for a run-of-the-mill local story, a
sharp rap on the glass wall that separated the photo lab from the
newsroom interrupted my work. I looked up to see Jackie's six-foot-
three-inch frame looming over me, dressed in a three-piece suit
with his arms stretched wide. Beaming from ear to ear with his
gap-toothed grin, his muffled voice rang through the glass: "Do
you believe in miracles?"

What a sight! That image is burned in my mind as clearly as
if I'd had a camera in my hands. I leapt from my desk and rushed
to greet him. We clasped hands, and I let out a howl. Editors and
writers glanced up and rolled their eyes at yet another disruption
from the free-spirited photo department.

He looked great. Since I had last seen him under the bridge,
he'd added a little paunch, a sign that he was getting proper nour-
ishment. His dark hair showed a light dusting of gray. His face
looked fuller. He'd lost the worried crinkle in his brow. His eyes
looked clear and bright.

As we talked, he exploded with the news. He now lived with a
real roof over his head. He had found work. He loved Baltimore.

He had charmed his way into the newsroom, past security
guards and receptionists, to invite Jimmy Smith and me to his
wedding. On December 5, 1992, Jackie Wallace and Deborah
Williams, now an executive secretary at Liberty Medical Center,
became man and wife.

JIMMY AND I couldn't attend the wedding, but we arranged a trip
in 1995 to mark the story's five-year anniversary and produce an

update for the newspaper. We arrived on a Friday and drove to Jackie's handsome two-story suburban home in north Baltimore.

We found the happy couple preparing for their annual July 6 rescue party, the day his story published in *The Times-Picayune* and his teammates pulled him from under the bridge. That year, they delayed the party for two days until Saturday so more friends could gather.

For the update, Jimmy described the house as a "big, gray vinyl-sided, almost antebellum-style home, four white columns framing a large veranda." Deborah had taken great care not to disturb a bird's nest near the front door.

They had only been in the house for a few weeks. Inside, a well-used Bible on the mantel lay open to Psalms 92–100. "Come, let us sing joyfully to the Lord," began Psalm 95. "Let us acclaim the Rock of our salvation. Let us greet him with thanksgiving; let us joyfully sing psalms to him. For the Lord is a great God and a great king above all gods . . . Let us kneel before the Lord who made us."

"Deborah and I read it every morning," Jackie said, peering over my shoulder.

He led me through the house, beaming all the way through

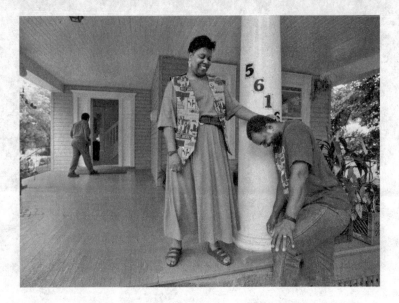

the four bedrooms, two baths, and across the half-acre lot. I shot a photo as he and Deborah joked on the front porch. His head bowed down in laughter as her hand caressed the back of his head.

As we walked back inside, he waved his arm around. "You see this? I appreciate this because it's something I haven't had for a while."

As Jackie opened a box of gifts from New Orleans—a box of pralines, chicory coffee, and red beans and rice—Deborah admitted that she hadn't fallen in love at first sight. "Jackie's a very complex person," she said. "There are times when he has a Jekyll/Hyde personality."

"You should have known me when I drank," Jackie, said, smiling as he bit into another praline.

"I'm glad I didn't know him when he drank," Deborah said. "I pray a lot for our relationship. I ask the Lord to help us. He's an A-type personality. He's critical, analytical, tears things apart. He's an extrovert; I'm an introvert. But our life has been good."

Jimmy scribbled his notes. I tried to imagine the two of them meshing as a couple. I loved that they could be so honest about their differences.

After the tour of the house, Jackie shuttled us downtown to the Baltimore Arena, where he had been working on the changeover crew, officially an "operations specialist," for the past three years. In a gray, purple, and gold St. Augustine T-shirt and a pair of dusty blue work pants, he showed us off to his co-workers while explaining the intricacies of freezing hockey ice. I took pictures as he and others moved plywood panels into place for that night's World Wrestling Federation show. His friends teased him about being a celebrity with his own personal photographer. One man looked surprised to learn of his NFL past. I smiled behind my camera as I watched him work.

The arena's executives praised Jackie's good nature, his easy smile, and his generosity. The office receptionist told how Jackie surprised her with a visit in the hospital after knee surgery the year before. "Today, he left me a lollipop." Meanwhile, the general manager dismissed any concerns about his ongoing battle against abuse, something we had been worried about since we'd gotten to Baltimore. "He's been wonderful," she said, "a real pleasure. He'll say the sweetest things, and that comes with having a good heart."

Jackie led us to the centerpiece of his tour: a small concrete-block room just past the employee time clock. A line of beige lockers, much like you'd find in a high school hallway, stood against the wall.

"Guess which locker is mine?" he said.

I didn't have to guess. Newspaper clippings covered locker number 47. One told of a Baltimore drug raid where Deborah's brother had been arrested, and an older clipping of the death of former Saints and Colts linebacker Steve Stonebreaker. We all knew the story: police had found Stonebreaker inside a locked Metairie,

Louisiana, garage with his head cushioned on a pillow near a car exhaust pipe.

Jackie jangled off the padlock and opened the locker. "I had gotten to that state. I just didn't have the courage to kill myself."

He pulled out a 1976 Baltimore Colts team photo. Fifth from the left on the second row, Jackie sat with perfect posture—looking determined and stone-faced in his blue number 20 jersey—surrounded by Bert Jones and Lydell Mitchell. He flipped the photo aside and opened a gray briefcase with a blue folder marked "Bridge Pictures, July 6, 1990." He pulled out the pictures I'd taken of him sleeping under the bridge five years before, along with news clippings from his turning point, a shocking reminder of a former life.

"This helps me get back in touch with my God," he said as he flipped through his memories. "I read this story all the time. When things are going real good or when things are going real bad." He told me how he needed to see the photos every morning, how touching them gave him permission to remember. "It only takes one slip," he said, "and I'll end up right back where you found me. That picture you took, in the fetal position . . . I'm being born again."

Hearing that was the proudest moment of my journalism career. I kept the camera tight to my face to hide my welling eyes. For a moment, I couldn't focus.

On Saturday afternoon, a sizable number of recovering alcoholics and addicts from Weisman House filtered in among the party guests. After they sampled his New Orleans cooking, Jackie presented framed copies of his *Times-Picayune* story to the "new alcoholics" (as Jackie called them), hoping to inspire them to greater heights. "People hear my story, and they say, 'Yeah, right. Yeah, right.' Then I show them my story. And they can't believe it."

I was astonished to see Jackie in this place. Here, instead of an addict on a trash bed in the weeds, I saw a leader, a man taking care of his responsibilities, engaged and committed. He said he and Deborah were considering starting a family.

He turned to Jimmy and me and talked about that fateful day in 1990. "You know, I said at the end of that article that I was all right. But really, I wasn't all right. I knew if I'd get past that moment, though, that I would be all right." He quoted his favorite Bible verse, Hebrews 11:1: "Now faith is the substance of things hoped for, the evidence of things that are not seen."

He said he'd noticed that Baltimore had lots of bridges. "And they have a lot of rats under there. And it snows here. They've still got people out there on the street dying."

He smiled and made us a promise. "I'm not going back."

CHAPTER EIGHT

Triumphant

1995–2001

At the time of my visit to see Jackie in Baltimore, I was in the middle of an extensive, eleven-month project focused on the health of the world's oceans, in which I was teamed with three reporters to explore the overwhelming environmental challenges facing the world's fisheries. When I left Jackie's house, I drove to Ocean City, Maryland, to photograph a fisherman for the series. The project, called *Oceans of Trouble,* took me on a tour of the Florida Everglades, New England's Georges Banks, the bay of Phuket in Thailand, and the Tsukiji fish market in Tokyo. The eight-day series, which published in March 1996, broke new ground in the understanding of wetlands loss, ineffective regulations, overfishing, and pollution concerns. In May 1997, the series won the Pulitzer Prize for Public Service. Champagne corks flew, and a brass band pranced through the newsroom as we celebrated *The Times-Picayune's* first Pulitzer in the newspaper's 160-year history.

Due to the prestige that the award brought, I began traveling the country to talk about my work at conferences, conventions, and churches. I showed my photographs, and spoke about Louisiana's environmental disaster, but I easily pivoted to other topics such as poverty and homelessness. I closed each presentation with Jackie's story, which I believed to be the most meaningful of my career. The photos and tale of Jackie's redemption often brought audiences to their feet. He was my hero, the personification of the power of journalism and faith.

Meanwhile, Jackie joined his own speakers' circuit and gave his personal testimony for addicts at Tuerk House. Other groups booked him for inspirational talks. He traveled to the Midwest to speak to farmers and business leaders about his triumphant recovery. He accepted every invitation to talk to church groups and schoolchildren. He joined the Baltimore mayor's advisory committee for mental health and substance abuse.

I RECEIVED THE first phone call in the fall of 1996, as I watched the Thanksgiving Day parade. I picked up the phone expecting to hear my brother's voice, making sure we'd be on time for lunch at his house. Instead, Jackie's buoyant voice rang out, "Happy Thanksgiving. This is Jackiewallace. How you doing?"

We didn't talk long, nor did we say much when we did—Jackie mostly wanted to thank Jimmy and me, as if to fulfill the day's overriding theme—but what I didn't know then was that the call would become an annual ritual, like clockwork, each Thanksgiving morning. "From the waist to the taste," he'd say, whenever he'd call every year, and I'd look forward to these check-ins. In some way, it felt as if our roles had become reversed.

More specifically I stopped thinking of him as the homeless man in the weeds or a sharp-dressed man in a three-piece suit. He became my friend, Jackie.

I enjoyed knowing that his time in Baltimore had gone so well. He had learned how important it was to stay on his "medicine," his word for doing the right things to stay sober. "Everybody that's ever been through treatments knows what the right thing is," he said. "That means, you go to these meetings, you get you a sponsor, get you a home group, go to church. You get people who you're going to listen to that's going to tell you the truth, and you do it." The "medicine" produced profound results.

The Early Bird group became his second family as he devoted more time there. He often presided over the AA group meetings. He enjoyed the new friendships. He benefited from the stories he heard from the men and women who drifted in each week. Everybody had a story to tell, but they all started the same way:

"Hi, I'm Barbara. I'm an alcoholic."

Barbara first connected with the twelve steps after she drunkenly crashed her car into a police cruiser. Step number four of the plan forced her to make a "searching and fearless moral inventory" of her life, revealing her darkest secrets to a confidant. She thought her group leader, Jackie Wallace, talked too much about football, but nevertheless she found him to be the perfect person to talk to. Before long, she began advising him to clean his own house. "Any leftovers will eventually reappear," she told him. "There's no wrestling with God," she said. She could see he was holding something back.

"Hello, I'm John. I'm an alcoholic."

John, a second-generation addict, tried to suffocate himself one night with a plastic bag outside of a bar when he was thirty-nine years old. His suicide attempt failed because he was too drunk to hold the seal around his neck. The attempt frightened him into Weisman. His first meeting at Weisman frightened him, too, as he sat against the wall, one of only two white people among a sea of black faces. He understood that he needed help, but he wasn't as bad as this room full of inner-city losers; addicts, criminals, thieves, and skid-row prostitutes. He had a respectable job making good money. He lived in a nice neighborhood. In other words, he resented being lumped in "with the dregs of Baltimore."

John tamped down his anger enough to tolerate the speaker's remarks, but he didn't really see the point. When Jackie mentioned football, though, John sat up. He scanned Jackie's size. He looked closer at this face. Then it hit him.

Jackie Wallace! Of course!

Unknowingly, John had just spent fifteen minutes mostly ignoring one of his Colts heroes.

John was one of the rabid fans that Baltimore likes to brag about and one of the drunks who dragged down the goal post in the legendary 1975 fog game. As a twenty-two-year-old, he was already a drunken mess when Bradshaw heaved the sixty-five-yard pass over Jackie's head in the '76 playoff game, a play that prompted him to take another deep swig of bourbon. He somehow survived his drive home that night, a drive that he can shake his head and laugh about now.

John suffered from a condition commonly known as King Baby Syndrome, where he felt as though he was better than everybody else in the room. The term originated from Freud's paper "On Narcissism" in 1914. "It's a sick, twisted thing," John said. His rational mind knew he *wasn't* better, but he felt like he *should* have been. Jackie exhibited many of the same traits with feelings of self-obsession, arrogance, vanity, greed, and an exaggerated need to be admired. Sometimes King Babies turn to rage.

John got sober in October 1993 and became a lifelong fan of the Early Birds. With Jackie's influence, John quit drinking for good.

John remembered one time when Jackie lost his temper in an argument after a meeting. He had to be restrained. John thought a man of Jackie's size could do some real damage if he couldn't learn to control himself. He also thought he could develop a little more humility.

SOME YEARS LATER, I don't remember how long, my Thanksgiving morning phone calls stopped. I didn't give it much thought at first; times change, and people move on, especially in my field of work. But somewhere around 2001, as my family and I returned home from our Thanksgiving feast, I began to wonder what had happened. I called Jimmy Smith to see if he'd heard any recent news from Jackie. He said he hadn't, but he'd make a few phone calls to follow up. We thought it would be fun to know how Jackie's recent years had gone—and if he was still working at the arena or if he'd moved on to better things. But when Deborah answered the phone, she told him that they had separated. She said they had argued and that Jackie had simply disappeared. She didn't offer any details other than to say she'd heard rumors that he had returned to sleeping under a bridge, but she wasn't sure. Jimmy and I were both stunned. Just like that, all the effort and energy that had gone into Jackie's recovery had failed. I found it hard to comprehend how he could crash so hard and so fast. There seemed to be no more information any of our contacts knew to give us. By the time we got the news of Jackie and Deborah's split, years had already passed. Whatever trail he left had grown long cold by then.

Jimmy and I both figured that he'd retreated to his comfort zone: New Orleans. I could imagine him again ragged and torn, wandering the streets between downtown and the East. The shelters knew him here, and most of his family still lived in Orleans Parish. Maybe he'd found a place with them. So, I started watching for him. Driving to assignments around the city, I tried my best to scan each homeless camp. As I waited at traffic lights, I looked deep into the face of each man begging with a cardboard sign, but I never saw him. For a story about the city's freeze plan, I visited the dormitory at Ozanam Inn, photographing men as they bedded down. I asked around the shelter if anyone had seen Jackie. Administrator Deacon Biaggio DiGiovanni told me that Jackie had dropped in a few nights the past winter. He'd heard he'd served time in Orleans Parish Prison. I searched public records and checked local prisons, but I couldn't find any trace. How does a man vanish?

Jackie Wallace hung in my gut like a dull ache. His disappearance bugged me, much more deeply than it should have. Photojournalists are supposed to use the camera to create an emotional barrier to grief and tragedy. We're supposed to maintain professional distance, to become mere observers. But not this time.

I couldn't understand why I cared so deeply. Drug addicts relapse all the time. Sweet stories turn sour on a regular basis. Pedestals crumble. Heroes disappoint. We all stand on feet of clay.

Perhaps ego and pride had gotten the best of me as well. Was Jackie's disappearance proof that my crowning journalistic "achievement" had failed? As if verifying this, my speaking engagements now ended with a desultory addendum. "Sadly," I'd say to my audience, "we don't know where Jackie is today," and I'd watch people's faces fall in disappointment. In some speeches, I considered dropping Jackie's photos and his story from my program altogether. I wanted my happy ending back. But for whatever reason, I kept them in. I kept telling his tale and trying hard to keep his memory intact.

But as the years passed, I found it harder to remember which NFL teams he'd played for or to remember Deborah's name or in which housing project he'd grown up. My mind had started to detach from him, and the lapses made me feel guilty. But this is exactly what journalists are supposed to feel in order to keep a healthy dispassion from our work. *Let it go,* I'd tell myself. But the more I tried, the more I realized that Jackie's life had profoundly intertwined with mine. I felt as though I should do more.

Ancient sermons and countless devotional readings flooded my conscience. What am I supposed to learn from the parable of the talents or the sheep and goats? What is the whole purpose of man? Am I my brother's keeper? These scriptures were meant to be more than motivational quips or philosophical exercises.

I wanted to know more, to feel more, to dig deeper. I didn't want dainty Sunday school answers to my problems. I could already see how God had used experiences to shape my faith—the doors that had already opened before me and the people I'd met. Like many Christians I knew, I yearned to communicate more directly with God—to sense His guidance more clearly through prayer. But despite my desire for clarity, I know Christians are called to live by faith. The crossroads in my past represented critical choices and circumstances that had led me to profound discoveries and opportunities, like my decision to move to New Orleans in the first place. Meeting Jackie represented an important crossroad. I could see how it changed me. A life of faith also meant that the future was intentionally left murky.

But there were many other experiences that helped shape my view of Jackie Wallace. Looking back, two critical landmarks helped me understand why a simple country boy from Mississippi wanted this one homeless man to be OK.

I found the first one in a place called Desire.

Like St. Bernard (Jackie's childhood home), the Desire Housing Project was named after its central street—the same street that Tennessee Williams immortalized in 1947 with *A Streetcar Named Desire.* The street cut a depressed, violent path through the project's core. The street is surrounded by other streets named Abundance,

Piety, Industry, Pleasure, Humanity, Benefit, and Treasure—all of them reduced to mockery by the social and economic conditions endured by the people living along those roads.

Back in 1989, my editor had given me a clear mandate: to melt into this fabric of violence, crime, and urban decay until my photographs could clearly show how people survived this place. I arrived with a head full of remedies for the education and salvation of the poor. I self-righteously believed that all the poor needed to get ahead was honesty, hard work, and faith. I believed the cliché: that the poor could and should pull themselves up by their own bootstraps. But in Desire, I saw no bootstraps—only bare feet and tattered sneakers. I saw a grade school without books and apartments without running water. I asked one mother what she'd like to see different in her life in five years' time. She simply replied, "I want my windows fixed."

The Housing Authority of New Orleans built Desire with federal dollars in the mid-1950s atop an old garbage dump in a cypress swamp. "It's a dog," said Ed Arceneaux, a housing specialist with the department of Housing and Urban Development during an interview in 1989. "This is only my personal opinion," he said. "But I think . . . it wasn't designed for people to live in. It was designed, rather, as warehousing for the city's poorest residents." There were plenty of facts to back his viewpoint: The buildings were built to minimum standards and had begun to crumble from soil subsidence, even before the first tenant settled in. The structures were densely packed—1,860 housing units on one hundred acres—built on the edge of the city, far removed from job opportunities, stores, churches, and even bus routes. One federal housing official called it "The Reservation" because, he said, residents had been removed from society and made dependent on the government support.

As I explored the neighborhood, I was shocked by the poverty and social isolation. Bewildered children rubbed my arms and stroked my hair as if they'd never touched a white man before. I watched rats rummage through my camera bag while I tried to sleep on a borrowed couch. Roaches scrambled over the lips of kitchen pots and pans, overwhelming the baits and traps. From a second-floor bedroom window, I watched teenagers pass drugs to buyers in expensive cars. In an ink-black stairwell at 2:00 A.M., slivers of light reflected off assault weapons balanced on the hips of teenage lookouts.

Each Sunday morning, when I worshipped safely in my own neighborhood with my family, I read familiar scriptures in a new light. The once-soothing sentiments now demanded holy obligation. I read the words of Jesus again: "For I was hungry and you gave me nothing to eat, I was thirsty . . . I was a stranger . . . I needed clothes," and "Whatever you did not do for one of the least of these, you did not do for me." According to these passages, I photographed into the eyes of Christ each day. Did I recognize Him?

I reread my favorite scripture, which I'd underlined in my Bible: "Commit your works unto the Lord and your thoughts will be established." In other passages, I read words I didn't want to believe. "If a man shuts his ears to the cry of the poor, he too will cry out and not be answered."

When I first entered Desire, I had subconsciously prayed, "God, this is what I'll do for You. Please bless my efforts." By week four, I was praying, "God, show me the way, and I will follow—regardless the cost." After that, I tried to make images that would touch the most critical skeptic's heart. Some days I left so angry and frustrated that I slammed my cameras into my trunk. My editor suggested that maybe I'd been on the assignment too long.

One afternoon, as I photographed little girls jumping rope in a courtyard, gunfire erupted around the corner. We all dove into the stairwell and waited for the melee to clear. After a few minutes of quiet, I peered out—with a five-year-old over my shoulder to check the scene. We didn't see any dead bodies or debris. We heard

no wailing or screams, so *she* declared it to be safe. The children reclaimed their rope as if nothing had happened.

As I began to edit my collection of photographs back in the darkroom, some of the images startled even me. One showed an infant as she stared into my lens from her crib with a backdrop of a U.S. veteran's casket flag. Rosary beads and a tiny crucifix dangled between two embroidered stars. Another closeup portrait showed a mother's eyes as she kept watch for trouble through a peephole in a steel door, her address crudely stenciled in white paint: "3665 DESIRE."

In yet another, a young boy recoiled in disgust as he carried three dead rats from his house to the garbage cans.

During the weeks of this project, my wife, Nancy, worried about my safety. She knew I sometimes risked too much for my photographs. I thought most of her concerns were out of proportion, but I couldn't argue with her feelings. I felt that most of my

risks were calculated and reasonable. I didn't talk about the few
that weren't. But they were impossible to hide. The evidence was
printed in the morning paper.

I shot one photograph at the Guste High Rise that showed
a young girl on roller skates as she stared at the lifeless body of a
murdered teenager, his blood trickling away on the concrete. In
1994, I photographed the funeral of Mikey Stewart, a four-year-
old gunshot victim—the city's first recorded drive-by shooting.
His family paraded his miniature casket through Central City in a
horse-drawn funeral coach as his young brothers, sisters, and cousins trailed behind with placards that read, "THOU SHALT NOT KILL."
New Orleans had become more violent with each passing year. In
1994, 424 people were murdered in the city—a record high.

For an earlier series on the escalating crack cocaine epidemic, I
took the calculated risk too far and hid in my trunk to get a picture
of drug dealers. I'd spent weeks shadowing narcotics officers on
drug busts and house raids. I made pictures of drug-related violence and close-up photos of rocks of crack in detectives' hands.

But despite it all, one important picture evaded me. I couldn't seem to get the actual moment of purchase on the street.

With a Sunday deadline looming, Friday morning found me desperate. By Friday afternoon, I had an idea. If I removed my car's taillight, I should be able to photograph the dealers through the empty hole. I knew my editors wouldn't approve, so I kept my plan from them. I recruited two co-workers willing to drive me to the target intersection and leave me to my fate. We communicated by two-way radio as they stood watch from two blocks away. There, alone, I waited for what seemed like an eternity.

Finally, a dark sedan pulled tight against the curb—exactly where I thought it would. The driver turned off his headlights. Three men sauntered over and leaned in with hushed tones. The streetlights gave me four perfect silhouettes. I held my breath and delicately squeezed the shutter release as they transferred cash for crack. I had the frame.

Dealers like these men controlled the streets with violence. They arrogantly taunted cops. They preyed on the weakest and the oldest as they chose their territory. Grandmothers retreated from their porches. Young parents cowered like hostages in their own houses. Dealers hid their guns and their product in the bushes or under houses until needed, so they wouldn't be caught holding when the cops came questioning. They dared anyone to mess with their stash, but even the children knew where the hiding places were.

Some have the courage to fight back. A few tried, but they mostly ended up in a shadowed heap on the evening news, a warning for others to mind their own business. Mothers pulled their wide-eyed boys from the windows and drew the curtains—afraid that they'd learn too much, that they'd fantasize about fine shoes, expensive cars, and the fine women that fistfuls of money attract.

But the children learned. A few can't wait to hold a gun—usually at twelve or thirteen years old—a twisted, warped rite of passage.

I watched through the lens as the men pocketed the cash and retreated into the night.

My editors were eager to get the pictures for the layout. Nobody asked what it took to get the photos. They didn't care as long as the images were ethical, truthful, and in focus, in that order. By Sunday morning, a seemingly simple photograph of a street-level drug deal anchored the front page. But the photograph could never show the fear I felt or how three men leaning into a car were destroying an innocent neighborhood, the lives of addicts as well as the future of the next generation. And it couldn't show why a thirty-two-year-old white man from McComb, Mississippi, would risk his life for a snapshot of life so distant from his own. The photo couldn't show why documenting the lives of the poor had become such an important part of my dedication to God. The photo couldn't show it in part because I still couldn't see myself. God was preparing me for something far beyond my vision.

CHAPTER NINE

Even a Dead Man Leaves a Trail

2012–2016

In the summer of 2012, the newly named director of the New Orleans Mission, David Bottner, spearheaded a $6 million renovation of its property, located just a few blocks from the Superdome. Bottner wanted to transform the mission from an "overnight respite" to a place that could change lives. He refocused the mission's priority on spiritual formation, which he believed was the key to long-lasting recovery. Bottner, a devout Christian, had given up a highly successful and lucrative career as an entrepreneur, motivational speaker, and nationally recognized sales trainer to work with the homeless.

The shelter's one-hundred-year-old building was in paltry shape, so bad that many homeless claimed that they preferred living under the bridge to dealing with the rats, cockroaches, and filth. By the fall of 2014, interior renovations brought substantial structural improvements, but it didn't stop the street critics from complaining about the living conditions. They were entitled to this perspective, of course, but Bottner believed their claims were simply excuses for avoiding serious help. He figured that if he could

provide a better "product," the homeless would have no one else to blame but themselves. "That's when people are most likely to face their inner demons," he said. To discover the truth about the shelter's state of repair, a reporter named Richard Webster suggested a deep-dive feature on the facility. I eagerly signed on. Bottner agreed to our simple proposal: To get a realistic understanding, Richard and I would go through intake. We'd eat, sleep, and live side by side with the homeless and addicted. We'd openly introduce ourselves as journalists and would openly carry the tools of our trade, but otherwise, we would attempt to experience what the residents did.

We arrived at 5:00 P.M. with the crowd of hungry men and women and underwent the same screening they did, which included a humiliating hour-long interview. I answered a litany of difficult questions about some very personal things. I guess I passed, because the volunteer screener approved me for a twenty-one-day stay. He told me I'd be kicked out if I didn't submit to a TB test within seven days.

The shelter required everyone staying overnight to bathe.

Some came only for a meal. About 40 percent were white. Over 90 percent were men.

None of them were Jackie.

At 6:00 P.M., the intake closed and the front doors locked, signaling the men through the double doors for a required one-hour chapel service. The sign on the wall read, "You don't have to pray to stay," but you had to be in the same room. Regardless, most of the men

and women eagerly engaged with the singing and preaching. Many praised God with raised hands and erupted in shouts of "Amen!" Those who weren't singing, and there weren't many, slept or read beat-up paperbacks in the back of the room. One man, sitting alone, told me that he *was* Jesus, possessed by Satan. "I know this sounds crazy," he said. "It's been a little Armageddon going on in my head."

The doors to the dining hall opened after the final prayer. Everyone filtered inside and found a chair among the thirty-foot-long tables while male, female, and children volunteers brought Styrofoam plates of corn and beans, ham and rice. I intentionally arrived hungry so I would force myself to eat.

After dinner, many filtered back outside and slowly disappeared down the street. Some bowed in the doorway before they left and prayed with counselors for a safe night. Others trembled and shook as they walked away looking for their next hit. One minister, Johnny Lonardo, joked that they wanted to build an electrified fence to keep the addicts from the dealers who lurked just a block away. "But that wouldn't work either," he said. "When an addict wants what he wants, he'll do *anything* to get it."

As we waited in the chapel for bedtime, a television connected to a laptop played *Old Yeller.* I saw several men wiping tears.

At 9:00 P.M., the dorms opened upstairs. Once most of the men had bedded down, I asked a solitary straggler if I could photograph him while he brushed his dentures. He looked me over and said, "You need a better job." I continued to shoot for an hour or so in the shadowy darkness as men snored and staggered to the bathroom. I noticed the shadowy silhouette of a man as he sat in his bunk. I approached through the darkness and asked him if he wanted to talk. He quietly introduced himself by his nickname, Tatonka, as he stared despondently at the cell phone in his hand. He'd just gotten word that his daughter had died in

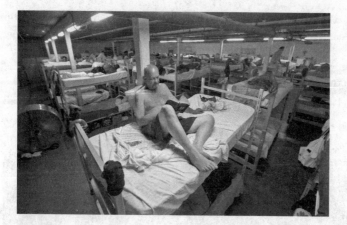

a car accident. He'd also lost his brother to illness and his son to suicide, all in the last thirty days.

Tatonka had been raised in the swamps around Dulac, a small community in extreme south Louisiana. He learned the rules of life from his father, a Mafia man who taught him to use knives and guns to get what he wanted. Tatonka came to the mission directly from Angola after serving a decades-long sentence for rape. He'd left prison with the intent of tracking down and murdering

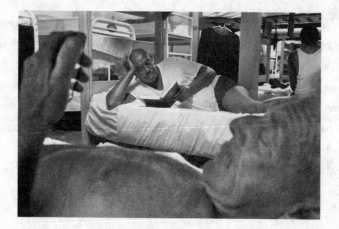

the woman who ratted him out. But to his surprise, the mission smothered him with a forgiving love that he'd never known. He said he'd found redemption and had decided to focus on building a better future for himself.

I shot a portrait of him, illuminated only by the light of my cell phone's screensaver.

When I finally lay down, I wrapped my camera in a towel and tucked it under my head for a pillow to keep it secure. In the darkness, an industrial fan rumbled a heavy rhythm as someone sang, "I'm sorry, Christ." I closed my eyes and prayed for those men. I prayed for God to use my hands, my eyes, and my camera to help them and others like them. I prayed that Tatonka could find peace and remain committed to the programs that the mission offered. I wondered about their life stories. I wondered how they arrived at this place. I prayed for the other men who I'd watched fall asleep reading their paperback Bibles.

I prayed for Jackie.

I wondered where he was. As I stared across the warehouse of broken men, I suddenly felt a burden that I'd never known before. I realized that I'd passively looked for Jackie for over a decade, but my "searches" had been opportunistic and superficial at best. The mystery of Jackie's circumstances burdened my sleep. It wasn't that I *wanted* to find him. I *needed* to find him. I didn't want to admit it to myself, but deep inside, I believed with all my heart that he was dead.

THE PRAYER AND inspiration couldn't have come at a more perfect time. They coincided with new opportunities emerging in the newsroom.

Carolyn Fox, the new director of content, represented a bold change at NOLA.com | *The Times-Picayune*. Her young and fresh approach came to New Orleans after an impressive stint with *National Geographic*. She challenged our entire staff with innovative strategies to reinvigorate the downward trend in our circulation numbers. The same numbers and the massive changes happening in the news industry left us feeling uneasy about our futures, despite assurances from our editors.

During a staff meeting, Carolyn challenged the photo staff to pitch ideas for serious, long-term personal projects that we cared deeply about and would like to work on. I pitched my top two notions: a ninety-year-old Cajun woman mourning the loss of her ancestral cemetery in Leeville due to environmental abuse—and, of course, a full-bore search for Jackie. Prompted by the detailed back stories, Carolyn and my photo editor, Andrew Boyd, approved both ideas and agreed to cut me loose for research. A few weeks later, I drove deep into the south Louisiana marshes to meet the feisty Cajun matriarch.

I honestly had no idea where to start with Jackie, so I enlisted help from two colleagues to search databases for prison and death records, but the searches returned nothing of value. I scoured the usual haunts under the bridges, even returning to the spot where I'd found him twenty-six years before. I walked the streets and knocked on doors. My search felt like a maze, every turn a dead end. But even a dead man leaves a trace. Right?

In October, I stopped by the Ozanam Inn, where I'd found my last direct clue a decade before. At least I knew the administrator, Deacon Biaggio DiGiovanni, would know who I was talking about. I had to try again.

I arrived before dinner, when I knew the courtyard would be full. I talked to a handful of men, lined up on a bench, who were talkative but had no useful information. DiGiovanni stood in the back corner, assisting with clothing requests in the yard, when I ambled over. He couldn't remember the last time he'd seen Jackie, but he singled out a few homeless men who had been around long enough to have crossed paths with him. I stayed optimistic, but I had tried this tactic many times before with no results.

One longtimer, dressed in a white undershirt with a seven-inch flip knife hooked into his jean pocket, politely gave me the same, tired answer that I'd heard for years: "Sorry, but I can't help you." But before he walked away, he introduced me to Joe Banks. I asked again.

"I'm looking for a man named Jackie Wallace," I said. "Ever heard of him?" This time, the answer floored me.

"Yeah, I saw him a few weeks ago," he said. "He looked good."

What? This was my first inkling that Jackie might be alive. But looking good? That didn't seem possible.

"I saw him in the store getting his shrimp loaf," he said, "at the seafood shop at Broad and Banks. He seemed happy, energetic, moving around. He looked like Jackie. I was really glad to see him." He said he thought he was staying with a relative or a friend in Mid-City.

Joe remembered the day he met Jackie, during a program at the shelter. "We hit it off, and talked, and he'd tell me about his football days, and you know, just trying to encourage me, and tell me to get my life back right. He's real sincere, from the heart. That's what I like about him."

I said that's what I liked about him, too.

"It's a possibility you could run into him at that store," he said.

At the seafood shop, I passed Jackie's photo around, but if the cooks and the owner recognized him, they were reticent. Men loitering on the corner outside said he looked familiar and promised to call the number on my business card if they saw him. Movie cops make it look so easy.

With this vague bit of information and a reported sighting, I asked crime reporter Jonathan Bullington to do another database search. This time, Jackie's name returned with an unlikely address in Harvey. His age seemed correct or close enough, but the item was four years outdated. My heavy schedule prevented me from driving to the Westbank straightaway. An assignment to photograph floating tourist cabins on the bayou in Westwego a few days later gave me a chance to drop by.

October 27, 2016

The address led me to a row of cookie-cutter quadplexes in Harvey, an unincorporated area that marked the southernmost tip of metro New Orleans. Developers built this neighborhood on reclaimed swampland less than a half mile from the wetlands protection levee. From there, only twenty miles of marsh grass separated these homes from seasonal threats from the Gulf of Mexico.

I scanned the numbers on the mailboxes as I crept along in my car. Every eye followed me as I passed. Near the end of the block, the numbers matched my notes. There I found a man sitting alone in a plastic chair, idling, staring at nothing in particular. I pulled to the curb and wondered where the next few minutes might lead. At best, I had hoped to find a relative, a friend, or a tenant who might remember a homeless man's name.

"Hi," I said. "I'm looking for a friend. I'm hoping you might know him." I gambled on the word "friend." Would a cop ever use it? I hoped not.

"Yeah? Who is that?" he said. His eyes were fixed on something beyond me.

From my years of listening to police scanners, I knew this area had seen its share of trouble, and I knew this man had little reason to trust a stranger. I watched his eyes carefully. If he recognized the name, I expected at least a twitch.

"His name is Jackie Wallace. Do you know him?"

His eye twitched, ever so slightly.

I felt a sudden rush. He looked me over, and then to my disbelief, he casually motioned to the door on the right. Almost on cue, the door cracked open and a big man appeared.

"What are you telling that man about me?" he shouted, perhaps belligerently. I reactively broke into a grin. I recognized the face immediately. I couldn't believe my luck. "Are you Jackie Wallace?" I said, already knowing the answer.

"Who wants to know?" His large frame overwhelmed the narrow space.

"When I tell you, you're going to smile." I approached within arm's length. "I'm Ted Jackson."

His wrinkled brow immediately broke, and his eyes lightened. Jackie shoved the door aside and engulfed me in a massive bear hug.

He had been thirty-nine when I found him under the bridge twenty-six years before. Now, at age sixty-five, his hair was snowy white, his face a little broader and filled out. His grin was just as gap-toothed as I remembered.

We fell effortlessly into a sea of questions and stories. He showed me around his apartment, proudly explaining how it was part of an addiction recovery program, Gateway Recovery Systems. He introduced me to his housemate, a recovering addict who rented a bedroom upstairs. Within fifteen minutes, Jackie and I had hugged five times. We shot a quick selfie with my iPhone. He said he'd been clean and sober for nearly three years.

He led me down the hallway to his bedroom with a labored limp, swinging wildly from side to side, touching the wall for stability. It was painful to watch. Seven years in the NFL can do that to a body. I told him I couldn't stay long but that we really needed to sit and talk for a few minutes. He was eager to sit.

He moaned as he lowered himself into a desk chair. This room was his private sanctuary. His bedroom walls were neatly decorated with inspirational posters, birthday cards, and *Star Wars* photos tacked over a Native American rug.

A framed team photo of the 1974 Minnesota Vikings seemed out of place on a plywood desktop set across milk crates. The desk was neatly arranged with a Bible, a heavily marked calendar, a perfectly arranged set of colored markers, reminder memos, and a handful of trinkets. Another frame grouped seven smaller photos in a collage—Roland and Audrey at the center surrounded by six smiling children in high school caps and gowns titled, "The Wallace Family." A 1969 newspaper clipping of a young St. Augustine quarterback with coach Eddie Flint, Ronald Arceneaux, and Eric Forest served as a bookmark for pages in a book of devotionals.

I couldn't hide my excitement over seeing him again. I asked if he'd be willing to talk with me about his missing years since Baltimore. I'd like to do a follow-up story for the paper. His eyes glistened in agreement. "Of course," he said.

I felt elated, but I couldn't be late to the Westwego assignment. I told him I'd return as soon as I could. He gave me his cell phone number, and we hugged again.

As I drove away, I pulled over to the curb and texted the news to my photo editor with the selfie—date stamped: 10/27/2016 12:43 P.M.

"Look who I just found!!!"

"Wow. Mr. Wallace?"

"Yes!!!"

"Alright! Looks like you just found your next story."

CHAPTER TEN

"Four Score and Seven Years Ago"

2016

"OK. Tell me everything."

It had taken me two weeks to get back for an interview, but now that I had Jackie within inches from me, I couldn't waste any more time.

When I arrived to Jackie's apartment in Gateway, I found him sitting in the front yard in two stacked plastic chairs in the shade of a cypress tree. He wore knee-length blue jeans, a blue T-shirt, and a pair of black Crocs. As he stood to walk inside, he lost his balance and nearly fell back into the chair. "I'm scheduled to see the orthopedic," he said. "He's going to tell me when I can get a total hip replacement."

Once inside his house, we passed the living room television, which was broadcasting *Judge Judy* as she attempted to rule over a dog custody case. I pulled a chair into the bedroom and set up my tripod while Jackie rolled his desk chair closer to his bed. I hit record on my video camera and asked for a mic check. At first, he struggled to keep his eyes open, but he looked straight into the camera lens.

"Four score and seven years ago . . ." He laughed.

I marveled that an addict, now sixty-five years old, still had both a sharp mind and a sense of humor. Then he completed two long lines from the Declaration of Independence perfectly—"We hold these truths to be self-evident, that all men are created equal, that they are endowed"—before giving up. "That's about it," he said. "That's what the concussions and the age has knocked off. I might remember a fourth of that. I might remember half of that."

He rambled as he talked. Distractions came easily. At times his speech slurred. I tried to keep him focused on the missing years, but when I raised general questions, he often reverted back to his health issues.

"Let's start with football," I said. Suddenly, his posture stiffened and his watery eyes twinkled. He turned into a virtual stat machine, highlighting his performance in his first Super Bowl with the Vikings.

His sharp focus was starting to eclipse the real reason I had come. "Tell me about the earliest thing you remember under the bridge," I said, hoping to lead him back to rehab.

He talked about the photograph I'd shot that day. "I was

reborn again," he said. "When you come out of your mother's womb, that's what that was like for me. It's been a long and uplifting journey. At that juncture when y'all found me, I didn't have a clue of what was going on with me."

Truth is, I hadn't realized what happened to Jackie after 1995, and it was this fact that haunted me. His time in Baltimore was a blank to me. I wanted to know what had happened between him and Deborah. I wanted to tell him how disappointed I was that he'd returned to sleeping under a bridge. And why hadn't he tried to get in touch with me in the past twenty-one years? Why had he let this happen? Did he know that most of his friends in Baltimore thought he was dead?

It was easy to conceal my frustration with my fascination in the moment. I felt like I was talking to a ghost—an interview with a man who had been resurrected from the grave.

As I gently guided him through the years, a rough road map slowly took shape.

AFTER I'D SEEN him in Baltimore in 1995, Jackie had continued to work on rebuilding his social life. He bought a used pickup truck. He often invited homeless and street addicts to join him in his new obsession, the Early Bird AA group. The program staff loved him, and he loved them back.

He found new friends among the recovering addicts, especially a man named Ed McFadden, who had an apartment on Greenmount Avenue at East Biddle Street. They enjoyed hanging out together. He reconnected with a few of his Colts players and friends, including Lydell Mitchell, who, like Jackie, had also played his final year with the Rams. He worked as a Colts game analyst with WBAL radio, even though the team had moved to Indianapolis. Neighbors remember a sign draped in the yard to promote the shows. He volunteered for charity flea markets at the Episcopal church down the street, waving signs and attracting motorists along the Alameda.

As he had done in L.A., he kept his home life private. Neighbors didn't see him or Deborah in the yard much, but the couple gave all the appearances of a happy home. Three dogs scampered about the house and frolicked in the yard. Deborah cooked stuffed peppers, Jackie's favorite. On weekends, they enjoyed board games, with Jackie usually winning easily at his favorite game, Scrabble. He teased her with outlandish mathematical formulas for his theory of infinity. They enjoyed their time together.

Jackie renewed bonds with his dad and his siblings. Roland shipped a box of his old news clippings, cards, letters, jerseys, and souvenirs to Baltimore, sensing that Jackie, finally, could be trusted to take care of his stuff. He tucked them in his attic for safekeeping.

At the same time, Jackie applied for and started receiving his NFL pension, which he qualified for, beginning at forty-five years old. As an early pensioner, he received only $650 a month instead of the much higher payout he would have received if he'd waited until his full retirement age of sixty-five.

Once a year, Jackie and Deborah took a trip south for visits. Deborah didn't care much for Mardi Gras, but she enjoyed the French Quarter and the romance of the city. She also enjoyed Roland's gumbo and the chitlins. Jackie's family and Father Verrett continued to encourage him to put his degree to work, but he enjoyed the simple labor of moving chairs and building stages at the arena.

As time passed, Jackie spent more time at Weisman House. He'd leave home at 6:00 A.M. for the Early Birds, go to work, come home, change clothes, and head back for another AA meeting. It seemed noble for a while, but, over time, Deborah began to feel abandoned as she sat at home alone. She noticed a difference between his sweet, charming nature in public events and his increasingly sour mood at home. What once seemed like normal machismo behavior gradually turned aggressive against her, especially when he didn't get what he wanted. She shared these observations with him, which only further set him off.

The late-night arrivals crossed into early mornings until finally, he didn't arrive home until 5:00 A.M., with no explanation for where he'd been. A dark cloud developed over their relationship. A surlier, more unstable demeanor began to emerge in Jackie.

Deborah didn't know how to respond. She wondered if he might be cheating on her or, maybe worse, using drugs again. He swore he was doing neither. But he lost interest in church and even scoffed when she read her Bible, making her feel betrayed.

Sometimes Jackie seemed to be confused, which made Deborah wonder if he might be suffering from the long-term effects of repeated blows to the head. He struggled to control his impulses and his hostility. When he couldn't adequately explain himself, Jackie began to worry, too. They took a trip to meet with officials at the NFL Players Association in Washington, D.C., to seek answers, but research at the time was scant. The NFL wouldn't acknowledge the link between head trauma and football until 2016.

The lack of answers, combined with the NFL's reticence, didn't assuage his fears about his condition. He wondered if he had made the right decision to play football in the first place. If he'd chosen a different path, he thought he probably would have ended up like Louvinia, "a wonderful little schoolteacher" in New Orleans. He remembered his time in Arizona when he camped in the mountains around Tucson. He remembered admiring the Arizona wildlife agents as they drove their company trucks, wearing respectable uniforms, helping campers, and earning an honest wage and a good pension. He thought he would have enjoyed a job like that.

In a 1997 interview with Jimmy Smith, Jackie said he'd enjoyed the glamour of the NFL, but he found that he wasn't prepared for the "highs and lows" of football. The fan base—and society in general—expected football players to be gentlemen, knights in shining armor in public, and "then the next day be a crazy brute." He found it difficult to maintain the dual personalities. He felt that his football career never allowed him to be a normal member of society, and it hurt him in the long run. He thought of himself as normal, but football never allowed him to be normal.

Jackie's old nemesis Terry Bradshaw, who finished his career with four Super Bowl rings, talked with Jimmy about the same intense pressures of playing championship games. "You think as much about losing it, if not more, than you think about winning it," he said. "Winning it just seems unreal. So, you have to deal with that, and that wears on you as an athlete. Super Bowl week is easily, for me, the worst experience of my career."

Living up to impossible expectations set by the NFL was tenuous at best.

Only a precious few athletes earn long-term glory. Even fewer get the glory and the riches: Ahmad Rashad, Lynn Swann, Jim Brown, Gale Sayers, Michael Strahan, Joe Montana, Brett Favre, John Elway, and Roger Staubach are among such rare exceptions. But many other players have had to find a way to adjust to an ordinary existence after football. Likewise, burning too bright for too long can destroy a man. The adulation, the hero worship, the entitlement mentality can corrupt an otherwise sane mind.

As Jackie tried to make sense of his shifting personality, Deborah's friends quietly warned her about other NFL players who had lost their healthy perspective on normalcy. The women obsessed over one extreme example in O. J. Simpson.

Born to poverty, Simpson excelled in football and earned his way to the top with a Heisman Trophy, a slew of NFL records, and the adulation of NFL fans. Like Jim Brown, he transitioned from football to acting. He got his mansion in California and the glamour that came with it. But somewhere along the way, he came to believe that the normal rules of life didn't apply to him. He had it all, until his young wife, Nicole Brown Simpson, grew tired of his emotional and physical abuse. America was watching as the story unfolded.

So was Deborah.

On June 17, 1994, "the Juice" famously led authorities on a low-speed car chase through Southern California after he'd been charged with the murders of Nicole and her friend Ron Goldman.

The drama transfixed the nation, as did the 474-day legal saga that followed. Deborah and her friends couldn't help but draw a similar—although vague—parallel. She worried about the latent violence of football—pent-up emotional energy waiting for an outlet. She wondered if she had made a mistake by marrying an addict and former football player. Her friends warned her to be careful. She felt debilitated by fear.

Jackie worried about his behavior, too, but he thought his wife's comparisons with O. J. were ridiculously overblown and told her so.

As the couple grew more distant, Jackie engaged even more with his adoring public through social events. In Baltimore, he helped with a myriad of team functions, charity balls, and speaking engagements. For a casino night charity, he served as a celebrity card dealer. He flew to New Orleans to join his 1967 teammates for a reception at St. Aug's gym to commemorate the thirty-year anniversary of the integration of the Catholic League.

He felt good about being back in the spotlight. But just like Mary before her, Deborah didn't care for Jackie's celebrity. She thought he took it too seriously, and besides, maybe he was getting too old to prioritize football-related events. Like Mary before her, Deborah saw a different man at home.

Jackie also began spending more weeknights and even weekends with his Weisman friend Ed at his apartment in downtown Baltimore. Ed was a short man with a big gut and a "chicken arm"—a withered and disfigured hand from a childhood run-in with a wringer washing machine. The two men bonded over their childhood injuries (Ed's arm, Jackie's foot), their uncommon intelligence, and their growing arrogance over their years of sobriety. Jackie had now been sober for nearly nine years, Ed for seven. Their Weisman friends remembered how close they became. Where there was one, you saw the other. They mostly found them in the run-down neighborhood along Greenmount Avenue.

As Jackie spent more time away from home, Deborah started hearing rumors about a new friend at work. She never heard her name, but friends said he'd started driving a woman home every day. Another friend told her she'd seen them walking together in the mall, with her children, looking like a happy family. Her name was Taris Whitley. She worked in arena hospitality.

Deborah never mentioned her suspicions, at least not to Jackie. She knew it would only irritate him.

One night when Jackie and Deborah sat down to dinner, instead of serving her typical fine cooking, she served warm SpaghettiOs on one of her fine china plates. "Here's your food," Jackie remembered her saying, bluntly.

"Deborah," he said, looking up at her, "we could have gone out to eat if you didn't feel like cooking."

She mumbled something, and Jackie lost his temper. "Something snapped," he recalled years later, and he called her a bitch. He took the plate and hurled it in her direction. It shattered, and the food spattered the wall. Suddenly, Jackie's memory flashed back to his mother throwing the lamp at his head. Deborah's flashed to O. J. Simpson. "You ain't going to do that to me," she screamed, and ran out of the room.

She felt like his erratic behavior had crossed a line. Her fear drove her to get out while she could. She packed her car, drove to her office, and left a quickly scribbled note of resignation for her boss. She drained the bank account and drove to Florence, South Carolina, where she moved into a safe house for women. Jackie figured Deborah would eventually calm down and return, but when she didn't, he called her pastor and her friends. When no one could tell him anything, he reported her missing, but he didn't tell anyone why she had left. He searched for weeks but couldn't find a trace. In South Carolina, Deborah tried to imagine what she would do if he suddenly appeared and tried to approach her, but no scenarios eased her mind. She tried to forgive him, but she couldn't push the fear from her mind. She felt traumatized. She had quit a good job, left her home, and driven seven hours to hide, but she still didn't feel safe.

The whole situation infuriated her. Why did *she* have to leave while *he* stayed in the house? After five months, with the financial and emotional support of the shelter, she drove back to Baltimore and "flipped the switch" on him, as she called it. She filed for and was granted an ex parte order, an urgent directive to prevent impending violence.

On the advice of the Baltimore Police, she surveilled the house from a distance until she saw his truck pull into the driveway. Then she summoned an officer, who quickly arrived and summoned

Jackie to the door. As the officer explained that he needed to vacate the house, Deborah walked confidently into the yard. With the officer between them, Deborah told Jackie that she was tired of being physically abused. The officer kept his hand on his gun in case of trouble, but Jackie dutifully retreated into the house to gather his things. "Now you know how it feels to be put out of your house," she shouted after him. Deborah and the officer watched from the porch as he loaded his truck and drove away. It was June 1999.

That night, he slept under the I-83 overpass in Baltimore.

BACK IN NEW ORLEANS, as Jackie told me about the scene on the porch years later, his thoughts leapt from Deborah to football to his mother's death as if someone were flicking a remote control in his mind. The breakup with Deborah and Audrey's funeral passed like a blur, he said, "as fast as Super Bowl XIV." He recalled the day his mom died and how his sister Margo blamed him for their mother's death because he had fetched her cigarettes. "You killed Mama!" she had screamed. Jackie hated disobeying his mama. He couldn't release the pain of that moment.

That's when he broke down, tears welling in his eyes.

"I always had that insecurity that I wasn't good enough. When I told you about Wanda's mama saying I'd be good for nothing, and stuff like that . . . I always had that old insecurity that no women liked me. I never looked at myself as being a big, handsome person. I never looked at myself as being smart. I always looked at myself as being awkward. And now, I'd lost the one person I knew I could count on. I knew my daddy loved me, but that was a different type of love.

"My mama used to do one thing that I used to always love. My mama would put us on her lap, she'd take a hair pin, and dig down in there and get the wax out of our ears. I used to love that.

When she would do that, my whole life lit up. I mean it, lit up. The other time my life would light up is when she'd say, 'Boy, you!'" He smiled and then shook his head. "She never knew my name. 'You boy, you know who I'm talking about. You, boy.' When I made the potato salad. I always felt good, especially around Thanksgiving and when we'd have our Christmas dinners and stuff. 'You boy. You're making the potato salad. Go get your stuff.' I used to love that. I used to love that."

And on and on it went. I noticed a pattern. His cycle of loss and recovery always revolved around women. His insecurities and his dependencies were broader than I thought.

The day after the breakup, he moved in with Taris Whitley, the co-worker he'd been spending time with.

All these revelations about Jackie left me feeling conflicted about our relationship. I had never met a man so complicated and yet so simple—so charming yet so dark. A benevolent friend and a thief. An addict, an abuser, and a pilgrim. A selfish philanthropist. A humble narcissist bent on self-destruction. But I had also never met a man more honest in his conversation. Deborah called him a broken human being and a con man. I didn't know what to believe or whether I was talking to him as a friend or a journalist anymore.

But regardless of what I had learned, football fans around the country continued to cherish Jackie Wallace as a one-dimensional caricature who could run fast and jump high enough to change the numbers on a scoreboard. To them, he remained hidden behind an impressive set of numbers on a statistic sheet.

On September 19, 1998, 52,634 proud fans screamed their approval as the University of Arizona unveiled its new Ring of Honor on the facade of the west grandstand of the school's football stadium. Of the twenty-one names unveiled, a handful needed no introduction, their deeds burned indelibly in the hearts of diehard fans and longtime ticketholders. Among them, in bold white block letters, centered on the 50-yard-line, read: "JACKIE WALLACE—1970–1972."

TARIS FELL IN love and fell hard. She was thirty-nine. Jackie was forty-seven. To Jackie, the relationship felt like a fresh start with an additional bonus: a ready-made family like he'd always dreamed of. Taris's three boys (two teenagers and a nine-year-old) loved how he indulged them with gifts, games of football, and trips to Mc-Donald's. The boys enjoyed the new father figure in their lives, and it was clear that Jackie enjoyed the new mother figure in his. Her extended family adored him, too, especially Taris's mother. Everyone thought of him as a great inspiration for the kids.

Not long after, Jackie started a new job with a company that specialized in building and mending fences. It came with better opportunities and more money. He also encouraged Taris to improve her own opportunities and badgered her to fill out an application for a job opening with the city. When she finally broke down and walked in for an interview, Jackie had already paved the way through his contacts. They hired her on the spot.

Taris thought that she and Jackie were the most beautiful couple ever. "Like the Huxtables," she told friends, referring to Bill Cosby's TV family. Jackie played the role of a good husband. He went to work, brought *all* the money home, and made sure the family was taken care of. He planned something for every weekend—fishing, beach trips, cookouts, movies. She bragged to her friends about her great new life. She also bragged about Jackie's nine years of sobriety. Before long, they began thinking about getting married.

With everything going so well, Jackie scaled back his involvement with Weisman House. He thought he'd outgrown the need. At first, he missed a few meetings, and then a few more. Before long, he'd broken the habit. After many months absent, an Early Birder named David spotted him driving downtown. He described Jackie as having waved big, as if to say, "Hey, I don't need y'all anymore. I've got the girl. Got the car. Got some stuff. I'm doing OK." When Jackie wasn't with Taris or at work, she could usually find him at Ed's apartment.

One Friday, about three years into the couple's relationship, Jackie didn't come home after work. By Saturday morning, Taris was worried sick. She called everyone she could think of, including her mother, for help, but no one had seen him. She searched all weekend, growing more panicked each day. On Monday morning, Jackie arrived promptly at work as if nothing had happened. Taris was happy to see him when he returned home that night but demanded answers. Where had he been, and who had he been with? He confessed that he'd partied all weekend at Ed's apartment. And yes, there had been women there—naked women—but he swore he didn't go for the sex. He hadn't been unfaithful to her. He had, instead, smoked crack with Ed, seduced by the moment. He said he couldn't believe it either. He'd been clean for eleven long years. How could he have been so weak? He swore it would never happen again.

He returned to the Early Bird meetings, and the other residents welcomed him back, but he mostly resisted their overtures. His pride got in the way, group members said. He didn't want to hear, "I told you so." They understood how embarrassing it was for an addict who relapsed after eleven years sober. And besides, they'd seen this coming. He showed the classic signs. He got comfortable with his sobriety, he stopped going to meetings, and he started hanging with old friends again. They peppered him

with the slogans he knew by heart—"It works if you work it"—
and that continued progress was more important than perfection.
They tried to draw him back in to the circle.

For a while, he clawed his way back to a sober mentality. But a
few months later, he slipped away again. This time Jackie missed
a whole week of work and lost his job. Taris called his boss and
begged for a second chance. The boss agreed, on the condition that
he get treatment. He went through the motions, but his efforts
were mostly a farce. He didn't really want help.

Once again, he blamed everything on his mother's death. Taris
tried to reason with him. "At some point in time," she told him,
"we all lose our parents."

His Early Bird friend Barbara told him that he always seemed
to be in a speed racer mode, hurrying from place to place. "What
are you racing for? Death?" she asked him point-blank. "Have you
forgotten about the pain and the misery?"

Other residents suspected that Jackie's friendship with Ed was
the problem. They believed that the two men showed all the signs
with their overconfidence. "They were too smart to get sober," said
one friend who wished not to be identified. "But I've never seen
someone who was too dumb to get sober." When the friend saw
Jackie and Ed together again on Greenmount Avenue, he told them
they needed to "dummy up" a little bit. Jackie told him to mind his
own business. The last time the friend saw Jackie, he wasn't looking so good. Shortly after that, he stopped going to the meetings
altogether. Everybody heard the rumors.

Several months later, Jackie disappeared a third time, but this
time, Taris knew where to find him. She took the elevator to
Ed's second-floor apartment and banged on the door. When Ed
answered, she said, "I want my husband." Ed disappeared into
the noisy and wild commotion inside and left her standing there

alone, feeling cheap and humiliated as the music wailed and the crude laughter wafted into the hallway. She'd couldn't believe that Jackie would waste their beautiful relationship on a raucous crowd like this. When Jackie appeared at the door, he turned his head away and blew out a mouthful of smoke. Since Taris knew how much Jackie despised cigarettes, she knew the smoke came from a crack pipe.

She gave him a clear choice. "You either choose this, or you can come home. Your choice."

She didn't wait for an answer, but instead turned and walked toward the stairs, bypassing the elevator so she wouldn't have to wait. When she reached the street, she glanced over her shoulder to see Jackie's dog-shamed face following just a few steps behind. As she walked to her car a half block away still burning with anger, she practiced what she would say on the ride home. As she inserted her key in the lock, she turned to tell him how much she wanted their relationship to work. But he was gone.

Her body went limp. She couldn't contain her tears as she stood in the darkness, alone.

"Christ!" she said. "Oh, my God."

She felt like she couldn't breathe.

Until that moment, she had no idea how powerful the draw of crack cocaine could be. Jackie had always professed how much he loved her. She never dreamed that he was capable of loving crack more.

WHEN HE CALLED a few days later, she shot down his empty promises. She'd had enough. Handwritten love letters arrived every day for a month, then once a week, then once a month for over a year. The last one arrived in 2001. She threw them all in the trash and never spoke to him again.

"He was a great, great person," she whispered through tears years later. "I truly loved him. My mother and family were all crazy about him. For him to go back to that life, I don't understand. I didn't understand.

"I loved him. Really did," she said. "I think mostly because he loved me so much. He's the only man I know that truly loved me."

JUST WEEKS AFTER Jackie had disappeared back into Ed's apartment, the Early Birds group got the news that Ed had collapsed and died. Most of Jackie's Baltimore friends believed that Ed had died of an overdose. They had no proof, but they talked about it that day as if it were fact. They had become numb to overdose deaths—one of the realities of the disease of addiction. "People live and die all the time in that world," they said.

Most of the old friends blamed Jackie's relapse on the friendship. But Jackie recoiled at the claim. The suggestion left him agitated. "No," he said. "What drove Jackiewallace down was Jackiewallace . . . Jackiewallace don't follow nobody, and Jackiewallace does what Jackiewallace wants to do and when Jackiewallace wants to do it, regardless of what the consequences are."

As Ed's family made arrangements for the funeral, Ed's sister called to ask Jackie to say a few words. It would mean a lot, she said. But Jackie told her no. He didn't want to look at his dead friend in the casket. That would have been too much.

Jackie didn't attend the funeral at all. He withdrew into what he called his "vortex of darkness," which began to spin faster and faster. Without Taris and without a job, he drifted away to "little spots" around downtown Baltimore until he returned to a space beneath Interstate 83. There, he poured all the money he had left into crack. For twelve months he survived under that overpass, bearing the cold through the winter of 2001. After that, he survived and smoked crack on his small NFL pension check.

Once Jackie's crack dealer discovered his NFL connections, he falsely assumed that Jackie had millions of dollars stashed away from his career. He suggested a scheme to use Jackie's name as collateral to get other dealers to give them a bigger supply of drugs.

That's when Jackie knew he'd had enough. As much as he loved Baltimore, it became clear that staying would get him killed.

He signed divorce papers with Deborah in June 2002, and soon after, he walked into a homeless service and asked for a bus ticket. The woman working the desk recognized him. "Jackie Wallace," she said, which brought a smile to his face and the charm back to his countenance. The clerk knew that he had money, but she gave him the ticket anyway. She watched as he climbed the steps on the bus. He settled into his seat, and the bus pulled away from the curb.

Old friends at Weisman say they heard that he'd left for Minneapolis. Others heard he'd headed back South. He was fifty-one years old.

"ONE SLIP," HE had told me back in his locker room at the Baltimore Arena. "It only takes one slip, and I'll end up right back where you found me."

As I continued to ply him with questions, I looked around the bedroom to draw back my emotions. I checked the focus on the camera. Yoda and Darth Vader battled with light sabers on the wall. A poster over his shoulder read, "You are my sunshine." I checked the lapel mic while Jackie Wallace shifted in his chair.

CHAPTER ELEVEN

So Damn Smart

2002–2014

It had been a twenty-four-hour ride through the South—with transfers in Richmond and Mobile—when the Greyhound bus pulled into the New Orleans station on Loyola Avenue at 7:00 A.M. Jackie crossed the street and walked under a bridge to join the city's homeless population. The sidewalks felt harder against his old bones. His feet ached. The damp, Southern cold settled deeper into his NFL-battered joints. So, instead of staying with the tent people, he checked himself into the New Orleans Mission. If he were going to live homeless, he told himself, he wouldn't live "ugly homeless."

It was 2002, and Louisiana's flamboyant governor, Edwin Edwards, had surrendered himself to authorities to begin serving a ten-year federal prison sentence for racketeering. Work crews demolished the Desire Housing Project because of the "indecent, unsafe, and unsanitary conditions" there. And despite an adoring fan base, the New Orleans Saints had yet to win a divisional playoff game in thirty-five years.

After Jackie's thirty-day voucher at the New Orleans Mission expired, he moved to the Salvation Army, then to Bridge House, and then to the Ozanam Inn. Meanwhile, he poured his pension payments into drugs. His $650 monthly check wouldn't pay for a room and food, he reasoned, but it would go a long way toward keeping him high on crack. "With the checks coming on the first, or the third, I'd get loaded. So, from the fourth to the twenty-eighth or the twenty-ninth of that month . . . I knew I was going to be poor. But around the thirtieth or the thirty-first, I'd start perking up because I knew my money was going to be there."

He called it "the twenty-eight-day game."

CLARENCE ADAMS KNEW all the games. In his eight years managing the front office at Ozanam Inn, he'd seen dozens of scams and hustles. Many volunteers helping the homeless find the manipulation of goodwill and services discouraging. But Clarence never let cynicism defile his compassionate heart. Instead, he used his growing insights to hone a more effective outreach.

To understand Clarence's heart for ministry and cheerful optimism amid such a depressing environment, you need to know that members of the Society of St. Vincent de Paul—the guiding force behind the charity—think of themselves as *servants* of the poor, not saviors. The philosophy derives from the fourth-century reasoning of the archbishop of Constantinople, St. John Chrysostom: "The poor are the physicians of our souls, our benefactors, our protectors. You give them less than you receive from them; you give them alms and you receive the Kingdom of Heaven."

"You have to experience it," Clarence told me in 2019. "We all know that it's better to give than to receive." But the homeless gave him something he didn't know he needed. "I found love here," he said. "Beyond that, how else could I do this for the money I'm paid?"

The Ozanam Inn, originally called St. Vincent Hotel, has

helped the unemployed and unhoused of New Orleans since 1911. In 1954, the directors secured and repurposed a three-floor boarding house on Camp Street in the Central Business District and renamed it. For sixty-five years, the Ozanam Inn continued to operate there, surrounded by some of the best art and history museums in the city. The ragged clients of "The Oz," as it's commonly referred to, stood in stark relief as they bumped shoulders along the sidewalks with the wandering tourists and art aficionados, especially during the most elegant gallery event of the year, White Linen Night.

Clarence remembered Jackie from childhood as a football star and had followed his story of addiction and recovery in the newspaper. He even considered himself casual friends with some of Jackie's relatives. Louvinia taught him math at Southern University at New Orleans as a freshman. "She used to always have a story about Jackie to tell," he said. The last he'd heard, Jackie was living "happily ever after" in Baltimore.

In the fall of 2002, as he prepared to go home on a Saturday night, Clarence spotted a gaunt and weary Jackie milling about in the food line.

"What are you doing here?" Clarence asked. "I thought you were living in—"

Jackie quickly cut him off. He explained that he'd split with Deborah and had returned to his old habits.

As Clarence watched Jackie move from the serving line to the tables and among the men, he could still see his potential. Even in his haggard state, Jackie still had a light in his eyes. He hadn't burned out as so many others did, with their dull expressions and pitiful stares. As the weeks passed, Clarence tried to draft him for his in-house volunteer work team. Jackie, however, said he wasn't ready to commit.

A few months later, he changed his mind, and Clarence assigned him to work with the front office staff. If he stayed off drugs, he could live, eat, and work there at no charge for up to two years.

The front office served as the inn's triage center. Jackie had a knack for assessing an applicant's needs, and he could defuse tension with a light word or a gentle joke. Some folks walked in confused. Some arrived with impossible, irrational, and insufferable demands. Many suffered mental illness. Jackie accepted them all. His mellow demeanor calmed anxieties and soothed frayed nerves.

He understood the rules and ran the office so well that many thought he was a paid staffer. If he didn't know an answer, he could find it. Clarence often found him on the back patio, counseling groups of addicts who'd listen to him because his reputation preceded him. He made a lot of fans among the staff, especially seventy-six-year-old Anastasia Hammond, a retired government research lab technician who had volunteered in the front office for over twenty years. Her son Lonnie had played football for Clark High School—a star running back—a year behind Jackie. Because of that, Miss Annie and Jackie constantly sparred over high school bragging rights.

For six months or more, Jackie served as a model reformed addict, so it came as a shock one morning when Clarence checked in for work and found Jackie waiting, sitting on a bench by the elevator with the bad news. "I just want to let you know I'm leaving," he said. "I don't want to waste your time. I'm not ready to do right." Clarence could see that Jackie's conviction had left him. The fixation of the disease was taking over. With a handshake and a hug, Jackie buzzed himself out and left. As Clarence watched his friend walk away, Jackie turned with a parting word: "Sorry to let you down."

"One thing about drug abuse," Jackie had told me over and

over back on the porch in Baltimore, as if still reeling from the memory. "It will wait on you."

He returned to his twenty-eight-day game—one week of abuse followed by three weeks of poverty. But, eventually, he needed more. He tried odd jobs, passing out flyers and light construction work. He moved into a shared efficiency apartment in Mid-City and lived for a while with a group of hustlers who stole checks for a quick buck. They forged Jackie's name on the payee line and then sent him to a French Quarter branch bank to try his luck. He believed that his education made him smart enough to get away with it. "So damn smart," he said years later.

He found it surprisingly easy the first time he conned the bank and thought he'd beaten the system. His arrogance grew with a few more easy runs. Then he got greedy. When he showed up again, this time with a handful of checks, the teller grew suspicious and secretly summoned the branch manager, who invited Jackie into his office for a cup of coffee. Jackie was still sipping when the officers walked in.

At the trial, the judge convicted and sentenced him to twelve months in Orleans Parish Prison. In August 2005, in the dog days of summer, Jackie watched from his prison cell as Hurricane Katrina slammed New Orleans and floodwaters began to rise.

"Wake up. The levees have broken."

Eliot Kamenitz, a fellow photographer kicked my feet and jostled me from my sleep on the floor of the newspaper's library. "Jesus Christ!" shouted a far-off voice. As we scrambled into the newsroom, another voice responded, "Even Jesus can't help us now."

On Sunday night, August 29, 2005, 240 people had huddled inside the *Picayune* building, including eighty working journalists and a sizable group of non-working employees seeking shelter from the storm with their children, parents, and grandparents.

All night long, Hurricane Katrina battered the Mississippi Gulf Coast and mostly passed to the east of New Orleans. I and other *Picayune* photographers spent Monday photographing the breached levees and people clinging to their rooftops in the Lower Ninth Ward and St. Bernard Parish. By the time the rain stopped, it appeared that the city itself had escaped with minor wind damage and street flooding.

But by Monday evening, it became clear that multiple levees had also failed in Lakeview and Gentilly. By Tuesday morning, we all knew the truth: the water wouldn't stop rising until it evened out with the swollen Lake Pontchartrain. New Orleans would flood like a bowl. Our front page carried a one-word banner headline: "Catastrophic."

After Eliot woke me, we watched as the floodwaters crept up the steps of our office building at a rate of an inch and a half an hour. It was too late to get our vehicles out. Now, we all needed to be rescued, too.

In a desperate move, publisher Ashton Phelps hatched a plan to evacuate everyone in the backs of the paper's circulation trucks. A sports editor began forming a small detachment to stay behind to continue reporting on the storm.

We mumbled our darkest thoughts to one another. Rumors spread through the newsroom that Orleans Parish Prison, just a block away across the expressway had either seen a massive prisoner release or a massive escape. Suddenly, we weren't sure about leaving a contingent of journalists behind. "What are you not telling us?" someone shouted. "Have the prisoners escaped?" Phelps ordered everyone to the trucks.

"Take only what you can put on your lap," he said. "Go now! You *cannot* stay in the building!"

I didn't know what to think. I just knew I didn't like the truck plan.

I slung my two cameras over my shoulders and stuffed my laptop, my cell phone, and a small bag of food into my backpack. I scurried down the three flights of stairs to the main corridor toward the loading dock. I glanced to the front door. The water had now crept up to the top step. An inch more and it would be inside the building. Phelps stood in the hallway like a field marshal, herding the last of the stragglers. "Get to the trucks," he told me, and hurried off through the packaging center.

I glanced to the back door. To my surprise, I spotted an aluminum johnboat pulled up on the landing, presumably left behind by a more prudent employee. I thought, *If there's a motor or paddle,*

I'm going to take it. But instead, I found a broom with ink-stained bristles. The wooden handle had broken in half. I stowed my gear and shoved off, paddling with the broom into the flooded parking lot. All alone, I crossed over a six-foot-tall chain link fence and stopped for a minute beneath a weeping willow to compose myself. As I watched the *Picayune* trucks filled with my colleagues and their families plow away through three-foot-deep water, I doubted that I had made the right decision.

After five hours of paddling through open threats and flooded mayhem, my boat finally found shallow water and scraped against

concrete at Causeway Boulevard in Metairie. Before nightfall, I photographed my drowning city from a National Guard helicopter.

My career had taken me into war zones, earthquakes, and more hurricanes than I cared to count—not because they number in the hundreds but because, after a while, they all run together. That's not to say I don't remember the individual stories, the faces, and the fear, but my mind has jumbled them into a file labeled "Disasters." But seeing my neighbors and friends trapped on rooftops and watching dead bodies floating down grand boulevards sucked the spirit out of me. I felt gutted. Even weeks later, my wife would describe my face as a blank slate with a wide-eyed stare. In less than twenty-four hours, the floodwaters had ruined us. I heard from colleagues that some among us had mentally shut down. Most of us continued to work on autopilot. I kept moving to keep from crying; I photographed in self-defense.

As we evacuated the newspaper building, Orleans Parish Prison guards ferried prisoners from their flooding cells to the Broad Street overpass (which turned out to be the source of the escape rumor). Over two hundred officers corralled them with shotguns. By afternoon, Jackie sat crammed shoulder-to-shoulder among more than 3,500 agitated, angry, and desperate inmates on the scorching concrete. Some testified later that they'd languished for four days in the ninety-five-degree heat without food or water before deputies erected scaffolds to get them to the buses on the interstate below. Many citizens would later say the prisoners got what they deserved. Others across the nation thought New Orleans, Sin City, got what it deserved, too.

Eventually, Jackie's bus transported him to Hunt Correctional Facility, an hour upriver in St. Gabriel. Two weeks later, Hurricane Rita forced authorities to relocate the prisoners to Calcasieu Correctional Center in Lake Charles.

Jackie watched the unfolding story of the New Orleans disaster on television. Time seemed to drag on. After ten long weeks, a guard summoned him from his cell to a small booth. He had a visitor waiting. His sister Louvinia had driven for hours to tell him that his father had died.

Jackie didn't say much. He stared into the walls and then returned to his cell. He mostly felt numb.

His father had died at age eighty-six in Stockbridge, Georgia, where he and other family members had evacuated to Roland Jr.'s home ahead of Katrina. A few days later, the family gathered in the shade of a live oak tree and interred his body in a family crypt in a Metairie mausoleum. Eight hundred feet away, his mother, Audrey, rested in her grave. Jackie wondered if his family missed him in his absence.

THE FUNERAL FELL among a long stream of hurried memorials and burials after Hurricane Katrina, which claimed—either directly or indirectly—1,577 lives in Louisiana alone.

In the storm's aftermath, New Orleans felt like a frontier town. Caked and sun-cracked mud covered the deserted streets. Saloons—

one of the few businesses to reopen in the early days—catered to lawmen and a raucous remnant of outlaws and gunslingers. The city had fallen into social unrest. About 80 percent of the city lay in ruin. For over a month, authorities barred homeowners from returning to many residential areas. Some neighborhoods took six weeks to drain. Hulks of new cars rusted and cluttered the streets.

It wasn't until a month later, in late September, when soldiers allowed Clarence Adams through a checkpoint in Slidell to reopen

the Ozanam Inn. A debris field of bricks covered the lot from a collapsed building next door, but Clarence was happy to find his building structurally intact. Like strays returning to their families, homeless men had filtered in and slept in the courtyard.

Clarence's home in New Orleans East had flooded with over eight feet of water. It took four more weeks before he was able to start his cleanup. As he loaded a few desperately needed tools from the Ozanam supply shed into his truck for a day of cleanup, a familiar voice caught him by surprise.

"Do you need some help?"

He turned and found a smiling Jackie grabbing a handful of

shovels and rakes. He had been released after serving seven months in jail.

"I'm not doing anything," Jackie said with a laugh.

For three days, Jackie helped Clarence shovel out a lifetime of memories, broken furniture, and soggy muck from his molded home. He never asked for anything in return. Side by side, they shoveled and dumped. Clarence looked at Jackie and shook his head in disbelief.

ONCE THE CITY got back on its feet and the Oz had regained its footing, Jackie asked Clarence for another shot in the program. Clarence could see his determination in his eyes. As Jackie showed himself to be more and more responsible, Clarence thought he might be a helpful accompanist when he toured local schools speaking about the dangers of addiction. Clarence's solo presentations had always gone well. Students consistently listened politely, but they knew Clarence was no addict. He lacked the authoritative experience that came with the territory.

With Jackie accompanying him, Clarence started with three questions: "Who here is a Saints fan?" Every hand went up. "Who's your favorite Saints player? Can you imagine that person being homeless on the streets? Let me introduce you to a friend of mine."

IN DECEMBER 2007, Ozanam prepared for its annual $100-a-plate Century Club Gala at the downtown Loews Hotel. The benefit raised a significant portion of the shelter's annual operating costs.

Deacon Biaggio DiGiovanni and Clarence decided to take a gamble with the program and invited Jackie to speak to the packed ballroom of well-heeled New Orleanians. As servers darted from table to table, topping off glasses with iced tea, dignitaries and administrators spoke about the shelter's accomplishments. Finally, the master of ceremonies introduced Jackie to polite applause. He strode to the podium in a borrowed suit and tie. He'd picked his dress shoes from the Inn's donation shed. They were a snug fit.

Jackie told of his triumphs in football, his personal failures, and his long journey back home. He explained how his new mentors had nurtured him back to life. As he thanked everyone for their generosity, the room erupted in a thunderous standing ovation. Even the newspaper's society editor took note.

After the benediction, a few couples ventured to the dance floor as the bandleader crooned. Jackie accepted hugs and handshakes. Some people took him by the shoulders and thanked him through tears. Before the band announced their final number, and after many patrons had filtered out, Jackie asked his office co-worker, eighty-one-year-old Anastasia Hammond, to join him on the dance floor. The remaining patrons crowded around and cheered as the two stole the show, a scene etched in Clarence's mind.

That's why he was stunned a few weeks later when Jackie slipped away again.

LESS THAN A year later, September 2008, the law connected Jackie with another count of writing bad checks. This time, instead of jail, the judge sentenced him to drug rehab at Gateway Recovery in Harvey, across the Mississippi River bridge on the Westbank. For two months Jackie regained himself, the same way he had at Weisman House in Baltimore.

But in November, a new district attorney, Leon Cannizzaro, took office. While reviewing recent cases, his office discovered additional checks Jackie had failed to disclose in his hearing. The managers at Gateway allowed sheriff deputies to arrest him in the middle of a treatment meeting. This time a judge sentenced him to seven years with the Department of Corrections. The law's patience had finally run out.

For years, prison bars separated him from his drug supply and his family. When his cellmates asked why he had no visitors, he explained that his father had always told his children that if they went to jail, they shouldn't waste a phone call. Write a letter instead. Louvinia sent stationery and $10 spending money from time to time, but no visitors came.

During his jail time, Jackie didn't talk much about football. That seemed like another life to him now. He stayed away from the "jailhouse craziness," as he called it, and volunteered to counsel youths in the prison's outreach programs. His good behavior easily earned him an early release after forty-two months. When he returned to New Orleans, authorities remanded him back to drug treatment. His long, forced absence away from the drug should have cleared his mind and his desire, but it hadn't. Instead, he craved it even more, and he looked for any excuse to defend his impending collapse. He thought of how Gateway had allowed officers to arrest him during a session. His logic made no sense at all, and he didn't care. He'd found someone to blame. He said the addict's two-word prayer, "F— it," then returned to the street and got loaded. He had three and a half years of stored-up NFL pension checks to burn through.

He disappeared into the homeless network again, rambling from place to place, but this time, he'd wandered into a deeper addiction, a "deeper disease," as he described it: one without euphoria. There was no pleasure left in anything, especially the drugs. "The only purpose of the disease is to kill you," he told me. "That's all it wants you to do, is to overdose. That's all they want you to do, is to get to a point where you either kill yourself or you get killed in the cycle of the dope gang with boys shooting.

That's what's going on, because you'll notice, right before the first of the month, and right after the third or the fifth of the month, you get a lot of killings in New Orleans. That's because, we call them the 'dope boys,' are wanting their money. And when they don't get their money, they wind up killing people."

But since Jackie's dealer knew he was a former football player, he knew he had money coming in month after month. The famous twentieth-century outlaw Willie Sutton once said he robbed banks because that's where the money was. The drug dealers latched on to Jackie because they knew he had a renewable supply of cash. They loaded him with credit and controlled him with the constant threat of violence.

His appearance deteriorated beyond recognition beneath an unkempt beard and layered rags. His countenance grew scraggly and wasted. He was now living "ugly homeless" by his own standards. One of his lowest days came in 2013, while sitting at the corner of Martin Luther King Jr. Boulevard and Magnolia Street, where the addicts gathered. "We just sit out there and beg or wait for our relatives to pass," he said. He was hoping his sister Louvinia would drive by with a little food or cash. "The worst thing you can do," he said. "She passed and she saw me. She waved and she kept on going.

"I said, 'Wait a minute, what's going on? Why she hadn't stopped?' And I tried to put that guilt trip on her. That's what we do in addiction," Jackie said, "make other people feel guilty so they can take care of us."

Another day, she stopped and gave him nothing. Her emotions crashed between pity and disgust. She said she had nothing left for him but her prayers. "I'm putting you in the hands of God," she said.

Jackie suppressed his anger. He knew that she loved him and

kept reminding himself of that. He'd lost his self-awareness. He couldn't see how low he'd fallen. He'd gone from being an addict to a crackhead. Nothing else mattered. He started picking out food from dumpsters; he fell behind on his payments to his dealer. When his debt grew so large that repayment seemed impossible, the dealer turned matters over to his gunmen. He told his young crew the next time they saw Jackie, to "take care of him." The worst part was that Jackie didn't care.

Christmas was only a few days away.

THE BEGINNING MONTHS of 2014 brought fresh excitement to New Orleans as the city was showing signs of a rebound. Twelfth Night signaled the start of Carnival season and king cakes, which meant Mardi Gras wasn't far behind. On the first Saturday of February, I photographed Mayor Mitch Landrieu as he danced a jig in the Hyatt Regency ballroom, celebrating his reelection. The day before, I'd photographed his predecessor, Ray Nagin, as he arrived at federal court, indicted on twenty-one counts of corruption.

The week before, snow and ice had blanketed the parishes north of Lake Pontchartrain—an anomaly for southeast Louisiana—forcing closure of back roads and major interstates. While it had warmed considerably by Monday, I still bundled against the weather as I went out to photograph my morning assignment: the installation of a beautifully restored "Flying Tigers" model Curtiss P-40 Warhawk at the National WWII Museum. The crowd cheered as the plane slid perfectly into the slot left open in the second-floor siding. A sign in the background read: "Campaigns of Courage." I zoomed in and framed the best image I could.

Just a few blocks away, Jackie had decided.

He was one month shy of his sixty-fourth birthday. It had been thirty-four years and two weeks since he had trotted onto the field—a local hero—to the thundering applause of 103,985 fans for Super Bowl XIV. But on this day, February 3, 2014, he stumbled out of the New Orleans Mission, hungover from another first-of-the-month high. In keeping with normal mission rules, he had to leave the building after breakfast since he wasn't enrolled in a mentorship program. Most of the men would return for lunch.

Jackie wore three shirts to brace against the cold. As he wandered toward the Pontchartrain Expressway, a stiff wind hit him in the face. "To hell with this," he told himself. "I'm tired of this."

He pictured only three options: find recovery, go back to jail, or kill himself. He walked to an on-ramp and turned. He had no power over his legs or arms, but he trudged on, zombielike.

Walking up the Pontchartrain Expressway to the Mississippi River bridge isn't easy. I'd done it several times on assignments. Nothing feels right up there, each step unsure. The steel and the asphalt move with the load as if it were alive. Holding on to the railing makes it worse, inducing vertigo. The intermittent wind from the traffic pushes you toward the edge, and then the vacuum from speeding trucks sucks you back. The roar is unnerving, almost violent.

As Jackie crossed the last ramp, the Tchoupitoulas exit, he looked over his shoulder to dodge the traffic. No one slowed or blew a horn. Nobody tried to stop him. He was worse than a dead man walking. He was no man.

As he approached the superstructure, the bitter crosswind caught his face. Maybe it was the chill of death or the wing of an angel, he thought. Whatever it was, it woke him up.

He suddenly regained himself, then panicked. He told himself that he was crazy.

He headed down the ramp and walked thirty blocks to the Rebuild Center near St. Joseph's Catholic Church, where he asked to be committed. The staff at the center transferred him to De-Paul Hospital for an evaluation. The psychiatrist there told him he wasn't crazy. "You've got a substance abuse problem," he said.

This time, Jackie had scared himself. He'd never known such brokenness before. His bitterness and unresolved guilt had tortured him into his deepest state of despondency. He imagined how disappointed his mother would be. He wondered if God could redeem a man so worthless.

But first thing's first: the psychiatrist told him that nothing would change in the state he was in. He had to stay sober.

Jackie returned to treatment at Gateway. He didn't want to die; he just wanted to end the pain.

CHAPTER TWELVE

The Gateway

2016

I turned off the video recorder as I reflected on what Jackie had just told me. The room was quiet except for the occasional muffled movements from Jackie's roommate upstairs, and for a second I felt as if I was freeze-framed inside an image of my own shame. The years had been undoubtedly brutal toward Jackie, and I kept wondering why I hadn't reached out. But Jackie wasn't in a place to ruminate. Jackie was on the move.

He grabbed a Minnesota Vikings bucket hat off a nail in the sheetrock and pulled it low over his brow as he led me down the hall. He brushed against a cardboard street sign tacked to the wall that read, "NARCOTICS ANONYMOUS WAY." His gait had grown more unsteady since I'd seen him last, but he had adjusted to it through overcompensating. His doctor had scheduled him for hip replacement surgery in the coming weeks, and I worried about how he'd respond to the diamorphine that he'd need for pain management. He said he'd be fine.

Heavy storm clouds drifted to the northeast and filtered most of the sun over the lower end of Harvey. Jackie walked in silhouette as he led me down the alleyway past rows of town houses and stagnant rain puddles in the sunken concrete. He was taking me to meet Gateway's director, Darryl Chandler.

Jackie labored up a narrow flight of stairs to the director's office. A sign met us at the door: "Danger ahead—Packers Country."

Chandler, dressed in faded blue jeans and white sneakers, welcomed us into his casual but spacious office filled with rolling desk chairs. Tacked up calendars, notes, and schedules decorated the walls, along with a framed diploma from Southern University at New Orleans. Jackie labored as he lowered himself into a chair.

Gateway Recovery Systems bills itself as "a domiciliary intensive outpatient program" for adult males, focused on military veterans, court appointees, and indigent homeless people. They operate forty-five townhomes that house four people each. On average, Gateway helps 150 to 175 men deal with substance abuse, mental health, homeless status, finances, family counseling, anger management, and grief counseling. The vibe was less clinical and more relational than that of Tuerk House in Baltimore. There were no locked wards here.

When Jackie first arrived in 2014, Chandler and his team ran a full evaluation of Jackie's family relationships, his history of substance abuse, his medical records, his social interactions, and his mental status. They concluded, among other things, that Jackie suffered from some form of cognitive decline. Chandler suspected a connection with Jackie's football career and wondered if the cognitive issues had led to his substance abuse issues.

Regardless of the cause, counselors tried to help him recognize his behaviors and manage them when they flared up. "When he thinks certain things, or when he feels certain things," Chandler said as Jackie looked on, "he knows what it is. It's not just him being a bad person." Jackie learned to work with the medical team and the psychiatrists to stay balanced. "As long as he does that," Chandler said, "the chances of him using or being homeless again are very slim.

"I believe he listens to me," Chandler said. "I believe he respects me and understands what I'm telling him. But he's still human, and he has the right to make whatever choices he wants to make. But he needs to take charge of the consequences—positive or negative." Jackie knew from his Bible studies that a man can't continue to sow wild oats and never expect them to sprout. Eventually, a grown man must give up his childish nature and accept God's spirit of self-control.

Even though Jackie had officially finished his two-month treatment at Gateway, he'd taken Chandler's advice to continue to rent an apartment within the compound. That way, Jackie could still engage with the rehab program. "He still has access to the aftercare groups," Chandler said, "and twelve-steps meetings *if* that's what he chooses to do." He paused, and I sensed an uneasiness in the air, as if the subtle accusation had revealed too much. Chandler looked at Jackie as he continued talking to me.

"He comes when he wants to, and when he don't want to, I know he's doing *something*."

Jackie broke into nervous laughter. "Say what? Wait . . ."

"I know he's doing something that he knows we're not going to condone."

"Right . . . ," Jackie trailed off nervously.

Jackie had made steady progress, but Chandler emphasized that he was highly susceptible to relapse. He warned Jackie about the people he hung with. Staying in contact with former friends and connections are often a major stumbling block for clients like Jackie.

Chandler pointed me to a prime example. Weeks after entering

Gateway in 2014, Jackie took his first NFL pension check and caught the bus for Central City. He walked straight through the gauntlet of old friends and old enemies and knocked on his drug dealer's door to pay his debts. Jackie knew drug debts were deadly. He wanted to clear the ledger. Gateway's rules discouraged such encounters, believing they were more dangerous than the threats. Chandler warned him to cut all ties to his former life. If you're a drunk, you don't hang out in bars. If you're a drug addict, you don't associate with dealers.

But Jackie had known this dealer since childhood, and although he still considered him a friend, he knew that business was business. And he also knew that in the drug trade, a dealer can't show weakness. Jackie handed over the $700 that he owed with a smile. In this case, the dealer was happy to lose a customer.

He drove Jackie ten blocks to Felicity Street and introduced him to the ragtag army of enforcers, the "twenty-something-year-olds," as Jackie described them, "the boys that do all that shooting."

"Look," he told them, as Jackie remembered, "here's the football player I was telling you about. You don't have to worry about him anymore. Leave him alone. And if he comes back to buy drugs, don't sell him any, don't give him any. Send him to me, because I don't want him smoking nothing no more. He's looking good, and I want him to stay that way."

"Thank you for that one," Jackie said, and just like that, the contract was canceled.

The last time the two men talked—right after the 2016 NFL season and before the playoffs—the same dealer waved him down to get Jackie's predictions on the betting line. He wanted to put his money on the Cowboys, but Jackie told him to hold off.

As we talked, Chandler speculated on Jackie's current status. "I don't believe he's using no substances," he said, "but he's using something else . . . probably a woman, or something." Again,

Chandler shifted his eyes toward Jackie and then back to me. "He knows. We've discussed all these things. I can honestly say that he knows what he needs to do and what he doesn't need to do right now. So whatever choices he's making right now, he's making them on his own."

Jackie raised his eyebrows, nodded his head, and stared at the floor. "Yep, right."

He changed the subject.

"They got me down for early dementia," he said of another speculative diagnosis.

As Jackie heaved himself out of the chair, Chandler made a motion to offer help but stopped short.

"Take care, pad-nah. You know how it works."

Outside, one of the counselors met him with a handshake and a shoulder hug. As Jackie's arms wrapped around the young man's shoulders, I noticed a tiny gold ring on Jackie's pinky finger that I hadn't seen before: a stylized woman's ring, laced with tiny diamonds.

"Where you been?" the counselor chided Jackie. "It's been months since I've seen you."

"Everybody think I've left?"

"You been ducking out sometime," Chandler said.

"Gooooodbyyyye," Jackie joked, trying to dodge the next barb.

"Come see me. You know where I'm at," the counselor said. "Come get your medicine."

The counselor turned to me. "I've been here three years. When I first met him . . . he was signing the back of another client's jersey. I asked another client who this guy was."

"That's Jackie Wallace. The Minnesota Vikings' Jackie Wallace."

"*The* Jackie Wallace?"

"Yeah, 'The Headhunter,' the old safety Jackie Wallace."

He was shocked.

"I grew up in south Louisiana with my father telling me about players like him, and the Buddy Ryan defense of the seventies," he said. "Goes to show you that the disease of addiction can happen to anybody. To go from where he was at to where he's been and be back where he's at now . . . it shows determination, and what the program can do for people. And now, with a few years clean, he's a little crazy, but he's an inspiration to a lot of guys here. Not to mention he's humble. That's the most resounding thing about him. People around here don't know him as Jackie Wallace the Super Bowl guy. They know him as Jackie Wallace with a few years clean that comes into therapy groups and meetings and helps people. And behold, now he's a friend of mine. I love this man. Awesome dude."

Jackie and I walked back to his apartment together, passing a dozen apartments and a few old Fords, Saturns, and Chevys. Jackie's Crocs scuffled the loose gravel and sent pebbles flying. As he mulled over the counselor's words—"Awesome dude"—he chuckled. His gait seemed a little lighter, his smile broader.

"Let's meet again," I said, "when you're ready. What can I bring you?"

"I'd like a print of the photo you shot under the bridge," he said. "I need that to keep me encouraged."

"How big?" I asked.

He spread his hands out as far as they'd go, just as he'd done in the newsroom twenty-four years before, and said, "About like this."

CHAPTER THIRTEEN

The Damage Within

2016

Jackie didn't blame the NFL for his crippled body. Even as a teenager, he understood that he routinely could blow out a knee or break a leg. But, like the tens of thousands of other players who had ever played the sport at the professional level, he didn't know how badly football could hurt him into retirement. He'd never considered the long-term effects it could have on his brain.

Jackie first noticed a slight mental decline in 1979, when, as a twenty-eight-year-old, he started having trouble remembering names of friends and acquaintances. Over the next three decades, he came to rely on detailed calendars to keep him on track—even to remember his own siblings' birthdays. He kept journals and notebooks and used colored highlighters to stay organized. He kept legal pads filled with numbers. Sticky notes littered his room until there were so many they became almost useless.

Sometimes he confused his two ex-wives' names. "Mary was a good woman. You met her," he said in conversation, forgetting it was Deborah I'd met. Some might easily blame these little slipups on the normal confusion of an aging person, but these lapses in conversation and memory started in his early forties, just a few years following his treatment at Tuerk House. During this same time, his uncharacteristic incidents of agitation and aggression began—which eventually led to trouble with Deborah. When Jackie's mood shifted wildly into violence, both he and Deborah knew something wasn't right. This wasn't the Jackie she had married. For weeks on end, he'd be kind and considerate. And then, with no explanation or pattern, he'd suddenly become depressed, angry, and detached.

I, too, was worried. I remembered his spine-chilling nickname, "The Headhunter," that some fans called him and imagined all the hits he must have received to the head; more important, I imagined the number of hard hits he *delivered* to receivers and running backs.

Somewhere along the way, Jackie came to believe that he'd somehow lost his ability to check himself when making decisions. He had always been a straight arrow. He retold how in grade school, he considered touching someone else's pencil a form of stealing. "There was a time you couldn't get me to spit on the sidewalk," he said of his younger days. But now, seemingly without warning, he'd shift from his loving-and-giving nature into an egocentric selfishness. He could tell something was wrong. If he had reached out to someone—if someone could have connected the dots on his troubling patterns of behavior—his relationship with Deborah might have ended much differently. But few understood the effects of head injuries on football players at the time.

From 1966 to 1979, the span of Jackie's playing years, there were no concussion protocols in football. Players who suffered blows to the head were treated with smelling salts and sent back into the game as quickly as possible. I remember my own experience in high school of being knocked out, stumbling to my feet, and then wandering into the wrong huddle. I remember the violent tackles or blocks, when the back of my head smacked the ground. I remember the shock, the instant blackout, the flashes of light as my visual cortex concussed into the back of my skull. The ringing in my ears. We called it "getting our bells rung," or "getting dinged." We laughed it off, same as we did while watching a drunk stumble down the street.

Coaches taught players to use the crown of their helmets as a battering ram, to "put their hats on 'em," they said. We thought of our headgear as weapons—the tip of the spear. The harder we hit, the less we'd get hurt, our coaches said to us. We didn't know how our brains were sloshing inside our skulls, or how the linear and twisting forces were stretching and tearing our nerve fibers and destroying cells deep inside our brains.

Recognition came in 2002, when Dr. Bennet Omalu, a Pennsylvania coroner, recognized a correlation between the neurologic disorders associated with chronic head trauma during an autopsy of former Pittsburgh Steelers center Mike Webster. He named it chronic traumatic encephalopathy (CTE), the progressive neurodegenerative disease found in persons, especially athletes and soldiers, who experienced *repeated* head trauma. The long-term repercussions had been studied and identified as "punch-drunk syndrome" in boxers since 1928, but it wasn't clearly associated with football players until 2005. The blows—over time—cause abnormal protein called tau to form clumps and spread through the brain. The degenerated brain tissue can appear months, years, or even decades after the last brain trauma, long after a player's last game.

The progression of CTE is categorized into four stages. Tau forms around the brain's blood vessels in stage one, but there are no recognized symptoms. In stage two, sufferers exhibit rage, impulsive behavior, and depression. Stage three brings confusion and memory loss. Stage four brings advanced dementia.

Unlike normal progressions of dementia, which typically begin in a person in their mid-sixties, CTE symptoms often show up in athletes or former athletes in their forties and fifties. The impairments affect thinking and memory and cause impaired judgment, impulse control, aggression, depression, confusion, paranoia, and suicidal thoughts. Eventually CTE leads to progressive dementia. Jackie suffered from most of these symptoms. To further confuse a proper diagnosis, many of these same impairments can be reasons people turn to drug abuse, which in turn can lead to some of these same symptoms. So, which came first?

Four different observational studies conducted between 2009 and 2015 suggested a *possible* relationship between traumatic brain injuries in young brains and "increased problematic substance use." While CTE has not been definitely linked to drug addiction, it's clear that brain injury, physical injury, and an unhealthy buildup of tau certainly lead to brain dysfunction and affect self-control and lapses of good judgment.

When Jackie reentered Gateway Recovery in 2014, the psychologists working through his background histories independently recognized a troubling pattern in his ability to remember details and in his ability to control his behavior and emotions. The doctors saw the same patterns that Jackie had noticed thirty-four years before and in Baltimore in the 1990s. They wondered if CTE could possibly have played a role. With Chandler's help, Jackie secured an attorney in Boca Raton, Florida, to help him join a lawsuit against the NFL. In June 2014, Jackie became one of fourteen plaintiffs, including Hall of Famer Dan Marino, who filed against the league, joining 4,500 others represented in hundreds of other lawsuits of their own. The first lawsuit had been filed in 2011, when Jackie was in prison or crashed on the street. The suits claimed that the NFL had concealed the dangers of concussions from the players.

CTE made sense to Jackie. When he read about Mike Webster and Dr. Omalu's autopsy, he couldn't help but marvel at the similarities in their situations and personalities. Mike was a kindhearted, intelligent, and organized man whose celebrated career and beautiful marriage had slowly deteriorated into divorce and despair. He was eventually found alone, disoriented, and sleeping in a train station.

"I guess it's the oxymoron of living," Jackie told me as we talked. "When I read the stories of Webster, he had a semblance of order and a direction in his life. [But] wait a minute," Jackie said as he compared Webster's CTE diagnosis and ordered mind to the photo I'd shot of him under the bridge. "Here's this guy sleeping underneath the bridge, got his shoes lined up, got his things lined up, but he's underneath the bridge. That's what got me with the concussion thing. It was off."

He continued. "I believe that's the problem that's going to happen with . . ." Jackie paused as he struggled to pull a name from his memory. "Number 21 . . . with the Patriots," he said, clumsily transposing the numbers of the New England quarterback. "You know, Captain America!"

"You mean Brady?" I said.

"Yeah," he said as we broke into laughter over Tom Brady's polished image. But Jackie continued, remembering how Brady's wife, Gisele Bündchen, awkwardly leaked during a CBS interview about how often Brady had suffered concussions.

Then, as he's prone to do, Jackie abruptly changed subjects.

Though Dr. Omalu had uncovered the connection between football and CTE, the profound impact wasn't fully clear until 2017, when Dr. Ann McKee, a neuropathologist with Boston University, published the results of a study that examined donated brains of deceased NFL football players.

Of the 111 samples tested, 110 tested positive for CTE.

While the findings have been criticized for sampling bias, McKee said the study was never intended to be a random study. Family members donated the brains because the athletes had shown signs of CTE. But the results demonstrated a shocking truth, especially since there is no way to perform the same test on living persons. Another Boston University study in 2013 showed that half of former athletes with CTE engaged in physical abuse toward others.

As I watched Jackie's old game films, one thing kept nagging at me. While I saw many hard hits, I never saw him helped off the field with a concussion. Jackie had enjoyed a relatively injury-free career. Dr. Robert Cantu, clinical professor of neurosurgery at the Boston University School of Medicine, explained that I shared a popular misconception about CTE. The main culprit isn't the dramatic, game-changing collisions that we see in sports highlights, but rather the *repeated* brain trauma that often goes unnoticed.

A Stanford University paper showed that "in just one game, a football player can be exposed to 50 to 60 violent blows to the head." While quarterbacks and wide receivers get the most attention over dramatic collisions, the greatest at-risk players are, in order, linemen, linebackers, and defensive backs because of the repetitive hits. Surprisingly, the average hit is delivered with a g-force of 25.8, roughly the same as if a player had driven a car into a brick wall at 30 miles per hour. Unfortunately, as Dr. Cantu pointed out, many defensive backs like Jackie led with their head—for the simple reason that it works for them.

Jackie's cumulative brain trauma effect progressed through his three years in high school, four years of college, and seven years as a pro. According to Dr. Cantu, Jackie probably averaged eight hundred to one thousand violent hits to his head each year—or ten thousand to thirteen thousand damaging blows over his fourteen-year career. And as Cantu reminded me, "Just because you don't have CTE doesn't mean you don't have brain damage from football."

In recent years, the NFL has tried to reduce the number of repetitive hits by cutting down on the amount of head-on collisions during practices. NFL players today absorb less head trauma than they did in years past, but players are still vulnerable, and the danger begins when they're in high school, where practices are not monitored as closely as in the NFL, according to Dr. Cantu. The dangers increase as players become bigger, faster, and stronger. In the 1920s, linemen averaged 190 pounds. Now the average is 311. The average player for all positions is now 242 pounds.

Compounding the problem, the macho nature of football leads to a cavalier attitude about injuries. Players do whatever it takes to stay on the field, Jackie said. It's not manly to tap out—to leave the field because of an injury. As sociologist Michael Messner once wrote on the irony of macho sports, "Men must break their bodies in order to prove that they are unbreakable."

Jackie initially avoided football at St. Aug because he didn't like getting hit. But he adapted to the hitting culture when he transitioned from quarterback to defensive back at Arizona. Bud Grant, his coach, once told him to dial back his aggression. In 1978, the same year he set the Rams' punt-return record, he remembered blacking out when his head wedged between Earl Campbell's thighs. When Jackie returned to the huddle, he told teammates that he would let Campbell waltz into the end zone before he tried to tackle him again. But Jackie didn't get any sympathy from his teammates, especially from Jack Youngblood, the defensive end and team captain, who famously played three straight games, including in the 1980 Super Bowl, on a broken fibula.

The psychology of football demands physical intimidation. Hard hits demoralize opponents. Some casual fans refuse to believe that players intentionally target opponents for injury. But in 2009, on their drive to the Super Bowl, the New Orleans Saints allegedly paid bonuses for intentionally injuring opponents. In the NFC title game, defenders apparently tried to destroy Brett Favre's motivation to play. According to *Sports Illustrated*'s Peter King, as Favre lay crumpled on the ground with a sprained ankle, the result of a devastating, unflagged, high-low tackle, an unidentified defensive player could be heard over the on-field microphone saying, "Pay me my money."

After the game, I photographed a battered and bruised Favre—one of the toughest quarterbacks to ever play the game—as he could barely climb the two steps to the podium for the postgame interview. Before the next season, the NFL sanctioned the Saints in the scandal that became known as Bountygate. The NFL Players Association later published the NFL's evidence, showing how the Saints strategized on how to most effectively "Kill the Head," or destroy a player's motivation to play. According to the evidence, the defense especially concentrated on making quarterbacks, running backs, and receivers "mentally vacate the game."

Jackie knows all too well what football can do to the brain, but he loves the game and doesn't want to see it change too much. "Problem is," Jackie said, "they're regulating it so much that it's taking the fun out of the game. The violence is what people like to see."

In August 2013, even before Jackie had joined the lawsuit, the NFL and the retired players had agreed to a settlement: the league would pay $765 million for compensation, medical exams, and continued research into concussion risks. After U.S. District Judge Anita Brody expressed concerns that there wouldn't be enough money, the NFL agreed to remove the cap, which meant the payments would likely surpass $1 billion in the sixty-five-year deal. Even though the agreement involved more than 4,500 plaintiffs, each retired player would have to establish his own individual case.

Since CTE can only be conclusively diagnosed through post-mortem analysis, the settlement assessments would rely on testing. Symptoms for CTE reveal themselves in three ways: cognitively, behaviorally, and emotionally. And since behavioral and emotional symptoms are also revealed in many other conditions, Judge Brody removed them from the settlement discussion, making two-thirds of the "CTE triad" irrelevant. That meant players who couldn't prove cognitive impairment would not receive compensation.

As a first step in the process, Jackie took a ten-hour-long battery of tests to measure his learning and memory. The NFL coordinated the test, called the Baseline Assessment Program. If the test indicated dementia, he could file a claim. A board would determine compensation based on a player's total number of years in the league and his age.

If he failed, he could apply for a second opinion from a doctor of his choice. The NFL called this the Monetary Award program.

Once the NFL received a qualifying claim, they had the right to additional qualifiers, which could involve appeals, medical audits, employment audits, and a third-party sworn affidavit that attested to the player's cognitive decline, which included these questions:

- Was the player's coordination or their ability to concentrate as good as it used to be?
- Had they declined in appearance?
- Was there a loss of appetite?
- Who handled the family's money?

Without that third-party affidavit, it's impossible to receive the qualifying diagnosis. The NFL also reserved the right to investigate every job a player had worked, as well as every doctor the player had visited in the past five years. The NFL could also hire a private investigator to secretly follow the player to verify a suspicious claim.

Jackie knew the testing, diagnosis, and decision would be an arduous process, but he tried not to worry. As of August 2019, 20,543 class-action members had registered for the testing. The NFL had received 2,864 claim packages. A total of 956 awards have been paid, totaling almost $690 million.

But even as the awards were dispersed, plaintiffs complained that they were seeing little of the money. The settlement process "is revealing the underbelly of the legal system," wrote ESPN writer Mark Fainaru-Wada. He cited attorney retainer fees as high as 40 percent, lawyers poaching clients from one another, and "lawyers effectively threatening to sue former players to ensure they get their fees." On the other hand, the NFL has said that hundreds of the claims have been denied because of "unscrupulous doctors and lawyers" who helped players appear more mentally impaired than they were, according to the *New York Times*.

But surviving CTE sufferers had bigger concerns than money. CTE sufferers are different from Alzheimer's patients in one important way, according to Dr. Vernon Palmisano, a New Orleans area physician and LSU Family Medicine faculty member: they're aware of what's happening to their brains. They recognize their own decline. That may be one reason that suicide is common among them.

When four-time Pro Bowl safety Dave Duerson retired from football in 1993, he easily transitioned into the business world. With an advanced economics education from Notre Dame and Harvard Business School, he found success in the food-services industry and eventually launched his own food business. Ironically, he also spent several years representing the players' union on a six-member panel that ruled on disability benefits for former NFL players. The board was criticized for denying a large percentage of neurological damage claims.

Later, Duerson began noticing symptoms of CTE in himself. After his businesses collapsed and he was forced into bankruptcy, he complained more and more of a deteriorating mental state. His marriage shattered in the process. Just before committing suicide, he left a handwritten message to his family: "Please, see that my brain is given to the NFL's brain bank." He then shot himself in the chest, specifically to preserve his brain sample. He was fifty years old. Neurologists at Boston University soon confirmed that he suffered from CTE.

A year later, in 2012, forty-three-year-old San Diego fan favorite Junior Seau shot himself in the heart. His behavior had deteriorated into dramatic mood swings, depression, forgetfulness, insomnia, and detachment. Seau, who played for San Diego, Miami, and New England, was never listed by his teams as having a concussion. After an autopsy, the National Institutes of Health confirmed he indeed had CTE.

Jackie spoke often on Seau's experience when we talked as he reflected on his own struggles with depression.

Not surprisingly, considering Jackie's intelligence, his test results through the first round of the Baseline Assessment Program failed to prove his case. Most of Jackie's symptoms were emotional and behavioral and were therefore not qualifying. He remained optimistic for his second round of tests. He felt sure another doctor would find a link. But for now, he'd have to wait and wonder. The results wouldn't be back for weeks, maybe months.

"CTE would have made so much sense," said Deborah, his former wife. "Something broke him."

CHAPTER FOURTEEN

The Lombardi

February 2017

It was Saturday evening, February 4, 2017. Shimmering light from the setting sun painted Jackie and his new friend, Darren, in golden rim light as they walked along Willow Street in Central City. Darren sipped iced tea from a plastic Subway cup as the men talked about their week. Three warped and weathered crosses stood vigil from behind a dilapidated chain link fence as they passed, but they didn't notice. They remained focused on their mission.

Up ahead, low-level hustlers collected in the growing shadows between Martin Luther King Jr. Boulevard and Josephine Street, where they prepared for another big night of slinging rock. Jackie studied his walk—one step at a time.

But as he stepped to clear a shallow curb—a minor obstacle—his hobbled hip caused his foot to miss the edging. As he tumbled toward the sidewalk, a spray of hard candies shot from his hand and landed on the ground. Darren caught his arm and wrenched him back upright. With regained composure and a shrug, Jackie struggled on. A half block later, he grabbed a handrail with a death grip as he climbed the three short steps to a meeting hall. Darren held the door.

As he entered the room, Jackie flashed his trademark grin and bellowed: "What time does this five-o'clock meeting start?"

The gathering of Narcotics Anonymous drew about twenty-five men and women, middle-aged and older, and filled about half the room. The rowdy group began to settle down once the coffee finished brewing. Someone handed out slices of king cake as Jackie found a chair against the wall. Even in his worn and deteriorated condition, strangers collected around him as if he were a bona fide celebrity. They wanted to say hello, laugh in response to his jokes, or grab a quick selfie.

The group leader, known to all as Darryl P., began the meeting with a harsh reminder aimed at Jackie. "Here, you ain't nothing but an addict," he said. Jackie nodded humbly; he knew Darryl to speak truthfully, even if he delivered it with little grace.

The meeting progressed as most NA meetings do. The personal, anonymous testimonies were passionate and painful, sometimes vulgar. People with no last names can confess a lot of misery in an hour and a half. Jackie remained mostly silent.

As time expired, Darryl encouraged the addicts to call on one another whenever they felt the urge to use. But before dismissing the group, he asked Jackie to step to the front of the room. Holding his arm around his shoulders, Darryl proclaimed, "Three years sober!" and presented Jackie with a gold medallion, a small token to commemorate his achievement. On the face of the keepsake, the words circling a cut diamond read, "Time equals miracles—Recovery equals life."

The medallion might as well have been the Lombardi Trophy as Jackie raised it to show the room. When the applause erupted, Jackie couldn't hide his smile or the glint in his eye. Three years felt like a lifetime, and the medallion symbolized the first step of yet another beautiful year.

Three years sober. Three years—almost to the day—since he walked up the ramp.

No one left the meeting immediately. Everyone wanted to hug him or shake his hand. One man planted a big kiss near his ear. After the crowd finally scattered, another friend helped him outside and to a waiting car, which emerged with the authority of a limousine. With Jackie in the back seat, the car drove off under the ever-vigilant eyes of the dealers on the next corner.

Back home that night, Jackie thanked God that he hadn't ended his life like other NFL players who stood on the precipice of career success, only to lose everything to drug abuse. He frequently recalled Joe Gilliam, a quarterback who had just enough success with the Pittsburgh Steelers to finance a fatal cocaine overdose. Jackie felt blessed not to have made more money than he did. More success would have led to more drug abuse. He felt sure of it.

TEN DAYS LATER, on Valentine's Day 2017, Jackie was scheduled for a hip replacement. I asked if I could visit him in the hospital, but he said not to bother. He'd be OK.

After a couple of weeks had passed without a word or call, I decided to drop by for a visit. I thought he should have called by now. His neighbor Ronald sat out front cloaked in headphones. Once again, I felt like an uninvited intruder.

"Have you seen Jackie?"

Ronald shifted his headphones just enough to catch the essence of my words.

"He may be there, he may not," he said, barely looking up. "You're the man from the newspaper?"

"I just wanted to check on him."

"He may be there."

The stained doorbell appeared broken, so I knocked instead, repeatedly. But there was no response, no "coming," no rustling around, not a sound. I circled the block to the Gateway offices. Maybe Chandler could help. Surely, he would know if Jackie was in trouble.

Residents hanging out on the sidewalk seemed anxious and uneasy, as if I'd just walked up on a crime scene. One man scurried into the stairwell ahead of me, seemingly looking for a place to hide. "I can't believe it," he said breathlessly. "The guy said he was going to kill us all. He said he had a bullet for each of us."

Meanwhile, just outside the door, Jefferson Parish deputies had cornered and cuffed a man and were wrestling him into the patrol car. I couldn't see his face, but the commotion reeked of violence.

Finally, Chandler came upstairs through the back steps. "What can I help *you* with?" he said, clearly frustrated.

"I'm worried about Jackie, his pain meds and all," I said. "He's not returning my phone calls. When I knock, no one answers."

"I have no reason to open his apartment for you," he said as he plopped down behind his desk.

"Oh, gosh, no," I said. "Do you know how he's doing since his surgery? Have you seen him?"

Chandler reminded me of what I already knew. Jackie had finished the program. He was not required to go to meetings any longer, although he'd been encouraged to do so.

"He just rents a place from me now," he said. "I haven't seen him in a while, but he pays his rent on time. But it's interesting you show up today. Just Saturday someone else mentioned to me that they were worried about him. I'll check in on him. I'll let you know."

The courtyard was still abuzz as I walked back to my car. The neighborhood had seen its share of crime and shootings.

Since my early days at the newspaper, I'd witnessed the festering drug trade around this area during numerous ride-alongs with cops. I remember clearly a crop of run-down apartments nicknamed Electric Avenue that served as an incubator for young dealers, resulting in endless undercover stings, drug raids, and arrests. I once photographed a three-year-old child wailing as officers led away his cuffed father on dealing charges. I nearly cried when I examined the negative under darkroom lights—another innocent mind forever scarred, I thought. In the Harvey area alone, the intense drug culture created the need for more than twenty-seven different rehab facilities.

Drugs and poverty are often blamed as root causes for the intense street violence in New Orleans. The murder culture in the city is so vicious that citizens have become emotionally detached from the endless news reports. A rational mind can only take so much. In 2017, New Orleans police reported 157 murders—a murder rate of 40 per 100,000, ranking the city fourth in the country behind St. Louis, Baltimore, and Detroit, and far ahead of Chicago (number ten) in per-capita rankings. For thirty straight years, New Orleans had ranked in the top five. Correspondingly, in the same year, census data said that New Orleans led the nation among the fifty largest metro areas with an 18.6 percent poverty rate.

As I circled the buildings back to my car, the police presence reminded me of a crime scene I'd photographed just a year or so before. The driver of a florist's van was murdered only a few blocks away from Gateway. It seemed pretty clear that the victim wasn't there to deliver flowers.

I decided to knock once more on the door before I left. Again, no answer.

I walked away but turned with my camera to make a reference photo of the old, plastic chairs under the cypress tree. One frame, two frames.

Then the door creaked. A man poked his head out.

"Jackie? Is that you?"

"Who is that?" he said, sounding confused and weak.

"It's me . . ." I walked up into the porch shadow.

He held his hand out, and I took it. He looked terribly frail for such a big man, barely able to balance on his walker. He wore a pair of white gym shorts. No shirt. A red stripe down the shorts told me he'd had them awhile.

"It's not a good time," he said, never breaking his pained expression. "It's not a good time. This hip is acting up on me."

"I understand," I said. "I'm worried about you. You OK?"

"Yeah, I'm OK. Let's do this another time. How about in a week? I'll feel better then. Same time, same place."

"How about I bring lunch?"

"How about two all-beef patties, special sauce, lettuce, cheese . . ." We laughed.

I told him I'd be back the following week with a Big Mac, which I soon learned was his favorite meal.

CHAPTER FIFTEEN

Dreams About Heaven

2017

A few weeks later, Jackie woke from a dead sleep in a panic. A pain pierced the left side of his chest as if he'd cracked a rib, and he could hardly breathe as he struggled to untangle himself from his bedsheets. In the early-morning darkness, his oversize fingers stabbed out 911 on his flip-phone keypad.

Hours later, at a nearby hospital, a cardiologist diagnosed his new pain. He was suffering from stage-three congestive heart failure, a common malady among crack users.

Tests showed that his left ventricle was struggling to pump enough blood, all due to damaged blood vessels around his heart. His heart's efficiency rating had dropped to 25 percent. (A healthy heart pumps between 50 and 75 percent.) While the doctor explained the damage, Jackie remembered the photographs he'd seen at Tuerk House twenty-seven years before. He remembered the images of damaged organs that had once left him queasy. He remembered being warned that cocaine was the perfect heart-attack drug. But now—even though he was three years clean—fluid had surrounded his heart and collected around his lungs. His doctor explained that congestive heart failure had no cure but assured him that proper medication and a better diet could slow the decline. "It is what it is," he said with a sigh to his doctor.

As I visited during the coming weeks and months, I could see how Jackie's world had contracted around him. His deteriorating hip and heart had limited his mobility, but his increasing isolation and loneliness came from a different source: his sobriety. The longer he stayed sober, the worse he felt. In a way, his apartment at Gateway felt like a nursing home—a place where people came to die, a far cry from the vibrant social interaction of inner-city New Orleans.

Gateway offered him a safe environment, for sure. But sequestered from his former world, the hands on the clock seemed to drag. Jackie and his buddies passed the time with dominoes and video games. Daytime TV zapped his ambition. Perhaps for no other reason than my belief of what idleness could do to a person, I worried that the boredom bred temptation. I longed to see Jackie around more positive people.

Jackie's childhood Bible classes taught him to sense God's influence in his daily life. He often described himself with a guardian angel watching over his every move. As clichéd as it sounded, he enjoyed imagining the angel whispering into his right ear to counteract the devil whispering into his left. But his study of scripture also taught him that Satan roamed the earth like a roaring lion, searching for Christians to tear limb from limb. He saw nothing laughable in the two competing images. The forces of good and evil battled constantly. As a combative measure, he started each morning with meditation and ended each day in prayer. He prayed for "checks and balances" over his behavior, something he felt he'd lost when his parents died, or maybe it was the CTE. He prayed for wisdom. He bargained for strength and perseverance.

But an ache persisted in his gut. He heard Satan's voice whispering, "If you're going to use . . . then use. If not, then fine, but if you're going to use . . . then use." Over and over. If he slipped, he knew what would happen. His demise always started with one foot, then another, and seven steps later he'd be "talking crazy," as he described it. By then, there was no turning back. Two irreversible words would slip through his lips: "F— it," and he'd be gone.

His mind would be closed to any words of caution or wisdom. Sound logic would grate like fingernails on a chalkboard, and the slightest challenge would ignite his anger. His willful self-destruction would overcome his will to live. He would find a room, a bed, a floor, it didn't matter. He'd take the pipe and take a breath. His eyes would bulge, and his lips would grow numb. His throat felt cool as the smoke seeped into the deepest cavities of his lungs, filling him with what he'd missed. Once again, euphoria would float across his brain, each drag better than the last.

Figures would pass him in slow motion like half-blurred bodies in a photograph—darting, dodging, and sprinting away. He would chase some of them, while others would chase him. His cheering cloud of witnesses would fade into the background, muted into dull shadow. A sea of bodies would crash around him. His head would whip against the blows. His mind would go dark as he fell. Agonizing pain would surge as his vision slowly cleared. What had happened to the euphoria he had once felt? How could he have it again?

The rush and fall would continue until his pockets were empty. And slowly, ever so slowly, after two or three days without the pipe, his crack coma would finally fall away. His senses would recover. The path would become clear again, and he would wonder how he ever ended up in this place. He would find his phone and ask a friend for help. And then, life would renew again.

That's the way it had been before Gateway. That's how his sweet/vile seducer had broken his will over and over.

That repetitive knowledge should have been enough to keep him from succumbing. But it didn't stand a chance. Giving in to addiction had nothing to do with logic.

But today, for one more day, Jackie didn't give in. Today, in his bedroom, when his demons whispered and clawed, he got down on his knees and prayed. He allowed the Spirit of God to flow over him. Today, he passed safely.

Since that day on the bridge, he'd won 1,245 daily battles.

AMONG RESEARCHERS, TWO schools of thought have formed around crack addiction. Some believe it is a psychological dependence. Others believe it is a physical, chemical hook. But the American Addiction Center warns that either extreme is equally invalid and unrealistic. Believing that chemicals inside Jackie's brain physically force a reflex action is as wrong as believing that Jackie chose to become a crack addict in the first place. Sure, choices were involved, but as the addiction center points out, people don't choose to become an addict any more than a cigarette smoker chooses lung cancer.

ONE AFTERNOON, JACKIE and I sat in his apartment and talked about how unpredictable life could be. He slouched deeply into the sofa and stretched his lanky legs, seemingly halfway across the small living room. His sloppy posture helped ease the pain in his aching hip. He groaned and rolled onto the floor—down to his knees—whenever he wanted to stand. He then lifted himself in agonizing slow motion. His wild-eyed *SpongeBob* T-shirt seemed to espouse his inner scream. His walker always stood within easy reach.

A large blanket covered the sofa, soft and printed in poetry that read like a note from a girlfriend: "Live like there is no tomorrow. Laugh until your sides hurt. Love like you've never loved before." It reminded me to ask about the delicate ring on his pinky finger. He blushed when he admitted that it belonged to his new best friend, Yolanda Stewart, a woman he'd met at the NA meetings. He told me secretly that he planned to buy her a new one when he could afford it. One day soon he hoped to surprise her with it over dinner, on one knee.

When I finally saw the two of them together, I thought they resembled a couple of teenagers wrapped up in a schoolyard crush. She dressed with a smart fashion sense with matching manicured nails and styled hair worn just below her shoulders. Her glasses made her look trendy and somewhat younger than her sixty-two years, and much more vibrant than Jackie's sixty-five. He showered her with affection, surprised her with small gifts, and performed chivalrous acts like holding doors open and pulling seats out for her whenever they dined at a restaurant. Her quiet, sweet, and unassuming nature squared nicely with his enlarged personality.

She'd been sober for four years and intended to stay that way, staying true to her weekly NA meeting attendance. "Ain't nothing back there that I need to go back for," she said of the streets. Yolanda found strength in daily scripture readings and among dainty motivational cards and quotations. She sent me one that read, "Laughter is spiritual warfare." She loved to laugh.

Jackie called her a "liberated woman." She described herself as a free spirit, doing what she wanted to do when she wanted to do it. They almost always held hands when they walked.

Yolanda made Jackie smile and livened his spirits. But Chandler had warned him about getting too deeply involved in a romantic relationship—a red flag for a man trying to break the cycle of addiction. To that, Jackie just winked and smiled. He said he had it under control, although both Chandler and I knew that control was not one of Jackie's specialties.

Yolanda helped him stay disciplined. He adopted strict hours for sleep to avoid nighttime temptations. He applied strict behavioral rules during family holiday parties. In December, he accepted an invitation from his nieces to their Christmas party so he could introduce Yolanda to the family. But instead of joining in the living room celebration with the adults, he stayed in the kitchen with the children. Yolanda asked him why he wasn't joining the grown-ups. "Go back. You'll see," he said. "It's because they're having wine."

Yolanda added herself to his list of "accountability partners" who were assigned by Gateway to drop by from time to time, often appearing intuitively when Jackie needed one the most. Jackie kept their phone numbers handy if he needed an emergency visit. I told him to add me on his list.

But for the most part, Jackie seemed to be managing well. He'd even restored order to his financial life. He now received two NFL pension checks that totaled $1,242. Combined with his $970 Social Security check, he kept his modest bills paid in full and on time. He bummed rides or took the bus downtown for his weekly NA meetings since he didn't have a car. His bad credit prevented him buying anything on time.

He seemed comfortable, assured, and secure. "Life is good for me right now," he said.

JACKIE AND I drifted apart for weeks at a time. Newspaper assignments kept me distracted for most of the spring and summer: Mardi Gras, Jazz Fest, demonstrations, and near riots over the mayor's plan to remove Confederate monuments consumed the city's summer of 2017 conversation. At the same time, I began making plans to leave my job with *The Times-Picayune* to work on freelance opportunities. I had used my cameras to tell stories of the most amazing people for more than thirty-five years, but the newspaper business model was falling apart, due mostly to free access to internet news. Since Hurricane Katrina in 2005, the *Picayune*'s circulation had dropped from 257,000 to less than 85,000, and the dovetailing numbers forced round after round of layoffs and reorganizations. Our leadership continued to ask us to do more with less. Gubernatorial candidate John Bel Edwards had pointed out in his 2016 campaign the universal truth that if *that* were possible, eventually we could do everything with nothing. The writing on the wall was as clear as the inked newsprint that I had once held in my hands.

I notified my editors and planned my departure for the end of October, giving me a few months to finish reporting and photographing the story on the sinking cemetery. But finding Jackie and writing his story as my final project felt like a beautiful conclusion. Like icing on a cake. Jackie was eager for me to do it, too. As I left his apartment one day, he asked when I thought the story might publish. He seemed giddy with excitement. "I don't want to miss it," he said.

DURING ONE OF my earlier interviews with Jackie, six months after I found him at Gateway, we dug deeper into his personal motivations. I continued to be impressed with his honesty. But this time he seemed entirely without reproach: he admitted the only reason he told me his story in the first place was to win my sympathy and get a handout that he could use for another round of crack. Since he brought up crack, I told him I'd read somewhere that he'd pawned his Super Bowl rings for drugs, but he said that was a bad rumor—that he just never liked rings. He said he'd given them away decades ago to a charity in New Orleans East. "The game balls, too," he said. "I never kept any of that stuff. The kids on Rockton Circle got the game balls. Their mothers would come around to return them, but I said, 'No, these are for the kids.'"

"So, you kept nothing?" I asked. "Is there anything at all?" I thought an old helmet or a rookie trading card might make a nice detail photo for the newspaper. But he said they were long gone.

He did keep one or two old news clippings and his three-years-sober medallion. The medallion was prominently displayed on his desk. Other than that, he said he'd never collected trophies. But there was one he longed for—the ultimate trophy, his crown yet to come: he said he often dreamed about heaven.

"I don't know about the rest of these people, but it's about heaven and hell with me. It's about me living the proper way so I can spend the rest of my eternity with God almighty."

Jackie saw his addiction as a battle with the spirit. "I know I mess up, but I love God as much as anybody going. And God can use me wherever I am," he said. The last phrase seemed awkward to me. He seemed to be saying that he'd come to terms with his addiction—and that he'd accepted it. He believed that he was cursed to smoke the pipe. He saw it as a sin, but not as an act of rebellion. He called crack cocaine his thorn in the flesh and his cross to bear. But regardless, he believed that God could use him no matter what he was doing, and that assuaged his guilt. He felt somehow justified in his failings.

I knew his theology was off, a bit self-serving, I thought. But I weighed my words carefully before saying anything. I knew I was treading on dangerous ground. I knew that he and his sister Louvinia had disagreed and squabbled over spiritual matters like this. At times, Jackie talked as if he resented her for not considering his spiritual positions. But the more I thought about it, the more I felt compelled to say something. It seemed like an important distinction to make. "But we can't go on sinning so God's grace can increase," I said, quoting the apostle Paul. I continued: "Yes, God can use you wherever you are, but God also used Judas when he betrayed Jesus. You don't want to be Judas."

"No, I don't want to be Judas. But somebody had to be Judas. That's why God gave us all the examples in the Bible. Like King David. He loved David. And as much as God gave David, what did he do? David neglected going to war one time, stood on his balcony and saw Bathsheba. He had a kid by Bathsheba. But God turned all that around and made Solomon. God still referred to him as a man after his own heart."

"But David lived with the consequences of his sin," I said. "And doesn't grace have an expiration date?"

"On the street, yes. With God, no. A favorite saying of addicts is, 'God is married to the backslider.'"

I wondered if he was rationalizing his behavior or if he had tapped into something deeper. I wondered if it might be both.

"I'm not trying to justify my life," he said. "I'm a sinner. And I believe 100 percent that Jesus Christ is the son of God. Understand, I love God as much as you love God."

"I believe that," I said.

"It will be all right," he said. "No matter what, there's always hope."

For weeks prior to this conversation, Jackie and I had talked about the writings of a seventeenth-century monk known as Brother Lawrence, who believed and wrote that we could live so deeply and deliberately that our own personal pain or pleasure would become irrelevant. Brother Lawrence wrote: "Many things are possible for the person who has hope. Even more is possible for the person who has faith. Still more is possible for the person who knows how to love. But everything is possible for the person who practices all three virtues."

Anyone could see that Jackie was no saint. On the other hand, I knew that he wanted to be. He had come to terms with his lot in life and had adopted a simple prayer for his life—to be used by God.

As WE TALKED, Jackie's watery eyes grew tired and his stamina began to falter. By sheer force of will, he lifted himself from his chair and moved a couple of steps toward his bed.

"I'll let myself out," I said, apologizing for keeping him so long.

As gracious as ever, he thanked me for coming and for telling his story. He lay down and rolled over to face the wall. Before exiting the room, I turned one more time to check on my friend. He was now curled up in the fetal position I had first seen many years earlier. I noticed his sneakers neatly arranged by his bed, his clothes folded neatly nearby.

I squeezed against the wall and made a quick photo that mirrored the image I shot in 1990, only this time with Jackie in a bed with clean sheets and a folded pillow cushioning his aching knees. Then I turned out the light.

The next morning, I holed up at a corner table in the public library and began writing.

CHAPTER SIXTEEN

A Frame for the Wall

2017–2018

My editors planned to run my recap piece on Thanksgiving Day, which felt appropriate considering how holiday phone calls had sustained our friendship over the years. In October, I finished the first draft and sent it off to my editors. I felt especially proud of the final paragraph:

> . . . unlike that day I found him under the bridge, today's Jackie lives under a real roof. And today, he truly understands the war he wages. He has a great support system, with people constantly checking up on him, and he knows how and where to get his medicine. He lives with a renewed comfort in his spirit. His demons now struggle much harder to overcome him, and he knows his angels are just a call away.

As I waited for revisions to return from my editors, I remembered the promise I'd made to Jackie to deliver a photograph of him sleeping under the bridge. I ordered a print from the photo lab, as large as I thought was tasteful for his bedroom—sixteen by twenty inches—and assembled the mat and frame myself. I looked forward to seeing his face as we hung it on his wall together.

When I found time, I dropped by between assignments and rang the bell. No answer. I knocked again, but there wasn't a sound.

I called Jackie's cell phone day after day, hoping he would answer. I expected he'd apologize for being so unavailable, saying that he'd been busy with doctors' appointments or that he'd been feeling bad. But time after time, his voice mail played the same old line. All my messages went into a black hole.

On October 5, I dropped by his apartment again. This time, his neighbor's door was left half-open and I could see a shadow inside. He was rearranging stereo equipment. I tapped on the door and invited myself in.

"Have you seen my friend Jackie?" I said.

"He moved out," he said as he continued untangling speaker wires.

"What?"

"Yep. I don't know where he went. No forwarding address." He offered the name of a friend he thought Jackie might be staying with, but the name was a ghost; it meant nothing to me.

For Jackie to suddenly disappear certainly meant trouble. Despite the shortcomings here, Gateway was his only refuge.

As I drove away, I began frantically calling and texting. I wrote, "Jackie, I have a framed photo for you. I'd really like to deliver it. My story is finished. Give me a call when you can."

He texted back within ten minutes. "Mail it to Yolanda. Thank you." He added an address.

I wrote back: "I'd love to drop by to see you. Are you ok?"

"NO," he texted back.

I drove straight to Yolanda's address in Central City, which turned out to be an artist's loft apartment building with a secured entryway. With the large framed photograph in my hand, I rang the buzzer and waited. I looked into the security camera lens and became conscious of how concerned my face must have appeared. After countless rings, the call went to voice mail. I left a quick message for her to please call me.

Then the front door abruptly swung open as a young man hurried out and brushed past me. I instinctively grabbed the door and found myself standing inside the lobby—alone—with no receptionist or guard. I spotted the elevator and walked the long hallway until I came to Yolanda's apartment number. She answered immediately.

"What is this?" she asked, noticing the framed photo in my hand. I held it up for her to see. She'd never seen the photo of Jackie sleeping under the bridge. She sighed. I told her about my texts with Jackie, how he'd said "NO," he wasn't all right and that I was worried about him.

"He gave me your address," I said. "I assume because you could get it to him. Is he OK?"

"Jackie's gone," she said. "He's gone back to using."

She invited me in. Her apartment was small and dark—nothing like Jackie's light and airy room at Gateway. I thought her windowless space, and her mostly bare walls, felt depressing.

"Jackie cleaned out his apartment at Gateway," she said. The "drug boys" had gotten him, she said, adding that they would keep him until he received his CTE settlement.

Yolanda looked at the photograph, which I had propped up by a bookcase. "This is where he's headed," she said, and shook her head. She promised to get it to him somehow. "This might be just the thing to bring him to his senses."

When Jackie left his Gateway apartment, Yolanda told me that he took everything. "The only thing he left behind was the Narcotics Anonymous stuff," she said.

I asked about his three-years-sober medallion.

"Yeah," she said. "He left that, too."

I RETURNED TO my office feeling empty, as if I had somehow failed Jackie. "You won't believe what happened," I said while standing in the doorway of my editor's office. "Jackie's missing."

"You're kidding," Carolyn said. After repeating to her everything Yolanda had told me, we stared at each other for a few seconds while the implications sank in.

"Write it just like it happened," she said.

After conferring with our executive editor, Mark Lorando, the original Thanksgiving publication date was scrapped as we decided to wait to see if Jackie would surface.

I put my newspaper career to bed on October 27, 2017. Jackie's story would be the last piece of journalism I would submit to close my thirty-five-year career.

By January, more than two months later, having still not learned a single clue about Jackie's whereabouts, Mark and the publisher decided to give the story its own special section—eight full pages with twenty photos, timed to run on Super Bowl Sunday 2018. I continued to reach out to Jackie, hoping for the best while preparing my mind for the worst, but he still did not answer my phone calls or text messages.

I'M TYPICALLY EARLY to rise, and Saturday, February 3, 2018, was no different. Though I usually enjoyed sipping coffee on my backporch swing while watching the sunrise, the cold, damp Louisiana morning drove me back inside to my couch. My chocolate lab, Roux, nestled next to me with his head in my lap while I scanned the morning news sites, emails, and Facebook on my phone. A single lamp illuminated my corner of the room.

Shortly after eight, after the sun had begun to warm the morning air, my phone dinged with an email. It was from Carolyn: "Good morning, Ted, I wanted to make sure you saw we ran Jackie online this morning ahead of print tomorrow."

"Thanks," I wrote back. "I have not seen it yet. I'm so glad we were able to get this done. I hope it has a great impact. I still haven't heard from Jackie. Maybe he'll be in touch after this."

A text message from Mark Lorando followed: "You might want to monitor the comment stream. Add something if you are able."

I pulled up the story on my phone and immediately read through it again. I wondered about where Jackie was and what condition he might be in. Would he be able to see the story? If he did, would he like it? Would he feel I'd abused his trust? Would he call?

I pulled up my Twitter account and thumb-typed a simple promotional tweet. It was a recollection from my first-ever conversation with Jackie:

In 1990, a homeless man looked me in the eye and said, "You aught to do a story about me." I asked him why. "Because I've played in three Super Bowls." Now, finally, here's the entire story, 28 years in the making.

I pressed the blue button and returned to the news.

Ten minutes later, I looked back over the post to see if my social media team from NOLA.com had promoted my tweet. I noticed that I'd accidentally misspelled the word "ought" in the message, but as I went to delete the post and start over, I realized I already had over three hundred retweets. I didn't want to lose that, so I left it alone. To my surprise, the numbers climbed rapidly as the minutes and hours passed. By night, my message had been retweeted fifty-one thousand times. I was stunned by the interest.

The next morning, Super Bowl Sunday, the paper published the print story. The publication date marked the thirty-eighth anniversary of Jackie's first Super Bowl appearance and one day off from the fourth anniversary of the day he'd tried to commit suicide on the bridge, as well as the one-year anniversary of the day he'd received his medallion for three years of sobriety. Friends told me that the old metal newspaper racks scattered throughout the city had been picked clean.

Meanwhile, the retweets kept coming by the thousands. Nearly five thousand comments and emails clogged my inbox, including many from Jackie's old teammates and friends. One sent a photo of the game ball Jackie had given him as a child in New Orleans East dated 2/12/79 and inscribed to "Jackie Wallace, Rams 27— Vikings 21." I got comments and notes from addicts thanking me, saying the story would help them stay strong. Families of addicts wrote to say how Jackie's story helped them understand what their own fathers, sons, daughters, and mothers had gone through with

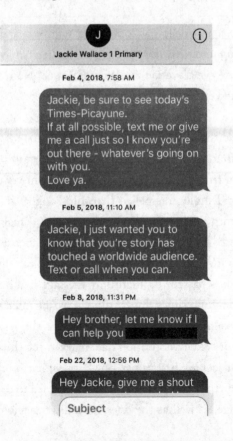

their addictions. One woman said she was picking up the phone to call her dad. She was inspired to shower him with renewed compassion and understanding.

And, of course, almost every single email, tweet, Facebook comment, text, and phone call included the same question. They wanted to know if I'd heard any word from Jackie and how they could help me find him.

I fielded phone calls from news outlets around the world, including local radio, television stations in Tucson, Canadian radio, ESPN, *Sports Illustrated,* and the BBC. I received comments and posts from sports junkies, sports haters; political and media celebrities; teens and the elderly; preachers, priests, and atheists; folks domestic and foreign; conservatives and liberals; grade school children, hipsters, and business executives. The story generated compassion even from a segment of readers who told me that their hearts were typically predisposed against the homeless and the addicted.

Within a matter of days, the story reached 1.47 million unique visitors and generated a surge of more than 8.3 million page views, more than the news site had ever seen. My original tweet was retweeted over 131,000 times, "liked" more than 279,000 times, and generated over 4,600 comments. While the original story in 1990 had touched the hearts of many, the added reach of digital media had surpassed and surprised almost everyone involved.

But there was no response from the person I wanted most to reach. Jackie.

I tried to keep up, responding to each and every email. For the thousands of Twitter comments, I created another tweet. On Monday, February 5, 2018, I wrote:

> Unreal response to the Jackie Wallace story. There are no real updates to report as of yet but I'm starting to get a few credible tips. Please stay tuned and prayerful.

SPECIAL REPORT

The search for Jackie Wallace

Jackie Wallace has lived a roller-coaster life. The New Orleans native played in two Super Bowls before ending up hooked on crack and homeless under an interstate overpass in the early 1990s. But he beat the odds and turned his life around. And now? *Ted Jackson*

A New Orleans football legend reached the pinnacle of the sport. Then everything came crashing down. This is the story of his downfall, redemption — and disappearance.

Ted Jackson *contributing writer*

One foot in front of the other, the hulking old man trudged up the ramp to the Pontchartrain Expressway. A cold wind stiffened his face, so he bundled tighter and kept walking. His decision was made. A life full of accolades and praise meant nothing to him now. A man who was once the pride of his New Orleans hometown, his St. Augustine alma mater and his 7th Ward family and friends was undone. He was on his way to die. The man was tired. In his 63 years, he had run with the gods and slept with the devil. Living low and getting high had become as routine as taking a breath. A hideous disease was eating his insides. He was an alcoholic, and he also craved crack cocaine. He was tired of fighting. He was tired of playing the game. He crossed the last exit ramp and continued walking the pavement toward the top of the bridge. He dodged cars as they took the ramp. No one seemed to notice the ragged man walking to his suicide. If they did notice, they didn't stop to help. Only a half-mile more and it would all be over. One hundred and 50 feet below, the powerful currents of the Mississippi River would swallow his soul and his wretched life. He dodged another car. But why did it matter? Getting hit by a car would serve his purposes just as well as jumping. How did it come to this? This

CHAPTER SEVENTEEN

The Tip

February–March 2018

Eighteen days after the story's publication, I received an unexpected phone call from a woman whose husband felt sure he'd run across Jackie in a downtown office building. The woman told me her husband, Mark, had encountered a stranger, limping with a cane. The man had initiated an odd conversation. He said, "Are you the man I'm supposed to meet about the money?"

The comment caught Mark off guard. "Excuse me?"

"Yeah, you don't remember me, do you? I loaned you $250,000, and you said you'd pay me back."

Mark thought he was crazy, but then the man said, "Yeah, I loaned you that money back in 1842." Then he laughed and opened his tote bag and pulled out a copy of *The Times-Picayune*. He claimed to be "the man in the paper."

"Really?" I said. "That sounds like Jackie's sense of humor." Mark continued to describe the man's height, build, hair color, and demeanor, which all matched perfectly.

"Where did this happen?" I said, thinking I might recognize a pattern, and maybe even discover a way to trace him.

But Mark resisted telling me more due to "privacy concerns." But he assured me, it made perfect sense for Jackie—if it was him—to be there. Out of respect for Mark's kindness, I didn't pressure him for more information. While I trusted his words and found comfort in them, his information gave me nothing that I could use. As it stood, I had no more actual *proof* of Jackie's true whereabouts or his condition than I had in October. And if Mark's story was true, then why hadn't Jackie called me?

I continued to watch my emails and text messages for more clues. A ninety-two-year-old woman called from Mississippi to tell me that an old man begging for handouts near her home was surely Jackie. She sounded sweet and concerned, but her description of a random beggar sounded nothing like the man I knew. I thanked her for her call.

Yolanda proved to be the most reliable source, unsurprisingly. She sent a text that hinted that Jackie was in detox somewhere and that she'd call me whenever she heard more. Her comment dovetailed perfectly with another woman who addressed an email to the newsroom to say that her company was in contact with him and that he was OK. Citing HIPAA privacy laws, she wrote that she had already said too much.

At precisely 6:46 P.M., Tuesday, March 20, almost two months after the story had run, my text message alert dinged while Nancy and I were relaxed on the couch. It was a note from Yolanda:

Here's Jackie's new phone number. He wants you to call him.

I jumped to my feet like a cat on fire. "It's Jackie!" I shouted to Nancy. Her eyes lit up as I darted from the room to the back porch, where I usually take important calls.

Jackie answered my call on the first ring.

He sounded good, his voice upbeat and bright. He was apologetic for not calling sooner, but I barely noticed. I couldn't help but laugh as we talked. I was so happy to hear his voice.

He had indeed been in treatment, just as Yolanda had said. I should have taken her words more literally instead of believing she was only trying to calm my fears. I would have slept better if I had.

Jackie explained that he'd been in a behavioral hospital. He told me that he'd learned how hard it was for him to accept help. "One of my downfalls," he said. "I want to help everybody else. I don't want anybody to help me, if you know what I mean, which is crazy. My relatives have been trying to tell me that for the longest. We'll sit down and do some real talking, if you have the time."

If I had the time? Of course I had the time.

The conversation lasted just seconds over two minutes, but I couldn't have been happier. As we closed, Jackie asked me to meet him for an appointment two days later at 3434 Prytania, 10:00 A.M. "I'll probably be standing right out front," he said.

"Make sure you keep your phone near," I said.

"OK. I'll keep it up high," he said. "I'll make sure I hear it ring this time."

I opened up my phone contacts and created a new entry. I labeled it, "Jackie Wallace New Phone."

ON THURSDAY MORNING I drove to the address, which turned out to be Touro Hospital. I slowed to a crawl as I drove by, but I didn't see him standing out front as he had suggested he would be. I circled the block, parked, and entered the hospital, where I searched the lobby and corridors with no success. Finally, I took the elevators to the clinic floor and ducked into waiting rooms until I came to an orthopedist's lobby, where I thought he might be. And sure enough, there he stood, pained and sad-faced as he checked in with a receptionist. He looked overweight and worn down as he rested against a cheap, bronze-colored aluminum cane. A wrist cord dangled from the grip like a tassel from a child's handlebar. His sweatshirt and pants hung on him loosely, and a band of dried salt stained his powder-blue baseball cap where the fabric touched his brow.

He flashed a smile when he saw me. We found two empty chairs and settled in among the other patients in the room. I wondered—if any of them had bothered to look up—if they would have recognized the man who had been reported missing by the local newspaper a few weeks before, heralded by a six-column photograph, no less. But instead, everyone kept their eyes locked on the pages of outdated magazines or their Facebook feeds. Their personal boundaries seemed boxed and fixed.

"So where were you when you disappeared?" I asked.

He lowered his voice. "Well, I went to the place I wanted to go. I went to the crack house . . . to get . . . to . . . to kill myself."

"To kill yourself?"

His voice grew quieter, faint. "By using crack. Every day. All day long. I went around the people that I knew would give it to me because they knew I was getting money."

"So why did you? . . . OK . . . ," I stammered in my own ignorance. "So, these people knew you, and they were welcoming you back?"

"Yeah. All they saw was a money thing and somebody using drugs. It wasn't a nice place. I disappeared from you, Yolanda, and my family because I didn't want nobody to see me in that state—including my family."

"Did you see the newspaper?" I asked nervously.

He reached into his bag and pulled out the special section. "I liked it."

"Did you see the *online* response?" He looked at me like I'd asked him about Venezuelan politics.

"Jackie, I got emails and comments from all over the world about you. This is the most-read story in the history of *The Times-Picayune*! Ever!"

Jackie tried to control his laughter. "Thank you, God."

"And the emails . . . this is what you and I have always been talking about! They say, 'Oh, my God, now I understand what my son . . .'"

Jackie could barely contain his excitement. "That's, that's . . ."

"Right?"

"That's what . . . remember, that was the original purpose . . . That's why we did it!"

"Yes!"

". . . right and they . . ."

"'. . . and now I understand my dad,'" I said, citing another one of the emails. "'I hated my dad and now I understand him better. Now I'm going to go talk to him again.' I got one comment Saturday morning when it first went up, from a man on Tulane's campus. He'd been clean for years and he was thinking about going back to using, it was so strong and powerful. He went to the chapel and prayed. He said, 'God, just give me a sign.' When he walked out of the chapel, the first thing he saw was *The Times-Picayune* paper box and your story. The story answered his prayer. Jackie, these comments go on and on."

"See, these certain things I have to do with my life," he said. "This supersedes football. Supersedes education. We need to share that we're not bad people. Your relatives are not bad people. We just need love and understanding. But there are times when we're not normal people. The time I was away from you, I was a devil. I need to know how to kill this evil that is inside of me."

The door in the corner opened, and a tech called out, "Mr. Wallace?"

"Yes, ma'am. Right here."

I had forgotten we were in the middle of the reception area until that moment. I stuffed my recorder back into my backpack, and Jackie grabbed his bag from the floor. "Get that hat for me," he said as he pushed himself up by the chair's armrests. He invited me to join him in the exam room. With a wink, he said I could be his caretaker. He introduced me as a family member as he limped past the nursing station. Nobody batted an eye.

While we waited for the doctor to come in, Jackie opened up about Gateway. "Getting clean brings it all back to life," he said. "Makes me more depressed. I'm so isolated, and I failed in so many ways. I became what Satan wanted me to be. When I get to heaven, I want to ask God, why did my life go like that?"

"Jackie, when you get to heaven, you won't care," I said.

"I like being around people who think like that," he said, laughing.

"People told me that the newspaper story made me look bad," he said. "People said I looked ugly. Even my relatives. I told them that's my true life. Now I need to see what good can come from it."

The orthopedist entered the room holding an X-ray of Jackie's upper arm, which he'd fractured in a recent fall. The doctor said it was nothing to worry about. It was healing nicely. And while the doctor looked at his aching, arthritic shoulder, Jackie told him about the cataract that was forming in his eye. He'd have to see his eye doctor for that, of course. Before we left, Jackie scheduled a hip replacement surgery for his right hip, a complement to his new left one. Jackie's body looked much older than his sixty-seven years.

As we walked out together, we passed through the lobby, where Jackie stopped a random woman. "Excuse me, ma'am. How you doing today? You don't remember me, do you? It was in 1842, I gave you $450,000 in tens and twenties and you said you were going to pay me back."

She nearly lost her breath laughing, unlike Mark, who felt taken aback by the random intrusion. Instead, the woman joined in the joke: "Can I borrow *another* $450,000?"

He took her hand. "My name is Jackie Wallace. I'm a retired NFL player. It's nice to see you smile."

As he climbed into my car, I asked if I could buy him a lunch.

"Yeah," he said. "Let's grab a McDonald's."

A few minutes later, as we drove away from the drive-thru, Jackie told me the details of his disappearance. He said bluntly, "You know, I was in the grip of the devil." As we drove toward Claiborne Avenue, he explained what he meant.

In August, seven months earlier, when his first-of-the-month

pension money posted, Jackie had borrowed a truck from a friend and driven away from Gateway without paying his first-of-the-month bills. He left with $2,300 in his pocket. He drove to a sprawling apartment complex in Harvey, where he knew a couple of crack dealers, and quickly blew through the wad of dough. When the cash was gone, he smoked another $2,800 worth of crack on credit. Then he skipped out on the dealers and headed to Central City to another crack house where he knew a woman. She had supplied him before and had heard through the rumor mill that Jackie had gotten clean. But when she saw his deteriorated state, she helped him in and showed him to a mattress on the floor.

Jackie explained to me that the woman ran the house much like a madam runs a whorehouse: "I don't know if you've ever been to one of those madam houses," he said, "where the house looked nice and clean, but what they're doing is despicable. That's the kind of house she had. It was a nice little double—a double shotgun. She had one side of it. The landlord was aware of what she was doing and why she was doing it."

She claimed Jackie as her john and put the word out to all comers, especially the Westbank drug boys, to leave her new client alone. No one would collect money from Jackie unless it went through her first. In a perverted sense, she became his protector, even as she supplied all his drugs. "She didn't allow any gunplay," he said. "It wasn't a Wild Wild West situation."

"Can you show me the house?" I asked as I drove along. But he declined, saying that it wouldn't be right to rat her out like that.

"Can you tell me what neighborhood it's in?"

"Just off Jackson and Magnolia. You know what kind of neighborhood Jackson and Magnolia is right?" I nodded. I'd worked many crime scenes in that part of town.

"I'll show you what I'm talking about," he said. "Make the

next right after the light. Like this neighborhood. This is considered a crack neighborhood. Most of the drug boys will be all out here," he said as he pointed. "There's a church right there. These people don't do drugs, but they're considered *in* the neighborhood. They work at the restaurants on St. Charles Avenue. That's why they have all the bikes. The lady over there in the white house is a minister. But this is where [the dealers] do their trade. The dealers don't live here."

"Is this madam a friend of yours?" I asked.

"No, I consider her for what she is: a woman who runs a crack house. I don't consider that a friend. What people in that world say is that she's your 'associate.' And basically, that's all she was, an associate."

"The money for the drugs came out of my monthly [pension] check and my Social Security. What I got paid, she would get all of that."

"Direct from your bank account?"

"ATM. She would do all of that. I didn't have to go nowhere."

"You gave her your PIN number?"

"Yeah. That's the way it works."

Just like Jackie's childhood home on Liberty Street, the layout of the crack house flowed from the living room in the front into the madam's room. She set Jackie up in the third room with a mattress on the floor. The kitchen and the bathroom were in the back. The whole house was filled with clutter, junked over with piles of discarded clothes, cardboard boxes, and papers, all pushed aside for a walking path. She cooked every day and kept the kitchen and bathroom clean. The junkies came and went all hours of the day and night, but she kept them corralled in the front room, away from Jackie.

"How many people a day would come through?" I asked.

"Sheeeeez, come on . . . How many people a day come through *The Times-Picayune*? It was constant."

"One every hour?"

"Constant."

"One every fifteen minutes?"

"Constant."

Of the never-ending stream, Jackie was the only one the madam allowed to take up residence. When a junkie finished his business, he left. There were plenty of women junkies, too.

As ALWAYS, JACKIE was a good client because he had a steady stream of money coming in. With access to his bank account, she kept the rock flowing. At one point, he told me he had a muffin-size piece of crack. "I smoked that by myself," he said.

Somewhere around December 8, his money ran out. That's when he became a desperate man, but to his credit, he never joined the business to support his habit. As a possible solution, he realized that his brother Roland Jr. would be coming to New Orleans to celebrate his birthday with his family, as he did every year. He would turn seventy in the second week of December. Jackie knew he could count on Roland for a little pity and maybe a little loan.

So once Roland got to town, Jackie called him and asked him to visit with him at the corner of Jackson and Claiborne Avenues. They met in the parking lot of a Dollar General store, four blocks away from the crack house. Jackie tried to clean up so Roland wouldn't know he was using again. But Roland wasn't fooled. He recognized Jackie's fidgeting when they talked. He could see the desperate restlessness that comes from his binges. He noticed Jackie's cracked lips, which came from sucking on the hot glass pipe.

He said, "Look, Jackie, we understand that you've got problems, but I ain't sending you no more money. It's good to see that you're still alive. But don't forget what Mama and Daddy always taught us. We can always go to God." Then he drove away with Jackie standing empty-handed, the same as Louvinia had done nearly four years before. Jackie's last hustle had run dry.

Jackie retreated to the crack house and sunk deeper into debt. There he could hide from the people who loved him. He hated for his friends and family to see him "messed up." In fact, when he left Gateway, he had made the breakup with Yolanda especially harsh so she wouldn't try to follow him. But even if she had wanted to find him, and even if she had known where he was, she'd have needed courage to knock on that door.

Jackie spent most of his time curled up on his mattress, but from time to time, he sat on the front stoop to feel the sunshine on his face. One morning, a man Jackie mistook for a stranger walked by and spotted him. "Yeah, look at you, Jackie Wallace, back down messing with that shit again," he said. The man told Jackie's niece Monique, who seemed to have a special love for her uncle Jackie. She asked for the address. The next morning, she, two other cousins, and an aunt found the address and knocked on the door. A stranger answered. He told them to wait. At first Jackie resisted coming to the door, but the stranger forced him to talk with his family.

"What do y'all want?" Jackie asked once he was pushed into the doorway. The women weren't intimidated by his belligerence at all.

"Jackie, we've come to get you," they said.

"Mind your own f—ing business. I'm fine." His voice raised in a menacing tone.

"Uncle Jackie, this isn't you!" Monique pleaded. "You smell like piss."

"We care about you, Jackie," said another.

But no words could persuade him. Still another asked him if he had an insurance policy.

"Yeah, why?" he asked.

"We just wanted to know so we'll have something to bury you with."

"Hey, I'm sixty-six years old. I'll do what I want!" he screamed as he prepared to slam the door. "Y'all leave me the hell alone and mind your own business." He left them to their tears.

But as days passed, he remembered their pained faces. He tried to forget, but Monique had gotten to him.

He thought of the shame he'd brought his family, his teachers, his friends, his coaches, his wives. He thought of all the chances he'd blown, the trail of disappointment he'd carved through so many lives. He remembered Dyan. He wished he'd married her. He regretted never having a son to nurture, to play with, to pass his skills and his name to. He had nothing to show for his life but misery and remorse.

Christmas 2017 passed like a dark cloud. On January 4, 2018, he opened a composition notebook and wrote his final regrets in large, flowing script:

> I Jackie Wallace suffering at Stage 4 of CTE disease is now accepting his death at the hands of ". . . . . ." drug dealer I met through living with ". . . . ." & ". . . . ." at . . . ., Harvey, La. I blame none of these people listed above. I could not commit suicide. My actions of billing up a $2800 crack debt smoked by myself, ". . . . . ." & ". . . . .," then running out on it is pronouncing a death sentence to myself.

I have no ill feelings about that. All I ask is mercy on them and help all that suffer through all stages of CTE & PTSD. I believe that they are close relatives to each other as Brother & Step Brother.

To My Immediate Survivors Brothers Roland Jr. & Donald Sterling and Sister Louvinia Elizabeth I love you. Sorry that I did not give myself opportunity to receive that Love you-all had for me. To My Sister-in-Law Debbie, you were a true Angel from God to me. Job well done. To all my other God Given Relatives, He truly loves you-all & So do I.

To My 2 Ex-Wives Mary & Deborah thanks for saying yes and being with me. From all my other relationships thanks! For two special ones Dyan & Yolanda, you two carried my heart & soul. I neglect to continue with it.

Now to end this! God has given me an outstanding life to serve Him. I believe that to the best of my abilities I have done His Will. It may not been done all the time. HOWEVER it was done. Now I know what a person who has incurable disease like CANCER feels like. One last thing many of you will say that I could have not had this happen like this *but my free will did it the way God would have had it done!*

Please again I know that "...... ...... " would execute the punishment just like the Romans executed their punishment on Jesus Christ My Savior. So like Christ I say "LORD FORGIVE HIM FOR HE TRULY DOES NOT KNOW WHAT HE IS DOING."

Again Praise, Honor, & Glory goes to God Almighty, His Son Jesus Christ & The Holy Spirit!

PLEASE READ AT MY FUNERAL

Jackie Wallace
3/13/1951—1/??/2018
PS I will not see February 2018

He drew a large star that took up the bottom half of the fourth page.

FOR TWO WEEKS, Jackie tried to overwhelm his weakened heart with a surge of more crack cocaine. He prayed that God would let him slip easily into unconsciousness and then into death. It was the only form of suicide he had left. He had tried before, and failed, on the Mississippi River bridge. He'd never been brave enough to pick up a gun or a knife. And when he failed to overdose on crack, he sat on the stoop and waited for his executioner to come. He expected to see a teenager stroll up with a pistol to extract revenge for his unpaid bills. Jackie envisioned himself getting down on his knees and closing his eyes . . . and waiting for it all to end.

But day after day, God refused to answer his morbid prayers. And day after day, his paranoia grew worse.

Thursday, January 18, was crisp, sunny, and cold, and Jackie lay crumpled on his bed. Just three days before, the city, and especially this neighborhood, had celebrated MLK Day with parades, days of service, exhibits, and block parties. Churches and their

—4—

Again Praise, Honor, & Glory goes to God Almighty, His Son Jesus Christ & The Holy Spirit!

PLEASE READ AT MY FUNERAL

Jackie Wallace
3/13/1951 ——→ 1/??/2018 PS

PS I will not see February 2018

ministers had extolled the power of perseverance in the face of adversity, but Jackie had wallowed in defeat. They had preached the power of God to deliver, but Jackie wondered where his God was—his prayers had been left unanswered.

Then, almost like a vision, Jackie remembered the faces of his nieces. He imagined them banging on his door, pleading with him through streams of tears—the faces of his angels, he thought.

In a clear moment of resolve, his spirit broke. He looked around himself with disgust and found himself praying again, this time for forgiveness. This time, instead of praying for God to take him, he prayed for God to send him. This time, he prayed—with every ounce of humility—for redemption.

Jackie reached for his phone, turned it on, and called Monique. She and her boyfriend responded immediately. They rushed him to a hospital, where doctors referred him to the care of a psychiatrist at Oceans Behavioral Hospital in Kenner.

AFTER TEN LONG days of rest and tender counseling, doctors released him into a transitional housing facility called No Place Like Home in New Orleans East, just a few blocks from the house he'd owned when he played with the Vikings, Colts, and Rams. There, he tried to mentally reengage the world.

On Sunday, February 4, 2018, he sat among other addicts on a beat-up sofa and balanced his breakfast on his knees. Over a din of loud chatter from the others, he directed the TV remote to Super Bowl LII pregame coverage. They watched interviews with the perceived stars of the game, and New England Patriots head coach Bill Belichick, another ghost from Jackie's past.

As he watched, one of the addicts came in with a copy of *The Times-Picayune*.

"Hey, Jackie," he said. "They're looking for you."

The front-page introduction referred readers to my eight-page special section on the missing football player. The headline read: "The search for Jackie Wallace," with a subhead, "A New Orleans football legend reached the pinnacle of the sport. Then everything came crashing down. This is the story of his downfall, redemption—and disappearance."

But Jackie Wallace, the pride of St. Aug, wasn't ready to be found. He still felt too fragile for the spotlight. And so he continued, day after day, to rest and recover and continue quietly with doctors' appointments in relative obscurity. He especially enjoyed returning to Kenner for his behavioral group meetings. Slowly, Jackie began revealing himself to the other patients and staffers, and then to strangers on the street.

On Valentine's Day, Jackie texted a photo of himself to Yolanda, looking healthier, clean shaven, and wearing a nice red-and-black polo shirt. He wrote, "Hello, text me whenever you have some GOD STUFF for me. thank you—"

He signed it: "JW 25@20."

On February 21, he introduced himself to a man named Mark as "the man in the paper" in a downtown Central Business District lobby. And on March 20, when he felt ready, he asked Yolanda to ask me to call him. "Give him my new number," he said.

CHAPTER EIGHTEEN

Love Letters

March 2019

Even after the story had published in the paper and online, even after the excitement died down, I couldn't stop reporting the story. But this time I was reporting it not for the paper but for myself, and what would eventually become this book: I wanted to fill the holes in Jackie's timeline and talk to the people I hadn't been able to find. One afternoon, I dropped by *The Times-Picayune* office and, with help from my reporter friend Jonathan Bullington, I looked through a list of Jackie's old addresses in Baltimore. On one page, a disturbing entry caught my eye. On January 26, 2000, Taris Whitley, the girlfriend who Jackie had lived with for more than three years in Baltimore, had filed sexual assault charges against him.

I suddenly felt a sense of betrayal. Why hadn't Jackie told me about this? And then came the self-reproach: Why hadn't I discovered it sooner?

It would be weeks before Jackie and I could sit and talk again, face-to-face. When we talked on the phone, I told him I needed to know more about his Baltimore days. He said he was looking forward to it. I wasn't. I knew it would feel heavy and stunted.

When we eventually did come together, we sat at the worn wooden table set near the patio door of the house. The old chairs creaked loudly, and at times, the man cutting weeds with a string trimmer outside nearly drowned out our voices. We talked and shared stories about some of his old friends still living in Baltimore and how he'd decided to leave the house on Purdue Avenue to Deborah. "It wasn't one of the good sides of my life experience then," he said.

"So, what happened?" I said, trying to ease into the topic. "There was an arrest record at some point. What was that about?" A look of confusion passed over his face like an ambling cloud. "Didn't have anything to do with checks or anything?" he said.

"Well, I found an arrest record that involved a sexual assault."

"Oh, you're talking about Taris."

Jackie didn't appear to be too alarmed. The public record, he said, didn't tell the whole story. He told me that he had come home agitated one night, high out of his mind. He pushed himself on Taris when she wanted nothing to do with him.

"But the charges she put on me were . . . ," He paused briefly, unsure of how to avoid sounding insensitive. "I felt like they were bogus charges. I'm not denying we had sex."

"But, Jackie. She charged you with *rape*," I said.

I searched Jackie's eyes for answers. He sighed, as if his next words were taxing his soul.

He said that after that night, after it happened, Taris didn't know how to respond. She had friends at the courthouse who convinced her to file charges. They told her that in order to get his attention—so it wouldn't happen again—she needed to throw the book at him.

In a matter of weeks, Jackie said, he and Taris had reconciled. But the charges had already been filed.

"So, what happened?" I asked.

"They gave me probation," he said. "And guess who brought me to probation every month?" He raised his head to watch my reaction. "Ta-ris," he said with a slight lift in his voice to emphasize his point.

"So, you stayed together?"

"Yeah, we stayed together for a good little while."

"So, what was your defense when you went to trial?" I asked.

"There was no defense," he said. "When [the judge] found out that Taris was still talking to me, that's when they asked me to plead." He said he took the judge's advice and pleaded guilty to sexual assault for a lighter sentence.

Jackie had never directly lied to me as far as I knew. Still, I didn't know what to believe. Once I returned home, I requested and received a copy of the arrest record from the Baltimore District Court and found contact information for Jackie's public defender. But I needed more information from the prosecution's side, too, so I booked a flight to Baltimore. Specifically, I needed to talk to Taris. I boarded the plane with nothing more than a twenty-year-old address and a phone number that had been disconnected.

DESPITE BEING NAMED the most violent city in America by *USA Today* in 2018, Baltimore has always supplied me with fond memories. Like Jackie, I loved its history, not to mention the crisp, cold air that smacked my face when I stepped off the plane on every previous trip. But this time my trip felt more sinister, more foreboding than those good visits that had come before.

It was still early when I drove my rental car down Lombard Street toward Patterson Park, scanning the addresses one block at a time on the stone and redbrick townhomes that looked as though they had seen better days. The numbers led me to a particularly handsome home near a tavern. As I walked up the cut-marble stoop, I prepared my inevitable speech and hoped that a woman named Taris would answer the door, and, more important, that she would talk to me. But instead, a teenage girl poked her head out of the second-floor window, catching me off guard.

She said, nope, she'd never heard the name Taris. Her mother verified this when she finally came to the door; she explained that they'd lived here for only a few years and was sorry she couldn't help me. But before I left, the mother remembered that she occasionally received errant mail for someone named T. Christian. Interesting, I thought, but not helpful. I thanked them and then knocked on neighbors' doors with no better luck.

I drove to the Baltimore criminal courthouse, where Jackie's public defense attorney now served as a judge. I told her I needed to know why a rape conviction resulted only in a sentence of probation. She said she couldn't talk about a case, even with Jackie's permission, even off the record. I phoned the state's attorney general's office to appeal, but they turned me down as well. I walked back to my car and sat there, staring at my cell phone, until an idea struck me: I typed Taris's old phone number into a reverse directory that provides matching addresses. A new address popped up, this one on the edge of town.

I found the house easily enough, tucked neatly in with more than 1,500 identical two-story redbrick row homes. Unlike the urban setting of Lombard Street, here barbecue grills and children's toys lined the edges of many of the small front porches. U.S. flags and religious statues adorned the fresh, trimmed lawns.

I knocked on the front door, but no one came. The neighbors on the left and the right didn't recognize the name. I left and returned multiple times until I found the front door open and music coming from inside. When my gentle knocks didn't work, I gave the screen door a sharp rap with my knuckle. From inside, I could hear a sleeping man rouse up from the couch. I had one chance to get this right.

I introduced myself as a journalist from New Orleans looking for a woman named Taris. If the strangeness of my quest hadn't hit me before, the ominousness did then. Here I stood, blindsiding a woman and her husband at their residence.

"She's not home from work yet," the man said. "But you can drop by later. What's this about?"

I told him I was looking for information about an old friend and that I had reason to believe that his wife might remember him. I left it there.

"This isn't about that football player, is it?"

"Yes," I said. Deep breath. Was this Taris's husband? Did he know about the alleged rape? I thought he might slam the door in my face, but he stood there looking at me, expressionless through the locked screen door.

"You can check back in thirty minutes if you like," he said. He introduced himself as Taris's husband, Steve.

I checked back as he requested, but Taris still hadn't arrived. I returned hour after hour until 8:00 P.M., when Steve, a bit perturbed by that point, said I needn't bother returning. "Trust me," he said, "I'll make sure she calls you as soon as she gets home."

After all my visits I worried about what he was going to say to Taris when she got home. Had I stirred up a bitter memory or a dark secret?

I LEFT THE residence and drove aimlessly north along Interstate 95 until, after ten miles or so, I spotted a coffee shop and took the exit ramp. That was when my phone rang. It was 8:30.

"Hi, this is Taris," she said. "You wanted to talk with me?"

Her voice was soft and delicate, almost angelic. "Yes," I said. "Would that be OK?"

"Sure. When can you be here?"

"About fifteen minutes. I promise not to take much of your time."

"And what is this about?"

"Jackie Wallace," I said. I held my breath as I anticipated the worst.

"OK," she said. "I'll see you in fifteen minutes."

Steve answered the door and invited me into their small living room. He offered me a Gatorade and led me past a big-screen TV that blared with cops chasing criminals through hails of gunfire and explosions. He pointed to a small kitchen table just off the edge of the sofa. "You can wait here," he said. "Taris will be down in a few minutes."

I couldn't see the TV, so I stared blankly at a goldfish who eyed me back. I watched the staircase, which descended across the room toward the front door. As I scanned the shelves, I noticed a pair of crutches and a power-lift rail mounted to the banister. Only then did I notice the wheelchair in the corner. Steve munched on his dinner of leftovers and continued to stare emptily at the screen.

Finally, the lift motor whirred and the chair slowly descended until it rounded the banister. I saw only one leg. She looked over her shoulder and smiled at me. Her kind face matched the voice on the phone.

She joined me at the table. We spoke in hushed tones, at times barely audible over the sound of Steve's television show. She told me about how she and Jackie had met at the Baltimore Arena and explained how their relationship had flourished from friendship. She told me how she wept after their breakup and how Jackie had chosen his crack habit over her. She talked about the yearlong barrage of love letters that followed and about her subsequent marriage to Steve.

I asked her if she'd kept up with Jackie since he left Baltimore—after the letters stopped arriving all those years ago. I caught a hint of wistful regret in her eyes.

"Yes," she said, but not entirely on purpose. "I saw him on TV. They were showing old Super Bowl games. They showed a game with him playing." She said the memories caught her off guard. "Oh, my God," she had whispered to herself. If Steve had noticed, he hadn't said anything. After the programming ended, and after Steve had gone to bed, she secretly Googled Jackie's name. My story from 2018 popped up. She read every word, plus every other story she could find, including Jimmy Smith's original story from 1990. When she read the ending of my story—and saw that he'd left Gateway and was missing again—she figured he had to be bingeing again. She knew he was probably still alive only because she couldn't find his name among obituaries. She checked regularly for updates.

She looked at me while we sat at the table. "I hope you find him."

"Oh, I know where he is," I said, apologizing for not already sharing that information. I had absent-mindedly assumed that she knew.

"Ohhhhhhhhhhh!"

I told her we were in touch again and he was doing relatively well. She seemed pleased.

"So, what brings you to Baltimore?" she asked. I was rather glad she hadn't asked sooner.

"I came specifically to see you," I said.

"Really? All the way just to see me? Did *he* ask you to come find me?"

"No, he doesn't know I'm here. But I'll tell him when I get back. I came because I need to know about the sexual assault charge."

Her voice went even quieter. "I don't want to talk about that. He . . ." She fumbled for words. "I don't know what was going on in his mind that day. He was just so mad. This is so personal. I don't want to embarrass him. I forgave him, and I don't want to embarrass him behind that."

She asked me what Jackie had said about the incident, and I told her.

"I've never talked about that, because it was . . ." She paused and sighed. "I was mad," she said. "Because he didn't have to do what he did. He scared me. I . . . and for Jackie to . . . it made me mad.

"I didn't think that he would hurt me . . . but his actions . . ." She stopped. Her voice suddenly grew bolder. "He was talking out of his mind . . . I don't know if he was high off his crack, and I got kind of scared. He was talking crazy."

"It was snowing that night."

"He was so sorry," she said. "He swore that it would never happen again. He begged for forgiveness. He begged for God to forgive him. He said he didn't know what was wrong with him."

Taris felt conflicted. Seconding what Jackie had told me earlier, she didn't want to press charges even though her friends and an attorney convinced her it was the right thing to do. She didn't think he'd try it again, but she wanted to make sure.

For a time afterward, Jackie lived with Taris's mother until a compromise was reached to avoid a trial. Jackie would plead guilty to assault and avoid prison. After the sentencing, Jackie and Taris returned home. She drove him to his probation hearings every month. The probation hearings gave her a sense of security, she said. "If you mess up with me," she had teased Jackie, "I'll call the probation officer."

They continued living together as close friends for more than a year, hanging out and taking in movies. Jackie continued to plan special outings for the family, but their romantic relationship never returned.

Six months after his conviction, he began missing work. That's when she caught him smoking crack with his friend Ed. After that, he disappeared to the streets. Even his parole officer didn't know where to find him. Taris could have found out, if she'd opened the handwritten love letters that showed up in her mail for over a year. But she didn't open a single one, deciding instead to throw them in the trash. The letters finally stopped in 2001.

"You forgave him?" I asked.

"I forgave him during the probation time and probably years after we broke up. It was after the letters stopped."

"Were you able to let it go?"

"He was my friend," she said.

"He was your friend," I repeated to confirm what she meant. "So, the most powerful part of the relationship was the friendship, right?"

"And I knew he loved me. He's the only man I can say that truly loved me." She started crying, wiping tears with her fingertips.

Steve walked into the kitchen and loudly dropped his dinner dishes into the sink. He stood looming over the table.

"You OK?" he asked.

"Yeah. It's a little hard," she told him.

Steve looked at me. "You ain't in here breaking up a home, are you?"

"What?" I said, surprised at the question.

He repeated himself word for word.

"NO, NO, NO, NO, NO, NO, NO!" I said in rapid-fire defense.

"If so, there's the door right there," he said.

While Steve sunk back into the sofa, I motioned to the wheelchair and asked her, "Do you mind if I ask what happened?"

"Not at all," she said.

"A motorcycle . . . speeding about eighty miles per hour hit me," she said. "I actually don't remember anything. My leg was amputated at the seam. I had a broken neck and a punctured lung. My right ankle was broken. My left wrist was broken, and part of my arm was taken off. I'm a survivor, thank God."

I told her about Jackie's health, his CTE concerns and his congestive heart failure. We talked about faith and the place for God in our fractured lives. "Jackie needs to learn to forgive himself," I said, and Taris agreed. Her eyes danced with encouragement. "I wish him the best," she said.

"It's amazing that you traveled this far," she said. "Like I said, I loved him. I really did. I think mostly because he loved me so much. He's the only man I know that truly loved me."

"What do you want me to tell him . . . if anything? I'll just tell him I saw you."

"Tell him that doctors had me dying in the night in the hospital. They didn't think I was going to make it. But I did. I survived. Tell him that."

CHAPTER NINETEEN

Giving Hope

2018–2019

Guilt.

The word tumbled in my mind with little satisfaction. But my visit with Taris had forced me to think deeper about humanity, about how resentment was burdensome. My memories flashed back to Jackie's walk onto the bridge to commit suicide. He'd carried a heavy burden up that ramp. What would it take to take his guilt away?

I remembered talking with Deborah long after their divorce and how she had openly wept over the pain that Jackie had put her through. I asked her if she believed there was a chance for redemption for Jackie. She said she believed that any soul could be redeemed, if the person was willing. She said she'd asked God to forgive him.

A week later, Taris called. She wanted to remind me, among other things, that Jackie had once told her that she wouldn't want to know him when he was on crack—and that he had been exactly right. When he was not on crack, he was as good as gold, she said. That's why, even nineteen years after their relationship ended, she still had a big part of him in her heart. "I will always be there for him," she said.

"You know, I still do care about him, because I know what kind of man he really is, and still could be without the crack in his life. I'm waiting to hear from him," she told me as we hung up. "I want to talk to him."

I TOLD JACKIE about my visit with Taris, but I stopped short of passing along phone numbers to either of them. I didn't want to play matchmaker. I only wanted to help Jackie overcome his addictions and resolve the guilt that continued to burden him. But Jackie's redemption had already begun some nine months before as he began to imagine a new future for himself.

Jackie spent the better part of the spring of 2018 keeping track of his datebook, bulging with doctors' appointments. Other than that, he focused on getting acquainted with his seven housemates at No Place Like Home. He shared a back bedroom in a nondescript ranch house with a big, friendly man named Reginald.

Jackie adapted easily to the house manager, Leon Courtney. Abrupt and blunt in conversation, Leon ran a tight ship. His discipline helped the men control their emotional outbursts—the "explosions" as Jackie called them—that often led them back to the streets.

He was eleven miles from Central City, which helped him avoid temptation. But No Place Like Home was no halfway house. There were no structured programs or lockdown requirements. The city bus stopped right outside the front door. With a transfer pass, Jackie could get anywhere he wanted to go.

Leon thought of the men under his care—and Jackie in particular—as fragile orbs in a game of marbles. His job was to keep them all inside the circle. But even so, he refused to be the men's babysitter. He told Jackie and the others to take responsibility for their own choices.

Jackie liked the facility, but he didn't know how long he would stay before he tried to get his own place. He felt like he lacked direction there, sitting around with the other addicts watching TV all day. He believed he still had something to give to inner-city youth groups. "Look at the murder rate," he said as he imagined the possibilities of telling his story to an audience again.

On June 22, 2018, I picked up a couple of sandwiches and drove Jackie north through the wildlife refuge at Bayou Sauvage. Even at seventy miles an hour, the swamp water under the bridges seemed higher than the roadway. We crossed the Twin Span Bridge toward Slidell. Sailing yachts danced on the sparkling, shallow waters of Lake Pontchartrain.

I drove into the piney woods, across old concrete bridges that reminded us of two-lane travel in the fifties. We talked about the days before civil rights. We were here to visit Giving Hope Retreat Center in Lacombe. I thought the director there, Johnny Lonardo, might offer Jackie a chance to speak to the addicts in his care. I also hoped he could offer him some advice to get his life on a solid footing. I'd met Johnny during my overnight stay at the mission, a man whose personality rocked with religious fervor and inspiration. I thought Jackie could benefit from a heavy dose of Johnny Lonardo, in addition to a heavy dose of religion.

The camp, set on fifty-eight acres deep in the piney woods near Lacombe, is a spinoff ministry of the New Orleans Mission. Jackie and Johnny had met there years ago, but I wasn't sure Jackie would remember. I expected a casual conversation, a tour of the cabins, and maybe even a walk around their serenity pond. The setting was perfectly peaceful. A large wooden cross fashioned out of two-by-fours sagged near the lily pads, shaded with towering loblolly

pines. As we walked across the front lawn, Jackie fed the remnants of his sandwich to a couple of rescue pups darting about the yard. They followed us into the lobby and settled in Jackie's lap.

After a short wait, Johnny welcomed us to his office. He was a big, muscular man with a full gray beard and a buzz cut. Greenish-gray tattoo ink covered his thick arms. Dramatic storm clouds artfully wrapped his right biceps to frame a crucified Christ. His forearm tattoo read "Surrender All" in elegant text. He spoke quickly but without feeling rushed.

The two men reminisced like old pals, laughing about their days at the mission, the food, and the chapel services. As they talked, I placed my voice recorder between the two men, sat down across the table, and tried to blend in with the furniture.

After a quick review of Jackie's background, Johnny got down to business. But instead of an item-by-item discussion about crack addiction, sexual assault, or CTE, Johnny drew Jackie back to his core beliefs. Johnny challenged the core of Jackie's conversion.

"When did you meet the Lord?" Johnny asked.

"I was baptized my junior year in college," Jackie said, a bit taken aback. He then confessed his faith: "I believe that Jesus is my Savior and that He died for the redemption of my sins."

"Did your life change after that?" Johnny asked. "I mean, you were in college, so you were partying, drinking, sex?"

Jackie swore his college experience wasn't like that. He attended church faithfully every Sunday. He did the best he could.

"Tell me about your first marriage," Johnny said. Jackie and I both suddenly realized that we had both unknowingly walked into a counseling session. But Jackie didn't seem to mind. He'd grown accustomed to, even comfortable with sharing the most intimate— even the worst—details of his life. And I could see that Johnny didn't lob softball questions. At times, I wanted him to throw even harder. Sometimes I was skeptical of Jackie's answers.

Jackie explained how Mary got pregnant.

"So, you're having sex outside of marriage? Were you conflicted about that?" Johnny asked. "I'm going somewhere here," he said as he leaned in and Jackie leaned back. "I'm trying to understand your thinking."

"I was a real infant in Christ then," Jackie said.

Johnny didn't let up. He said Jackie hadn't paid the price of discipleship. Obedience to God was a sign of strength, but that obedience had to come from a sense of love, not obligation. "We're grateful because we're going to heaven," he said.

Jackie agreed. He knew Johnny spoke the truth. He'd heard it since childhood.

Johnny asked Jackie about his NFL years. "Were you in any kind of fellowship or discipleship?"

This was the question I had hoped for. I believed that Jackie had ignored the importance of regular discipleship. In my mind, he had been spiritually lazy, making up his own rules as he drifted along.

Jackie admitted that he had fallen out of the habit once he entered the world of Sunday football games.

"That's a big, big issue for a lot of Christians," Johnny said. "That's why it's good to examine yourself. You can see the trend: no discipleship, no authority in your life. No accountability."

Jackie knew that, too. The same principle held true in Narcotics Anonymous. But knowing didn't always translate into doing.

Jackie tried to defend himself as he explained his own theories of God's love and discipline. He reached for his favorite example: David of the Old Testament scripture. Even after David committed adultery with Bathsheba and murdered her husband, Uriah, God still blessed David by making him a great King of Israel. Even after David had sinned, God still called him a man after His own heart. Even in David's weakness and premeditated rebellion, God still used David. In Jackie's logic, God could still use him, even in his sin.

But Johnny reminded Jackie that David's child died because of his sin. "Right? And when God granted David sincere repentance, David became grateful and contrite. He stopped sinning. He repented. He was broken. It's all about the fear of the Lord. When we finally face our sins, we say, 'Lord, forgive me.' That's when we become humble."

Jackie shifted in his chair, toward Johnny. "Now, there's another part you have to help me with," he said. "I play that little game with myself with Paul in Second Corinthians. God has put a thorn in [Paul's] flesh, and he prayed three times to release it. But [God] doesn't. God says, in my weakness—right?—I'm made strong. Crack is my weakness, but God won't release it. I use it sometimes to say, this is why I do this."

Jackie immediately admitted his own logic was self-serving.

"I know it's wrong," he said.

"Of course," Johnny said.

"I know it's wrong, I know it's wrong," Jackie said, shaking his head.

"Of course. You make up any excuse to do what you want to do. That's called deception—self-deception."

"Amen. . . . I'm glad you called me on that. Because I struggle with that. But if I don't have Jesus Christ as the author and finisher of that faith . . . I'm just pissing in the wind. And you know what happens when you do that," Jackie said.

"That's it, bro. There's no power in it."

Then Johnny confessed his own past. "I've been in rebellion to God for a long time," Johnny said. "And it's OK to say that. The deception is justifying that. We have to face the truth. Because if not, our bones ache, we lose everything, we hurt. God took me from the womb. Gave me talents and gifts. And I used it for myself for a long time."

Then Johnny pointed a finger to Jackie. "You knew the truth . . . when you were in college. [God] always had all these blessings for you. He had character for you. He had mission. He had purpose. Now I don't want to weigh you down with a guilt trip . . . but, listen. You blew it."

"The truth is the truth," Jackie said.

Johnny followed up quickly like a revival preacher. "Football players and presidents all need Jesus. We're all the same. I'm me and you're you, bro. So, you've got to say, 'God . . . I'm yours. I've blown it for twenty-eight years. . . But for whatever years I have left, let me love you with all of my heart. And *send me,* Lord.' That's it."

"Believe me," Jackie said. "I've done that. And that's one of the reasons we're sitting here today."

"When did God grant you real repentance over your sins?" Johnny asked. "When did you finally look at what you'd done?"

"Believe it or not, it was January eighteenth of this year," he said, referring to the day he called Monique from the crack house after his five-month-long binge. "I'd gone to all these treatment centers because I thought I had a substance abuse problem."

"But you didn't," Johnny said. "You had a heart issue."

"Thank you."

Jackie sat silently for a moment. When he finally spoke, he told Johnny how superficial his past attempts at sobriety had been. "It wasn't about getting clean," Jackie said. "It was like taking a shower. You might clean off all of this. But if you still have that dirt and nastiness inside, it takes more than just getting off the crack."

"Repentance," Johnny said.

"That's right."

"So, you feel like you came to the Lord in January and you really confessed *all* that He died for and received His forgiveness?"

"Yes."

"Hallelujah. Where do you live now?"

"In a shared living facility in the East. No Place Like Home. Ever heard of it?"

"Nope."

"I get enough money from the NFL for my own little place, but I knew I wasn't convicted enough to do that."

"You weren't ready," Johnny said. "That's good. That's wise."

"OK, we're late," Johnny said. "But we're here. Now it's going to be about consistency. Now we want to let go of the old Jackie."

Johnny explained how God—like coaches—only disciplines the ones He loves. "And, man, Jackie, you've been disciplined," Johnny continued. "So, what's it going to be? Is it going to be twelve years clean? Ten years clean? Six years clean? Is it finally over for you?"

Jackie stared into Johnny's eyes, but he didn't say anything.

"Are you connected to a group? Are you in a fellowship? Do you have a pastor? Are you going every week? Do you meet with those guys weekly, too?"

"Nope," he said. "That's the part I know I have to do. The same way when I played football. We knew what time we had to be on the field for practice—consistently. And of that . . . we became better and better."

"That's a great statement," Johnny said, his voice escalating in power. "You did it because football was important."

Johnny suggested that Jackie pray for God to help him change his heart to love Him more than the women, the sex, and the drugs. He told him to rely on God and not his own effort. "You know what I'm saying?"

"God doesn't respect persons," Jackie said, catching Johnny's fever. "But I think the only reason he allowed me to play football is to catch someone's eye. 'Oh,' they'd say. 'You're the football player sleeping under the bridge.' Yeah, but God saved me."

"Right," Johnny said, his voice growing more intense with each sentence. "And he could have used it back when you were in the pros." Johnny's voice reached a fever pitch. "He gave you a platform to share Jesus back then on TV. You blew it," Johnny said for a second time.

Jackie was stirred. "Yeah, you're absolutely right."

"But it's not too late. That's what we're talking about. You can do it now, bro!"

Jackie nodded his head and grinned.

"I'm glad you're alive," Johnny said. "A young man just left from here two weeks ago. They found his body in the woods—thirty years old. Another guy, at twenty-six years old, in and out of rehab for five years. He takes some prescription meds from some chick he was screwing . . . has a reaction and his heart explodes.

Dead. What???? BUT YOU'RE ALIVE, BRO! By God's grace, you have a chance to start another day.

"Pray about it," Johnny continued. "Say, 'I want to be disciplined. I want to follow Christ. I want to know more. I want to be accountable. I want to give up this world. I don't have a lot of time'—and you don't—'and I want to use it for the Lord.'"

Johnny rose from his chair as he continued to prod Jackie. "Right now, it's your time to grow."

He reached out and pulled Jackie up from his seat.

"Love you, man," Jackie said as the men hugged. "Thank you."

"Bless you," Johnny whispered. Jackie hugged tighter, with his chin across Johnny's shoulder.

"Thank you," Jackie said.

"God knew about this meeting back in July 6, 1990," Jackie said, referring to the day he was pulled from under the bridge.

"How about two thousand years ago?" Johnny said, referring to Jesus's crucifixion.

"Hey, hey," Jackie countered. "How about when He said, 'Let there be light'?"

The men exploded in applause and laughter.

Jackie beamed like I'd never seen him before. "You got me fired up. Yes, indeed."

"You should be fired up," Johnny said. "What's better than eternal life? You've got the light, Jackie. You still got the light! The light keeps the body light. It's in the soul here."

"I needed this," Jackie said. "Thank you."

CHAPTER TWENTY

The Sabbatical

2019

On a bright spring morning in 2019, almost a year after his meeting with Johnny, Jackie stepped out from his dingy bedroom dressed for another doctor appointment. His house manager, Leon Courtney, handed him $50 in cash like a parent ushering out a second-grader. Jackie tucked the bills into his pants pocket. "Don't go spend that on drugs," Leon reminded him. "Remember: $45 for the co-pay and $5 for the shuttle, got it?" Jackie nodded and waddled out the door to the curb.

Young seagulls darted and squawked overhead. Graceful pelicans balanced in a perfect hover on the breeze that blew from Lake Pontchartrain, only a block away. Jackie's hips ached as he watched the young birds, but he chuckled as he parodied God's voice inside his head: "I gave you two good legs. You're the one who messed them up."

When the shuttle pulled up, the driver glanced over his roster of passengers. "One of my friends, Mr. Roland and his wife, had a son named Jackie," he said. "He used to play football. Is he related to you?"

"I'm that son," Jackie said.

"How often do people recognize you these days?" the driver asked with an extended handshake and a smile.

"Pretty regular when I need it," Jackie said. "God has a way of knowing when I need it."

JUST LIKE LEON, I had developed a tenuous faith in Jackie. Not because he had earned it with his actions but because he'd demonstrated a basic goodness—an inherent loving spirit—that even the years of crack and blows to the head had not destroyed. Whenever we got to visit, we loved talking about discipline and personal responsibility—even more so since our visit with Johnny Lonardo. I tried to serve as Jackie's accountability partner as best I could. And when I wasn't around, I tried to keep tabs on him. Tasha, the director of No Place Like Home, assured me that Jackie was doing well, and Jackie assured me that he'd been clean for eleven months. I wished that I could find a way to verify his claim.

Jackie's doctor appointment today was routine. As the bus headed downtown, he entertained the other passengers with jokes and stories as they made stops at the various health facilities around town. Some of the men preferred to get their care at the state-of-the-art University Medical Center on Tulane Avenue, built to replace Charity Hospital after the flooding of Hurricane Katrina. The gleaming steel-and-glass structure had revitalized that section of Tulane Avenue but hadn't eradicated the prostitutes who once gripped the neighborhood. It had just pushed them farther down the avenue.

But Jackie stayed on the bus. He preferred his doctors at Touro Infirmary on the edge of Central City, even after they began marketing themselves—to Jackie's amusement—primarily to pregnant women with their advertising slogan: "Where babies come from." He kept the men laughing with his constant ironies. It was his nature. At the same time, Jackie's garrulousness could transform to charity. I've watched Jackie put his encouraging hand around a drunkard's shoulders. I've seen him take charge of a room with his larger-than-life personality, heard his gentle words leave a trail of encouragement.

On a crisp spring day, Jackie asked me to drive him to a house in Central City where he often sat vigil over a dying friend, a seventy-seven-year-old former NFLer who had never been able to kick his crack addiction. Jackie checked in on him at least once a week as his death drew near.

As we circled to the address through the one-way streets, Jackie warned me to stay aware of my surroundings. I reminded him of my time in Desire, and he reminded me that I should never grow complacent. He pointed out dealers both young and old as they paced the sidewalks. Some he knew by reputation. Others he had known since childhood.

Jackie let himself in through a front door, which had been left ajar, and introduced me to the big man laying half-covered in a neatly tucked bed. The room felt stifling hot. Jesse (not his real name) was bedridden, so Jackie pulled up a chair and struck up a conversation that seemed to be a mid-sentence continuation from the day before.

Jesse's voice was raspy and hoarse. I could barely understand him over the drone of the TV news. But Jackie seemed to anticipate every cue. Every time Jesse reached or stirred, Jackie's own crippled reflexes kicked in. "What do you need?" he said as he hobbled around to fetch a sip of water or help him find his slippers for a trip to the bathroom.

Their conversation was mostly banal—idle chatter about football trades, hip replacements, and the occasional remembrances about racism in the South. Jesse had grown up in Chicago. The two men's childhood stories sounded so dissimilar. "In Chicago, we drove the bus," Jesse said. "When I came South, I learned to keep my mouth shut." Taped to the wall were meticulously rendered charcoal drawings of Rosa Parks, Barack Obama, Frederick Douglass, Fats Domino. Jesus stood watch over them all. A tattered Malcolm X hung by one corner by three pieces of duct tape. Sometimes during his vigils, Jackie would fall asleep in the chair—sometimes all night. He just wanted to be there in Jesse's final days, as much as he could. He learned that from his father.

In a matter of weeks, Jesse was transferred to a nursing home, where he died.

Another afternoon, Jackie asked me to drive him to help a "sick" friend. "This is the Christianity I believe in," he said as he navigated me into Central City. Michelle (not her real name) was expecting him to drop by. She had called with an urgent need to talk.

She was manic when she welcomed us in, spinning and twirling around the sparsely decorated room and draping her bone-skinny body around Jackie while she chanted, "I want a big ol' hug, a big ol' hug, a big ol' hug." Jackie wobbled on his cane for a moment and then regained himself. "Be careful," he said, pulling her off him.

She retreated to a rumpled mattress pushed into the corner of her bedroom, where she sat cross-legged. Jackie pulled up a chair to face her. There, her conversation rambled and darted through her troubles for nearly an hour as drugs seized her. She fretted about the men who were trying to control her. She said this bedroom was her hiding place. Jackie promised that he knew how to deal with the men. I couldn't tell if these "men" were paranoid imaginations or actual threats.

Jackie and Michelle had met in a crack house, when he had gone missing in 2017. They bonded after Michelle used her confrontational boldness—or lack of verbal filters, as I called it—to protect Jackie from predators and opportunists while he was strung out. Now he was trying to return the favor. I couldn't tell what she was high on, but from what Jackie told me, crack was her drug of choice. I knew I was getting only half the story.

After an hour or more, she calmed, and Jackie felt she'd be OK.

"You're fine now?" he said.

"Yeah, I'm fine, I got a big ol' hug, I got a big ol' hug. A big ol' hug."

"Oh, Lord, here we go," Jackie mumbled to me. "It's time to leave."

As we walked through the front room, Michelle pointed at a small table with a crisp Bible laid open to Psalms 23. "That's beautiful, huh? Um-huh, so beautiful. That's my protection," she said. "God bless you!"

"Don't hurt yourself," he told her one last time.

She danced out to the ledge of her front stoop, silhouetted in a frozen pirouette as we drove away. Her whoops echoed behind us. The teenage drug boys working the street looked up but showed little interest in her antics. They were more interested in watching me. A subtle gesture would have indicated that I wanted to score. Instead, my glare proved that I was a cop.

"How y'all doing?" Michelle shouted as they hid their faces.

Later, I accompanied Jackie into post-operative suites, where he sat for hours passing ice water and fruit cups to a friend. I've seen him deliver hand-drawn get-well cards to the sick. He said the missions of mercy cost him nothing, but I disagreed.

It was easy to see that Jackie Wallace had a gift. He and I called it a blessing from God.

On May 10, 2019, a text message stirred me in the predawn hours. "I'm in Touro," Jackie wrote, "and I'm not having a baby." It had been over four weeks since I last talked to him, not that I hadn't tried. Those were the times that tried my patience.

I arrived as quickly as I could and found him alone in his fourth-floor room watching ESPN. He looked as though he wanted to apologize, but instead, he just smiled. His voice was weak and his breath labored. He confessed that he'd taken a "short sabbatical" in Central City—a spontaneous binge that had caused his blood pressure to spike and fluid to build around his heart. His chest, legs, and feet were puffed. His weight had ballooned from 240 to 261 pounds—twenty-one pounds of fluid. "We're gonna be all right," he said as I grasped his hand. With a forced smile he repeated, "We're gonna be all right." His doctor had told him that medication, which he hated taking, should stabilize him in three or four months—but that his heart couldn't take much more of this. One more "sabbatical" would probably kill him.

"Well," I said, "I'm on your side, man. You know that."

"I know. I know."

I had begged him so many times to stay strong. I told him how badly I wanted his life's story to have a happy ending. I described to him how horrible it would be to write his obituary, but as a journalist, I would have to.

But looking at him now, I was beginning to believe that we weren't going to win this battle.

I reminded him that crack could cause his heart to give out and echoed what a chaplain at the mission had once told me, "Just like on the street, grace has an expiration date. Every time you go out there, you roll the dice."

Jackie nodded his head that he understood. Jackie's problem was never cognitive. It was emotional and behavioral.

We discussed CTE, and I told him that all my reading on the subject inclined me to agree with his self-diagnosis.

"Yeah," he said. "But the only way you can be diagnosed is if you're dead and they cut your brain out."

I asked if he'd considered donating his body to science. It was an uneasy topic, but by now, we could talk about anything.

He said no, but he had signed up to be an organ donor. "They can use any part of my body," in any way they want, he implied.

He said that his CTE lawyer had called a few days before and had told him that he'd failed the second battery of tests. There would be no help coming from the NFL. He couldn't remember any other details.

"That's done." He sighed.

"You know, people aren't getting any money, anyway," I said. "Very little."

"I know," he said.

Privately, I wondered if Jackie was fortunate to have failed, even though I believed the tests were skewed against his deficits. If Jackie ever got his hands on a bundle of money, it would probably kill him. Of all the triggers that led him back to crack that I'd seen, the chief among them had always been disposable cash. Leon, the house manager, called Jackie's money, or rather his lack of it, his leash.

I could tell that I was wearing Jackie out. But before I left, he asked me if I would dig into his shoulder bag on a table across the room. "Look in there and pull that picture out. The one on the side between the two Bibles."

I dug past a worn-out copy of *The Times-Picayune* and a handful of his autographed Rams photos. Between the Bibles I found a photocopy of a photo montage of his mother and father, surrounded by six individual photos of their children in their high school caps and gowns.

"I remember this from Gateway," I said. "I was thinking about it just yesterday."

"Yeah. I've had that for a good long while."

He pointed out his siblings one by one. "That's Dabney, and that's Margo," he said. "They're the ones who passed. On the top left is Roland. He lives right outside of Atlanta. He's doing well. He beat cancer.

"Take that with you," he said. "Can you get a frame for me and bring it back when I see you again?"

I told him I'd take care of it and tucked it carefully in my backpack.

"I appreciate that," he said. "And tell your wife Happy Mother's Day."

JACKIE, ON HIS worst days, can be a burden for anyone who tries to help him, including his friends and his family. At times, I see subtle manipulation. At times, he's openly rebellious. He's like a swimmer caught in a riptide. There are only a few ways and only so much time to save a drowning man in that situation before he is lost. And Jackie resists the most when the rescuer finally reaches out to him. Even in his final gasp for air, he desperately scratches and claws against the ones who love him the most. His doctor asked him why he treated himself so badly.

Once Jackie returned home, I dropped by with his family photo. It looked much better in a new frame. As I looked over the faces in the picture, I couldn't help but imagine the sorrow, pain, and agony that he had put them through. Many times, they simply had to accept that he had wandered beyond their reach. They had to pray without reconciliation, except possibly through the peace of letting go of an addict that couldn't be cured, as Louvinia finally felt that she had to do. They prayed for miracles.

I stood in awe of Monique's courage for pulling Jackie out of that crack house. Her love for her uncle defied logic and reason. She kept fighting because she believed that it was the right thing to do, and because she believed that somewhere, someone would do the same for her.

As I left the house, I stopped to chat with Jackie's roommate, Reginald. From what I could see in my limited time with him, he was the most emotionally stable of the group. I asked him to take care of my buddy. Without hesitation—and with even less emotion—he said, "The only person that can help Jackie Wallace is Jackie Wallace."

I thought to myself, "And Jackie has not helped Jackie nearly enough."

Jackie's struggle to keep his life together didn't surprise his counselors. They were well acquainted to what they called the "yo-yo effect."

Actual success rates for recovering addicts are nearly impossible to quantify considering the myriad qualifiers involved, though most agree that they are extremely low. Some studies estimate that only 17 to 18 percent stay clean long-term after their first admission. For someone like me, who'd never dabbled in illegal substances, the solution seemed too simple. Just stop making bad choices. Ray Anderson, the chaplain at the New Orleans Mission, a recovering addict himself, explained how frustrating it is for addicts to be told by their friends and families to "just stop using," as if it's a switch they can turn off in their heads.

He also pointed out the hypocrisy of simplistic advice coming from people who have unresolved issues of their own. "It's like a person who is overweight telling me I can't smoke crack," he said. "Well, how much are you eating? Why don't you just stop eating so much? People smoke cigarettes when they know it's killing them. Just stop!"

He tells well-meaning but uninformed people to "check their own closets." Everybody is addicted to something, he said. "Check your closet," he repeated. "What are you hiding?" Addictions can involve sex, gambling, social media, the internet, pornography, sugar, or shopping. The possibilities are endless. Many people will confess secret addictions to chocolate or video games. Some will even brag about their harmless addictions. Even romantic relationships coupled with dependency can be an addiction.

My addictions to my smartphone and sugar are not illegal. Few people will ostracize me for them. They don't send me staggering down the street. They will likely never lead me to a homeless camp under a bridge or a prison sentence for altering stolen checks. My addiction may or may not prove to be harmless to me and to society. In fact, my addiction is encouraged by society and pushed, legally, by billions of dollars in marketing campaigns.

The point is that my brain and Jackie's brain are more alike than I care to admit. If we are honest with ourselves, we can all identify some action or behavior that controls us.

One of Jackie's counselors at Gateway suggested another approach to treating addictions that is being considered among clinicians. "If you really want to understand addiction," he told me, "check out a writer and journalist named Johann Hari." The counselor, who had not treated Jackie in over two years, believed this new approach could help him.

JOHANN HARI ARGUES that addiction may not be about chemical hooks in the brain at all. Instead, addiction may be an adaptation to a negative environment or situation. He argues that addiction is more associated with a lack of strong human connections than to the substances themselves.

In his book *Chasing the Scream,* Hari referenced a famous thirty-second television commercial that ran in 1980 sponsored by the Partnership for a Drug-Free America that showed a rat in an empty cage nibbling and clawing at a pellet of crack. The voice-over says, "Only one drug is so addictive that nine out of ten laboratory rats will use it, and use it, and use it, until dead." The harsh lighting and heavy piano notes dramatize the scene as the rat scampers around, stumbling over himself until it finally, with matted fur and glassy eyes, collapses and dies. "It's called cocaine," the narrator continues, "and it can do the same thing to you."

The ads mirrored studies performed by experimental psychologists in the 1960s to better understand drug addiction.

But Bruce Alexander, a professor of psychology at Simon Fraser University in British Columbia, Canada, noticed something odd. The cage in the television ad and the cages in the 1960s experiments were small and empty.

He wondered if the rats would react differently if the cages were larger and filled with toys, spinning wheels, tunnels, and, maybe most important, male and female rats. In a controlled experiment, he and colleagues built two sets of environments. One replicated the tiny, solitary confinement of the earlier experiments. In the other, they built a large virtual rat wonderland. Alexander named it Rat Park.

In both sets, the rats had two water bottles to drink from. Alexander filled one with pure water. He filled the other with water laced with morphine. The results were staggering. The solitary rats drank twenty-five milligrams of morphine a day. In their small, empty cages, they had nothing to do but get high and die. Meanwhile, in Rat Park, the rats drank less than five milligrams a day. Instead of lapping up the morphine, the citizens of Rat Park preferred to play, explore, enjoy the scenery, and have sex. In the isolated cages, nearly 100 percent overdosed and died as opposed to none in Rat Park.

Bruce concluded that the addiction and overdoses must be blamed on the rats' environment, not the drug itself. The addiction wasn't a disease, he said. It was an adaptation. "It's not you," he said. "It's the cage you live in."

Next, Alexander needed to prove that his findings applied to humans, too, and not just caged rats. Interestingly enough, there was a similar large-scale study being performed at the same time on humans. We know it as the Vietnam War.

In the sixties and early seventies, 20 percent of the young men fighting in Vietnam had picked up a heroin addiction as an adaptation to the isolation and horrors of the jungle warfare. People back home were rightfully concerned that junkies would flood American streets when the war ended. They believed in the pharmaceutical theory of addiction: the idea that addiction was primarily caused by the chemicals in the drug. But the archives of general psychology did an extensive study on the returning vets and found that 95 percent were able to quit cold-turkey within a year, with no withdrawals or cravings once they returned to their normal bonds and connections. They require no rehabilitation. Studies revealed that most of the soldiers who continued in their addiction had experienced miserable childhoods or had been addicts before they left for war.

As one recovering addict told Hari, "Addiction is a disease of loneliness."

In Baltimore, Jackie stayed clean for eleven years. He stayed clean for three and a half years in prison from 2008 to 2011 and three and a half more at Gateway. If Hari was right, then the chemicals in his brain didn't pull him back into addiction on the street. His isolation and miserable sense of self-worth did.

Hari suggests that we've been treating addicts the wrong way by isolating them.

The opposite of addiction is not sobriety, he says. "The opposite of addiction is connection."

CHAPTER TWENTY-ONE

Glory Days

May 2019

On Monday morning, May 20, 2019, as I worked at my desk, my phone screen lit up with caller ID: "Jackie Wallace New Phone." It had been only ten short days since our visit in the hospital and less than two weeks since he'd last dragged on a crack pipe.

"I just wanted to let you know that Burton Burns called today," Jackie said. "He told me that doctors put Coach Otis Washington on life support."

For a second, I reflected back on my brush with Jackie's high school coach. Only a year before, we had sat and talked in his living room in Baton Rouge, the day after I had met Jackie in the hospital waiting room—after he'd been missing for five months. I had told him that Jackie had resurfaced and that he seemed to be doing better. I remembered his relief. He, like many other friends, had spent weeks worrying and expecting newsmen to report that a male skeleton had been found somewhere in New Orleans. I had expected the same. Coach Washington and I had talked about how Jackie had helped shape his life and all those who surrounded him.

And now, on the phone, Jackie wanted to tell me how "Coach Wash" had changed his.

"It's not the people that you see every day that influence you and make the decisions. It's the ones that help you with some decisions that are life-changing. That's the two things that he did. He got me to play football, and he convinced me to look at Arizona."

"So, if something should happen," I said, "are you planning to go to the funeral?"

"Yeah, if something happens, maybe me and Burton can go together," he said.

"Do you think it would be appropriate for me to go to the service?"

"Well," he said, "we'll talk about it if and when it happens. We'll see. I just had to let you in on that."

Only four days later, Coach Otis Washington Jr. died peacefully in Baton Rouge at the age of eighty. The newscasters called him a legend, the winningest coach in St. Augustine High School football history. He had also coached the offensive line at LSU and led Southern University's football team after that.

I picked up the phone to call Jackie, but the call went to voice mail. "Jackie, I just wanted to make sure you saw the news about Coach Washington. Let me know if you want to go to the funeral."

I worried he might disappear again, considering his track record with funerals. I didn't feel better when he didn't return the call. He didn't text either.

That night, Nancy and I talked about what Jackie would wear to the funeral—that is, if he agreed to go. Everyone will be dressed in fine suits, I said.

"We should find him a suit," Nancy said. "We should buy him a suit."

"We'll see," I said. "I'll bring it up when he calls."

That night I prayed my most fervent prayer in years—the kind of prayer where my emotions and thoughts jumbled together without the need for actual words, with a groan that only God can hear. But I didn't pray for Jackie. I prayed instead that I might have faith in God's wisdom. I prayed for full trust in His will. I prayed for full peace—no matter what happened with Jackie.

On Tuesday morning, Burton called. He hadn't been able to get Jackie on the phone either, and he had the same concerns that I did. In big-picture terms, Burton had remained one of Jackie's most consistent friends from childhood. His role in escorting Jackie to Baltimore for treatment had formed a lifelong bond.

St. Aug scheduled the memorial for Thursday morning.

Jackie never returned my calls, which left me seething. Jackie was copping out, again. He was still blaming all his problems on his mother's death. I thought he was acting like a child. And now when people were trying to reach out and give him the support he needed, he was withdrawing. He should face the people who love him. He should at least answer my phone call!

I remembered my prayer from the week before. I tried to let the moment wash over me, but it was hard.

I decided to go to the memorial alone. I could meet Burton and pay my respects and pass my condolences to Coach Washington's widow, Linda.

But as I drove on, I faltered in my plan. For some reason I can't explain, I couldn't do it. At the very last second, I detoured on my drive to St. Aug and headed toward No Place Like Home. I figured it was worth a try. Then I decided to call the house phone instead of Jackie's cell. If he'd disappeared again, this call would confirm it once and for all. I hated calling the house phone for this very reason.

"Is Jackie there?" I held my breath.

"Just a minute."

Within seconds, Jackie was on the line.

"Who is this?"

"Hey, Jackie. This is Ted."

"Oh, hi. Sorry about not calling you, but my phone's been broken for days now."

"Actually, I couldn't be happier to hear that," I said. "Listen. Were you planning to go to Coach Washington's memorial service today?"

"That's today?"

"Yeah."

"Where is it?"

"At St. Aug. His body will be laying in repose from ten till two. It's a come-and-go kind of thing. You want me to pick you up?"

"I'd like that very much."

"Great!" I said. "I can be there in thirty minutes. Or we can go later."

"Let's go early—get in and get out."

"That sounds great. I'll be there in thirty minutes."

"I'll be ready."

Unbelievable. I leaned over my steering wheel, and I looked through the clouds. I couldn't help but smile.

When I walked in the door, Jackie was lifting himself up from a walker fitted with a fold-down seat. I instinctively scanned his attire from top to bottom. He stood with his cane, in dark work pants, blue slip-on sneakers, and a half-wrinkled white polo shirt with an ink pen clipped across the lower button. His thick head of gray hair extended too far over his ears. He looked fine.

He groaned and tugged as he climbed into the passenger seat. I helped him with his seat belt and his cane.

"How are you feeling?" I said. "How's your blood pressure?"

"One-sixty over about seventy-seven," he said, "which is real, real good."

"Are you taking your heart medicine?"

"I'm taking everything. And I'm taking it at the required time. My heart specialist said that if I continued living right, leave that stuff alone, and eat the right things . . . my health will get better. We're getting better."

I guess Jackie had noticed my darting eyes from the living room. "I thought about buying a new suit," he said. "But I figured, this ain't about me. I could have run out and bought me a nice little suit and shirt and tie, have rings and stuff, and go walking in that place looking like . . . whatever. But my purpose is to pay tribute to Otis."

"I think you look fine," I said.

Jackie refreshed many of his high school memories during our twenty-five-minute drive to the school. As we passed Holy Cross High School on Paris Avenue, I yielded to four young football players in practice uniforms as they crossed, helmets in hand.

"Look at those boys," I said. "Like they know what they're doing."

Jackie smiled. "Yes, indeed. That's what we used to do. We used to walk from St. Aug to Hardin Park. And those metal-tipped cleats clackety-clacked on the pavement."

As I drove on, I mused at how the city had changed in the twenty-nine years since I'd met Jackie. I wondered if those young men crossing the street could ever appreciate what men like Coach Washington, Jackie, and his St. Aug teammates had done to erase the racial barrier of high school sports in Louisiana. Far in the distance, I could see the hazy outline of the cityscape framed by the fifties-era frame and brick houses of Gentilly. Occasionally, on the neighborhood houses and businesses, I could still spot subtle visual remnants of Katrina—a faded watermark or a spray-painted "X." This area had been inundated with six to ten feet of water, or more. The storm left a latent mark of PTSD on everyone who was here. She almost ruined us. That can't be overstated. I remembered how we all felt reborn when the Saints won the Super Bowl in 2010. The fleur-de-lis became our symbol of recovery after that. It's amazing how the bond of sports can help us transcend our hatred and our pain.

I dropped Jackie at the front steps of St. Aug. He said he'd wait by the door for me to park. I could tell that he was nervous. I hoped people would see him the way I saw him: a man who sincerely wanted to be the man he once was, long before the demons got their claws into him.

Maybe no one would notice him at all.

But by the time I walked back to the front of the school, three alumni in expensive suits had already surrounded him.

"Jackie Wallace! Oh, my God! It's so good to see you."

"It's good to be seen," he joked.

"How are you doing?"

"Not bad for two hip replacements."

"Do you remember me?" a man said as they walked to the door.

"Ahhhhhh." Jackie laughed. "Now, you know my CTE ain't going to let that happen like that. Didn't I lend you $450,000 in 1842? Do you have that for me?"

"Yeah," one man said with a nervous laugh. "Let me get that for you."

"You know I don't take checks," Jackie said.

Two men held the front door as he hobbled through on his cane. He glanced around the school's walls at the mascot Purple Knights iconography, the religious trappings, and the medieval suits of armor. He took a deep breath and savored a long, lost aroma.

Student hosts directed him through the hallways toward the cafeteria, where guests were gathering. He stopped to sign the registry, specifically reserved for coaches and players from 1961–1979.

He could see a couple of dozen men milling about through the glass door.

When he lumbered in, a voice from across the room rang out as if Jackie had just trotted out onto a field of play.

"The-great-Jackie—Wallace!"

Another voice joined in to confirm as they ran up to greet him, "That's him! There ain't no telling where you're at. You're still the great Jackie Wallace."

"Yes, indeed, we're trying," Jackie said with a laugh. Then men enveloped him in a knot of hugs, handshakes, and backslaps. Cell phones suddenly appeared out of pockets. I volunteered to shoot the first group shot.

A big man took Jackie's face in his hands. "The most fearless man I've ever known," Byron Honore gushed. "You were like my uncle, my inspiration. You taught me how to be a f—ing man—how to be a f—ing person." Then he looked at me. "Jackie Wallace saved my life. He taught me to avoid the streets. To avoid the gangs." Then the tears started flowing. "I hate to cry, but I can't help it. I can never pay him back. It's impossible to ever pay Jackie Wallace back. It's impossible."

Jackie couldn't hide his sudden rush of joy either, but he deflected with an introduction to his friends. He pointed to me. "This is the man who found me under the bridge—" Another man cut him off. "Don't act like we don't know the story!" he said with a laugh. Everyone instantly lost themselves in talk of the glory days, game stats, favorite plays, and family.

"How's Donald?" one man asked, remembering Jackie's brother, the pitching legend.

"He's still driving the RTA bus," Jackie said.

"And Dr. Louvinia!" said another. "How's the best mathematician in New Orleans?"

"Doing fine," he said, smiling.

Before long, the men guided Jackie past the gathering of congenial men, past a mural of a heroic-size, meticulously painted Purple Knight in full battle armor. They led him down the long corridor and into the school's darkened chapel, which measured no more than thirty feet square. There, Coach Washington lay in repose. Two students dressed in full uniforms guarded either end of the dark-gray casket. Their steely eyes pierced the deep shadow from inside their perfectly gilded Spartan-style helmets.

Jackie stood between them in front of the casket and stared at the corpse of one of the most influential men in his life. He told me later he could still hear Washington's words wash over him, the words that set him on his path. "We're going to make a quarterback out of you . . . Jackie, you have to play like it's first and twenty-five . . . Have you considered Arizona? . . . Jackie, please keep in touch."

He regretted that he'd ignored the last words of advice.

When he turned, Linda greeted him.

"Jackie Wallace," she said as she wrapped him in a hug.

"I'm so sorry, Miss Linda." He took her hand and kissed it.

"I could just spank you right now," she said. Jackie knew that his former coach would have worded it differently.

She sat him down in the open chair beside her, and they talked.

"I'm OK," he said. "I'm getting better. It's going to be OK."

Linda's diamond-studded wedding band sparkled in the light as her fingers folded around his oversize hand. She held on until they finished their whispered conversation. Then he dipped his head, raised her hand, and kissed it.

He fumbled with his cane as he left the room. He passed a decorated memorial table of three state championship trophies, sideline photos of the coach, dainty pompoms, and two modern football helmets. The school logo, an interlocked "S" and "A," blazed over metallic gold. There, Jackie stopped to chat with a friend. "Did you wear one like this?" the man said as he pointed to the helmets.

"No, mine was leather," he said with a laugh.

Jackie, hips aching, found a wall to lean against. Friends continued to surround him. Men hugged and exchanged phone numbers and posed for pictures.

I caught snippets of conversation.

"I'm trying to move a barge over to Africa right now."

"No, I'm not a legislator. I'm Clerk of Court."

"Yeah," a father told his son, pointing to Jackie. "That's him."

By now the crowd had swelled to over two hundred. But the sea of men parted and every head turned when Burton Burns arrived and finally spotted Jackie. He bellowed out: "Jackie Wallace!"

"Oh, Lord have mercy," Jackie responded, just as loudly. The men buried their faces in the other's shoulders.

"You're looking good!" Burton said. "So, you got a new phone now?"

"I'll have one tomorrow."

"You still got my number?" Burton asked.

"Yeah, it's in there," Jackie said. "You know I have two hip replacements?"

"You know I have two knee replacements?" Burton laughed.

"Boy, I still remember that long flight we took that day," Jackie said.

"That was something else," Burton said. "That was the best!"

"Yeah, the first time I went to treatment in Baltimore. Best ride I ever had was that airplane," Jackie said. "And Father Verrett . . ." He trailed off. "We went to one little restaurant in Baltimore."

"Yeah, we ate good, whatever that was."

"Yes, you talk about nice!" Jackie said as the two men got lost in conversation. "Yes, indeed."

Jackie's high school wingback, Melvin Howard, helped Jackie as he walked. He had gone on to become a colonel in the Orleans Parish Sheriff's Department. "I had my men looking everywhere for you," he said, referring to the 2018 story in *The Times-Picayune* that ended with Jackie disappearing. The men traded phone numbers. "Man, I'm going to come pick you up," Melvin said. "We're going to go talk, eat, bring you to see the boys. We're going to take you out so much you'll be sick of it."

"Yes indeed." Jackie smiled.

Jackie leaned over to me. "I can see the bigger picture now," he said. "All that stuff I was going through . . . there was a purpose to it. I was so low. I said, 'OK, God. What you got now?' Now I see what he got. This is the whole picture, teammates, coaches. All these guys. We've never forgot each other. This beats going to treatment. This beats going to all of those Narcotics Anonymous meetings. I get around people that actually know me—know my character and my heart. That's what I need. They accept me for me, and they know they can help. It's my brotherhood. It's my team."

On the ride home, he said it had been the greatest day of his life.

THE NEXT DAY, Jackie caught the bus from New Orleans East into Gentilly to run errands. He rode through the neighborhoods where he was once forbidden to play in the mid-1950s. They're now over 76 percent black, as whites have continued to flock to suburbia to escape the crime and corruption.

The decayed and crumbling housing projects are all gone, too, razed and replaced with pastel-colored mixed housing in an effort to decentralize poverty. The noble experiment of a housing utopia for the poor had failed. The names "St. Bernard" and "Desire Housing Project" will soon fade into the collective memories of old men and dusty old photographs. The drug boys continue to drive misery and death in selected neighborhoods with revenge shootings, turf wars, and debt collections at the beginning of each month. As for now, Jackie was a survivor.

But today, May 31, 2019, Jackie stepped with a new bounce as he disembarked at Gentilly Boulevard and Elysian Fields and walked past the payday loans, beauty supply, and the Queen Nails to T-Mobile to activate a replacement cell phone.

There, he struck up a random, jubilant conversation with Phalynn Powers, a district executive with the cell phone company who had recently transferred to New Orleans from Georgia. As usual, Jackie shared a joke and an unsolicited snippet of his NFL story, complete with an autographed action photo. A cynic might say he could have been more modest. But as a sixty-eight-year-old man doddering around town handing out treats and tales from a cloth shoulder bag, he was charming.

As he talked, the woman's eyes welled with tears. She told him that her father had also played for the Vikings, a few years before him. He'd died when she was only twelve years old, but she suddenly realized that if he were still alive, he'd be about Jackie's age. They talked and shared stories for over an hour. They posed side by side as a clerk took their photo. Jackie's ragged and stretched T-shirt looked especially ragged next to her crisp purple polo.

In the picture, they both fingertipped the edges of a black-and-white eight-by-ten of the play that broke the NFL punt-return record. He signed it with the words "To Phalynn, Stay Sweet, Jackie Wallace #20." His unkempt gray hair fluffed out from the band of his faded blue baseball cap. His sweat-soaked V-neck and matching gaunt face were eclipsed by his broad smile. His eyes literally sparkled.

Due to the searing heat, she gave him a ride to his next errand:

the drugstore to buy a pair of slippers for his brother Donald's sixty-sixth birthday present on Sunday. She left him with a hug, a small gift for brightening her day.

After she drove off, she Googled his name to confirm the unlikely tale that he had told her. She sat there lost in his story as she read my article from 2018. She cried again after she read the last paragraphs. She found my email address in the postscript and wrote to say that she'd found a new friend. "He was a ray of sunshine," she wrote me.

Meanwhile, back at the drugstore, Jackie paid for his purchases from a damp knot of small bills and walked to the nearest bus stop. There he waited in the shade for his ride home. He boarded one stiff leg at a time behind the other passengers.

The bus jostled through the potholes as it turned back toward New Orleans East. Jackie watched through the window as athletes gathered on ball fields, laughing and shoving and bonding as bands

of brothers. He glanced around at the other riders, some mingling in lively conversation and some sitting quietly, draped in earbuds on another random Friday afternoon.

He glanced at the bus driver in the mirror and thought of his brother Donald—an RTA bus driver himself—and how great it would be to celebrate with his family on Sunday. He hoped that his nieces would be able to attend. He had so much to tell them after his day at St. Aug.

He settled back in his seat and opened his crisp, new phone to check for any missed calls. He found thirty-two new voice messages, mostly from his old friends inviting him to lunch, coffee, or to watch their sons' football games. He gripped the phone tighter and smiled, then stared out the window as Gentilly blurred by and whispered to himself, "Thank you, Jesus."

Epilogue

As the months passed, friends and former teammates continued to reach out with phone calls, text messages, cards, letters, and visits. They seemed to arrive with precise timing. Chuck Foreman, Brent McClanahan, Steve Holden, Glenn Doughty, Freddie Scott, and Maureen Kilcullen, as well as Colts quarterback Bert Jones checked in from time to time to encourage him and wish him well. One card read, "Please know that you're surrounded by a cloud of angels who are cheering you on." Jackie couldn't stop talking about them.

He randomly bumped into Tony Dorsett on Magazine Street. Together on the sidewalk, they recalled the plays of the NFC championship and divisional playoff games in '79 and '80. In a way, reliving his past reconnected him to his future.

Taris stopped short of reestablishing a romance, but she wanted me to tell him she still loved him and always would. I chose, for the time being, to let that alone. Deborah, on the other hand, told me that she never wanted to see or hear from him again, but she still prays sincerely for his soul.

I pray for Jackie every day, too. And I ask him to pray for me. It took me some time to realize that I needed his prayers as much as he needed mine. Life is a tenuous trail. We never know where our paths are leading us.

Many times, I wondered why I was so driven to search for Jackie after all those years. I knew it wasn't just for the sake of journalism; it had to be something richer, more profound.

Let me be perfectly clear. Jackie is not a man to be idolized or championed. He is a deeply flawed and broken man—a cautionary tale if I've ever known one. Deborah was right when, as early as 1995, she described him as a Jekyll and Hyde personality.

Even so, my time spent trying to understand this man has enhanced my appreciation for my home, my family, my faithful friends, and my blessings. It has given me a deep insight into my own weaknesses and prejudices. I've come to a fuller understanding of the insidious nature of addiction and sin. I now know that recovery and salvation have little to do with personal willpower. Salvation is God's business. Our job, though, is to accept or decline the gift. The process of recovery is a progression that rarely follows a linear path, and it never has an end. The goals we reach are often found at the end of a long, ragged trail—if we can reach them at all.

Many friends say I've wasted my time and energy with Jackie, saying that addicts are manipulative and untrustworthy and will always be hopeless. They may be right. No, they probably are right. I have to admit, my relationship with Jackie has been torturous, maddening, and depressing. But I didn't choose Jackie. For some extraordinary reason, God laid Jackie at my door, and I've tried to answer that call.

TODAY, THERE ARE few physical reminders of Jackie's career. There are no jerseys tucked away in an attic, no helmets or boxes of memorabilia. And many of the venues of his most glorious memories are now transformed into other purposes. Minneapolis's Metropolitan Stadium is now the Mall of America. The site of New Orleans Super Bowl IX is now student residences, a parking garage, and an activity field. Baltimore's Memorial Stadium is now a Little League ball field.

Jackie's house in Baltimore is falling apart from rot and neglect. His house in New Orleans East flooded in 2005 and has since been torn down and replaced. His Super Bowl rings are long gone, either given away to children or, as some still believe, pawned for drugs. There is, however, at least one decorated game ball from 1979 that remains in the cherished collection of a man who grew up in Jackie's neighborhood.

I still have the original black-and-white proof prints that were marked and sized for publication in 1990. I keep them in a special folder along with yellowed newsprint pages from a great newspaper. My original negatives are carefully sleeved, catalogued, and cared for by the Historic New Orleans Collection. Jackie still carries a small stack of autographed eight-by-ten prints that he hands out to unsuspecting strangers. I suspect one day soon I'll have to order a new batch.

ONE NIGHT, I dreamed of Jackie walking out on a field before a crowd of spectators. Instead of wearing pads and a helmet, he stood dressed in his typical polo shirt and tattered cap, surrounded by a supportive squad of teammates. He smiled like only Jackie can and thanked the group for their kind welcome. His body looked whole and strong again. He captivated the folks sitting along the front row because they were the brokenhearted, the abandoned, and the most hardened, despicable addicts. He spoke primarily to them, saying, "Don't give up on me, and I won't give up on you."

His gentle words inspired them more than any interception or punt return had ever inspired before. His compassion eased their guilt. They felt encouraged, knowing that he was on his third, fourth, or maybe even his fifth chance in life. In his example, they found comfort, understanding, and, maybe most important, hope.

As he finished speaking, Jackie watched as families reunited and friends welcomed back their own lost souls and redeemed their walking dead. Daughters reconciled with their fathers, and mothers wept over their sons. And standing there, Jackie knew—possibly for the final time—that he'd found his place in the world. Not only had he been used as a lesson—he'd been used up.

Acknowledgments

I would imagine it rare for a random conversation with a homeless man to result in a book. But when Jackie Wallace and I met in 1990, he believed he had a story to tell even at the expense of exposing his deepest and darkest secrets. He believed his story could help others if he could get someone to tell it. Thank you, Jackie, for trusting me.

There are many others to thank for their support along the way including, first and foremost, my dear friend Jon Eig. I shared with him my desire for this project over a decade ago. His friendship and advice brought me to the starting gate and his encouragement helped me across the finish line.

Many thanks go to Rica Allanic, my wonderful literary agent at David Black Agency, who parsed through my intentions and discovered a story worth telling. More than that, thank you for believing that I could tell it. And I'm thankful for my steadfast editor, Matthew Daddona of Dey Street Books, who read my proposal and believed the world needed to hear more about friendship and redemption. Thank you, Matthew, for your patience as you helped me craft a story worth reading. Thanks also to Ploy Siripant and Paula Russell Szafranski for your beautiful design work and Elissa Cohen for your keen legal advice. Andrea Monagle, your extraordinary copy editing is simply amazing. Thank you, everyone at Dey Street and HarperCollins.

I am grateful to all those who took the time to share their stories, beginning with Joe Banks, who first gave me hope that my friend was still alive. And to Gateway director Darryl Chandler and staff, who proved priceless in my understanding of Jackie's struggle. Much appreciation and admiration go to David Bottner and Johnny Lonardo for the work they do at the New Orleans Mission and Giving Hope Retreat. Thank you for granting me full access to your wonderful, giving staff, especially chaplain Ray Anderson and his wife Kathy Anderson. My thanks and admiration go to Deacon Biaggio DiGiovanni and Clarence Adams and the other tireless workers at Ozanam Inn, and all my new friends at Alcoholics Anonymous and Narcotics Anonymous who welcomed me into their meetings in Central City. Particular thanks go to the Early Birds: David, Rhonda, Barbara, and specifically John, who guided me around Baltimore and into the inner workings of AA with your time, phone calls, books, and even a visit to New Orleans. I admire your sobriety, dedication, and perseverance. Your insights and kindness opened many new doors, as did the many anonymous health care workers who courageously kept me pointed in the right direction.

And many thanks to the recently deceased Coach Otis and his gracious widow, Linda Washington, who welcomed me into their home for my first interview for this book. Thanks to Burton Burns, who gave his time and heart to help Jackie in all the seasons of his life. Thanks to Jackie's former coaches and teammates Eddie Flint, Chuck Foreman, Bert Jones, Dale Brock, Sam Castle,

Nate Wright, Frank Corral, Glenn Doughty, and Jackie's friend Dr. Jacqueline Hern Bell-Jones for enduring my long interviews and conversations.

A special credit is due Maureen Kilcullen, formerly of the Baltimore Colts, who contributed her valuable time to help me understand Jackie's experiences with the team and with the city. Your heart is golden. I've never known anyone more connected and eager to help a stranger.

And thanks to Deborah Monroe for unlocking your door and heart to me. You didn't have to and I know that. And even though I never met him, I want to thank Father Joseph Verrett for making it your life's work to help Jackie and the thousands of others like him. And to the staff of Tuerk House and Weisman House, your hospitality and openness gave me great insight and details into the struggles of addiction. Taris Whitley, you are an angel. I could hear it in your voice when I first talked to you on the phone. I pray this book is a blessing to you.

I am grateful to the librarians at the New Orleans Public Library who helped me filter through the maze of records and microfiche, and to Leon Courtney and Natasha Lawson at No Place Like Home for their hospitality. Thanks to my friend Ro Brown, who proved invaluable in helping me rest easier at night with his timely phone calls.

And thanks to Dr. Robert Cantu, Dr. Jeff Andry, Dr. Vern Palmisano, and Dr. Waylon Bailey, who were never more than a phone call away when I needed deep background or a quick reference. And I've come to rely on Richard Campanella for his incredible knowledge of New Orleans geography. I appreciate the tiny nuggets I found in interviews with Lonnie Hammond and Matt Wannebo. And my heartfelt gratitude goes to Yolanda Stewart for your well-timed texts.

Jackie's story grew out of decades of undying support from the wonderful people at *The Times-Picayune*, especially publisher Ashton Phelps, who went out of his way to let me know he stood behind me. Thanks to Robert Hart, who first hired me at *The Times-Picayune*, Doug Parker who edited me through two Pulitzers, Dinah Rogers who kept me on task, and Andrew Boyd who encouraged me in all things Jackie Wallace. Thanks to photo editor Kurt Mutchler who first dispatched me to the Carrollton underpass, and to Jackie. And I raise a salute to my comrades in arms, the photography and lab staff who not only taught me the profession, but also created for me a second family. Each and every one of you inspired me with your specialized skills and covered for me while I worked on projects. But I especially want to thank Kathy Anderson, G. E. Arnold, Bryan Berteaux, Norman Berteaux, Alex Brandon, Chuck Cook, Rusty Costanza, Michael DeMocker, Kathleen Flynn, Chris Granger, David Grunfeld, Eliot Kamenitz, Ellis Lucia, John McCusker, Cara Owsley, Pat Patterson, Susan Poag, Matt Rose, Thom Scott, Jim Sigmon, Robert "Bobby" Steiner, Donald Stout, Ariane Kodach Swisa, Irwin Thompson, Scott Threlkeld, Tyrone Turner, Jennifer Zdon, Alex Barkoff, Paige Hodgson Cliff, Joe Graham, Vickie Harper, Heldegarde Hard Horan, Sandy Maillho, Todd Melancon, and Jane Rolling.

And lastly, thanks to my dear friend Brett Duke, the one man I could always count on to pull me out of a jam.

I am indebted to many fine journalists that helped shape this book's path: my editor Jim Amoss, whose leadership and friendship took me far "beyond the wall"; Louann Dourough, who I can accurately say first encouraged my writing; Carolyn Fox, who challenged me to find my voice and my own stories; Mark Lorando, whose crucial advice and editing brought Jackie's story to life on

NOLA.com; Greg Lopez, the *Daily Iberian* columnist, whose beautiful writing and heart taught me to honor the people who trusted me to tell their stories; Jonathan Bullington and Richard Webster, whose dedication to compassionate journalism inspired me and proved instrumental in helping me find Jackie after his twelve years on the streets. And great appreciation and admiration go to my friend and colleague Jimmy Smith, whose words and compassion gave birth to Jackie's most successful revival.

Many thanks and fond memories are due to my friend Steve Gardner, who first introduced me to the camera, and eventually to journalism. And thanks to my journalism students in arms: Mike Barrett, Jamie Bates, Scott Boyd, Steve Coleman, Chuck Cook, Tim Isbell, and Dianne Laakso. We owe much to the dean of photojournalism, the incomparable Ed Wheeler. I also want to thank my friends Mo Leverett and Danny Wuerffel for their shared love for the children of Desire. Your influence is spread throughout these pages.

And to the McComb Church of Christ: You nurtured me to use my gifts for God's service. Thank you Norman Miller, "Brother Dale" Justus, and the entire McComb Church of Christ youth group, including but not limited to Marlin Bass, Eddie Cagle, Jay Justus, Joe Justus, Gloria Matthews Killeen, Ronnie Lofton, Sharon Stephenson Lofton, Terry Lofton, Brian Miller, Krista Miller Pendergrass, Steve Sims, Greg Smith, Mike Smith, Wanice Sims Smith, and many more who have gone before. Special thanks to my friend Eric Tooley.

And thanks to my friends who have prayed with me: Randy Patterson, Harold Bergeron, Ty Angeron, Billy Lambert, Dick Perl, Ambrose and Renee Ramsey, Mark and Carla Bundy, David and Becky Gilbert; and my Bible class at First Baptist Covington who encouraged me and prayed fervently for Jackie through the hard times, including Christie Andry, Jeff Andry, Karen Bennett, Natalie Brown, John Brown, Steve Coriell, Barbara Coriell, Diane Duncan, Marlene Haffey, Steve Hayden, Suzanne Hayden, Jennifer Higbee, Tim Higbee, Paulette Jones, C. J. Jones, Lou Kennedy, Ron Kennedy, Julie Liepelt, Mark Mauer, Dr. Vern Palmisano, Judie Palmisano, Linda Reagan, Tom Reagan, Bob Simmons, Mary Bess Simmons, Anita Soileau, Brad Soileau, Ellyn Sterling, Jerry Sterling, Beth Stire, Paul Tullier, Holly Tullier, Toni Twiggs, Lisa Varnado, Greg Varnado, Gail Zirkle, and Gary Zirkle.

And thanks to the men, women, and students of Parklane Academy. Your hard work and dedication to education overcame the dark days of racial struggle and nurtured and inspired me to reach higher than my own understanding. As Theodore Roosevelt said, "It is only through labor and prayerful effort, by grim energy and resolute courage, that we move on to better things."

And thanks and love to my dear parents, Hulene and Lenox Jackson for a lifetime of sacrifice and encouragement, coupled with the support of my entire family: Curtis Redd, Ruby Redd, Lucious Jackson, Bessie Jackson, Betty Gatlin, Charles Gatlin, Jeff Gatlin, Jennifer Covington, Don Jackson, Caroline Jackson, Jenna Valentine, Megan Warren, Ken Jackson, Jill Jackson, Hayley Hicks, Maggie Slaton, Jonalyn Clark, Randy Clark, Clare Clark Taylor, Mary, Jon, Garrett, and Caroline Jordan, a host of uncles, aunts, and cousins, and my dear mother-in-law, Mary Tatum, who believed in me against her good judgment. You all gave me the blessing.

I feel never-ending gratitude to my beloved children and their wives: Chris, Ashley, Jeremy, and Tami. You are an enduring anchor, inspiration, and source of pride. May our love never cease.

And to my grandson, Austin, who, upon learning that this book project was officially going forward, sent my first encouraging text reading, "Go Poppop!" You are an amazing and bright young man. I can only imagine where your paths will lead. And to my lovely Ava. Even at ten years old, you helped me write a sentence to help explain Louisiana humidity. And I'll never forget the day you eagerly joined me to drop off bags of clothes at Odyssey House. You walked bravely through those ancient, intimidating doors because, as you said, "I want to meet Jackie." You have the most beautiful heart.

And to Jackie's family members, especially Monique, Louvinia, Roland Jr., and Donald—who I never had the pleasure of meeting—I pray that you understand how much I love your brother. I pray that you discover our true purpose within these pages. With God, all things are possible.

Most importantly, this book is dedicated to my beloved wife, Nancy. You were the first to believe in my calling and you gave me the courage to pursue it. You graciously endured the decades of uncertain outcomes, the loneliness, worry, and acceptance of my domestic and foreign assignments. You more than any other understood that God's purposes are often revealed in times of trial and trouble. Your enduring love lifted every word in this book. God gave me a special gift when he sealed our vows and we've made it an adventure. I love you more than you'll ever know.

And finally, I thank Jackie, who once looked me in the eye and said, "You ought to do a story about me." It was a moment that God had planned before "Let there be light." May God bless you, my friend. Our works were not perfect, but we dedicated them to the Lord that they may be established.

Jackie, may you find peace and redemption in the grace of our awesome God. And may He use our story to inspire others to live a life worthy of His calling, to stay sober minded and focused on faith.

It's why we did it.

Credits

CHAPTER EIGHT
Page 150 Photo by Ted Jackson | NOLA.com | *The Times-Picayune*
Page 152 Photo by Ted Jackson | NOLA.com | *The Times-Picayune*
Page 153 Photo by Ted Jackson | NOLA.com | *The Times-Picayune*
Page 154 Photo by Ted Jackson | NOLA.com | *The Times-Picayune*
Page 157 Photo by Ted Jackson | NOLA.com | *The Times-Picayune*

CHAPTER NINE
Page 160 Photo by Ted Jackson | NOLA.com | *The Times-Picayune*
Page 161 Photo by Ted Jackson | NOLA.com | *The Times-Picayune*
Page 162 Photo by Ted Jackson | NOLA.com | *The Times-Picayune*
Page 163 Photos by Ted Jackson | NOLA.com | *The Times-Picayune*
Page 164 Photo by Ted Jackson | NOLA.com | *The Times-Picayune*

CHAPTER TEN
Page 172 Photo by Ted Jackson | NOLA.com | *The Times-Picayune*

CHAPTER ELEVEN
Page 194 Photo by Ted Jackson | NOLA.com | *The Times-Picayune*
Page 195 Photo by Ted Jackson | NOLA.com | *The Times-Picayune*
Page 196 (Top) Photo by Ted Jackson | NOLA.com | *The Times-Picayune*
Page 196 (Bottom) Photo by Mario Tama | Getty Images
Page 198 Photo by Ted Jackson | NOLA.com | *The Times-Picayune*
Page 199 Photo by Ted Jackson | NOLA.com | *The Times-Picayune*

CHAPTER FOURTEEN
Page 226 Photo by Ted Jackson | NOLA.com | *The Times-Picayune*
Page 227 Photo by Ted Jackson | NOLA.com | *The Times-Picayune*

CHAPTER FIFTEEN
Page 242 Photo by Ted Jackson | NOLA.com | *The Times-Picayune*

CHAPTER SIXTEEN
Page 250 Used by permission | NOLA.com | *The Times-Picayune*

CHAPTER SEVENTEEN
Page 257 Photo by Ted Jackson

CHAPTER NINETEEN
Page 282 Photo by Ted Jackson
Page 297 Photo courtesy of Jackie Wallace

CHAPTER TWENTY
Page 297 Photo courtesy of Jackie Wallace

CHAPTER TWENTY-ONE
Page 310 Photo by Ted Jackson
Page 312 Photo by Ted Jackson
Page 315 Photo courtesy of Phalynn Powers

About the Author

Ted Jackson is a freelance photojournalist and writer who spent over three decades exploring the human condition for the *New Orleans Times-Picayune*. In 1997, he was one of a four-person team that won a Pulitzer Prize for public service for "Oceans of Trouble," a comprehensive look at the impending collapse of the world's fisheries. In 2005, he photographed Hurricane Katrina, for which *The Times-Picayune* staff won a Pulitzer for public service.

His work has appeared in books, newspapers, and magazines around the world including the *New York Times*, *Washington Post*, *Newsweek*, *Time*, and *National Geographic*. He has appeared on the *CBS Morning Show*, ABC, NBC, CNN, Fox News, and NPR. He was one of three subjects featured in the Weather Channel documentary on Hurricane Katrina.

He lives in Covington, Louisiana.

See more of his work at www.tedjacksonphoto.com.

He can be contacted at Tedjacksonphoto@yahoo.com or through his website.